Jump-Start Your Career as a Digital Librarian

A LITA Guide

Edited by

Jane D. Mo

An imprint of the American Library Association

CHICAGO 2013

JANE D. MONSON received her MLS from the University of Iowa and is digital initiatives librarian at the University of Northern Colorado. She was previously digital projects librarian at Truman State University in Missouri. She has been published in *Computers in Libraries* magazine, is a book reviewer for the *Journal of Electronic Resources Librarianship,* and serves on the Library and Information Technology Association's Publications Committee.

Printed in the United States of America

17 16 15 14 13 5 4 3 2 1

ISBNs: 978-1-55570-877-1 (paper); 978-1-55570-881-8 (PDF); 978-1-55570-882-5 (ePub); 978-1-55570-883-2 (Kindle). For more information on digital formats, visit the ALA Store at alastore.ala.org and select eEditions.

Library of Congress Cataloging-in-Publication Data

Jump-start your career as a digital librarian : a LITA guide / edited by Jane D. Monson.
pages cm
Includes bibliographical references and index.
ISBN 978-1-55570-877-1
1. Library science—Vocational guidance. 2. Digital libraries. 3. Librarians—Effect of technological innovations on. I. Monson, Jane D., 1977—editor of compilation.
Z682.35.V62J86 2013
020.23—dc23 2012036377

Book design in Berkeley and Avenir. Cover image © Ohmega 1982/Shutterstock, Inc.

∞ This paper meets the requirements of ANSI/NISO Z39.48-1992 (Permanence of Paper).

Contents

PART 2
Practicing Your Career

Preface

The world of digital libraries is often a bit overwhelming. This is true even for those of us who make a living as digital librarians, but it's particularly so for professionals just entering the field. The skill set of the digital librarian is broad, intersecting with diverse subject areas both within library science (collection development, cataloging and metadata, archival management and preservation) and without (computer science, digital technologies, design and usability, copyright law). For the new professional, it can take significant time to find your bearings and understand how all the pieces connect. Where should you start? What are the topics that every digital librarian needs at least a basic understanding of in order to be effective in his or her work? This book is intended to provide you with answers to those questions, whether you are considering a career as a digital librarian or newly embarking upon one.

While many library and information science graduate programs now offer digital library tracks, it can nonetheless be difficult to gain exposure to all facets of digital librarianship in the course of two short years. Once you have that MLS in hand, you may still feel that there are gaps in your knowledge that need filling. At least, this was my experience, and there were often times as I started to put my training into practice that I wished for a road map to guide me or someone to sit me down and explain, in plain terms, the things that were still unclear (I sometimes still do). Some of us may be lucky enough to find an experienced mentor early in our career, but most must cobble together a cohesive understanding of this new and fast-changing field from disjointed sources. We may be the only digital librarian at our institution, expected to have all the answers but with no one to turn to with our own questions. Or conversely, we may be in such a specialized role that we have a hard time seeing the digital forest for the trees.

That's where this book comes in. It aims to be your mentor—or twenty-one mentors, to be precise, who present their collective wisdom to guide you through the first stages of your career and provide a clear, concise overview of the core concepts and competencies of digital librarianship. We don't assume you know much about librarianship at all, but also don't talk down to readers with experience. Are you thinking about going to library school, but aren't sure whether digital librarianship is really for you (or even what exactly it is)? This book can help you decide. Are you currently enrolled in library school and know that you want to be a digital librarian? This book can assist you in planning your coursework and getting a grasp of the field as a whole. Are you a new graduate starting out in your first digital library position, or a seasoned professional transitioning from a more traditional area such as cataloging or archives? This book will provide you with advice and best practices for succeeding at your new job duties. You may also be a librarian or information professional who has no plans to work in digital libraries per se, but you realize that knowledge of digital practices is of increasing relevance to everyone in the field. This book is for all of you.

Part 1 sets the stage with an emphasis on education and career planning. Chapter 1 begins by tackling the question, "What exactly is a digital librarian?" as the concept can be tricky to define. In chapter 2, we discuss tailoring your graduate degree in library and information science to give you well-rounded exposure to the theoretical and practical aspects of the field, preparing you to enter the job market and hit the ground running. Once you're ready to go after that first job, chapter 3 will give you realistic and useful advice to assist you in the process. For those readers who aren't new to the library scene but are facing a shift to more digital-oriented responsibilities in their current job (or are actively seeking out a digital library-related position), chapter 4 offers perspectives on making a smooth transition. In chapter 5, we present advice on advancing your career once you've established a foothold in the field.

In part 2, we roll up our sleeves and dive into more in-depth discussions of specific concepts and scenarios you will encounter on the job. Chapter 6 gives an overview of the basic technology competencies that every digital librarian should have, from HTML to XML. Chapter 7 is devoted to the fine art of managing digital projects. Chapters 8 and 9 talk about metadata, an essential topic for all digital librarians, beginning with a basic introduction and continuing on to a more practice-based analysis. In chapter 10, the changing world of scholarly publishing and the digital librarian's role in it are explained in straightforward terms. Collaboration being a key feature of many digital projects in libraries, chapter 11 discusses best practices for making these partnerships a success. Finally, chapter 12 offers an introduction to digital preservation, a topic of increasing importance in the digital library community.

These subjects are the ones we consider to be essential to understanding and succeeding at digital librarianship. It's true that there are others we don't cover, or mention only briefly—for example, digital humanities or the semantic web. However, a grounding in the above basics will provide you with the foundation you need to move on to more complex, specialized topics and emerging technologies. This touches on another issue faced by the digital librarian (and truthfully, most people with an Internet connection): information overload. Keeping up with new trends and developments and engaging in continuous self-education is essential for our line of work, and doing so successfully is one of the most important skills a new digital librarian can learn. But achieving this goal efficiently can be a challenge—sign up for a few random library blogs and discussion lists, and you could easily spend hours a day following (or simply being distracted by) the most recent discussion threads. To help you effectively target your learning, we recommend the most useful and up-to-date resources you can use to pursue further education on your own.

Finally, this guide strives to provide you with an accurate assessment of career realities for the digital librarian, which you may not receive from library science programs or other literature about the profession. Particularly in the current economic climate, it behooves one to enter the field with a pragmatic view of the challenges that may be encountered on the road to career success. Embarking on your new path armed with a realistic understanding of the library job market, common stumbling blocks to project completion, and expectations you will face from employers, will help you proactively plan your career and avoid unpleasant surprises down the road.

With that said, digital librarianship offers many opportunities for career satisfaction and growth, and you will find few other professions that combine involvement in cutting-edge technology with the gratification of working for the public good. We hope this book will prove to be a valuable aid in your exploration of this exciting field, and wish you much success in jump-starting your career.

Jane D. Monson

PART 1

Planning Your Career

Chapter One

So You Want to Be a Digital Librarian—What Does That Mean?

Jim DelRosso and Cory Lampert

If you've been to library school, then you've probably heard of S. R. Ranganathan and his Five Laws of Library Science: (1) books are for use; (2) every reader his (or her) book; (3) every book its reader; (4) save the time of the reader; (5) the library is a growing organism (Ranganathan, 1931). Times change, technology advances, but those laws remain relevant. Books are still for use, whether they're made of wood pulp, or read on an e-reader, or even if the "book" is actually a journal article, a blog posting, a digital image, or a sound file. Someone has to step up to connect these resources with readers, not just in terms of subject matter but also in terms of format. There is a glut of information available now, and as Steve Kolowich (2011) writes, even the "digital natives" need help sorting through it all. Someone needs to be there to save them time, and especially to save the time of those who have only limited access to those resources.

Ranganathan's fifth law—"The library is a growing organism"—is what this chapter is really about. Access to information has increased in amazing ways in the past couple of decades, and that doesn't eliminate the need for librarians; it gives us even more room to do truly staggering things. In fact, it's this recent explosion of information that has given rise to the newest iteration of our profession: the digital librarian. If you're reading this book, then you either are one of this new breed, or you want to be—or you suspect that you *might* be, and you're thinking about changing what it says on your business card. This chapter will set the stage. We'll define what it means to be a digital librarian and discuss the mindset, resources, and challenges specific to the role, as well as the connections it has to traditional librarianship and what sets it apart from what's come before.

DEFINING "DIGITAL LIBRARIANSHIP"

Defining the term *digital librarian* is not as easy as it might initially appear. You can't simply say, "It's a librarian who works with digital products or provides digital services," because digital products and services are a nearly ubiquitous part of the job these days. To further complicate matters, the job title *digital librarian* is often spotted in close proximity to a similarly hard-to-define term: *digital library*. There is a whole body of literature concerned with the definition of digital libraries and the issues surrounding the concept, and we will allow you to explore this research area as your interest dictates. But to help define the scope for this book, let's consider the two terms. While *digital librarian* often refers to the person (an individual and their work), *digital library* does a better job of getting at the larger impact beyond the responsibilities of digital resources and their management, encompassing the philosophy and practice of digitization, the infrastructure (technical and organizational) around the digital library, the functions of the library itself, and the users that form the digital library community. Certainly digital libraries are repositories of digital content. And yet, they are so much more. Digital libraries provide rich value-added services around digital content, they foster communication and interaction, and ultimately they are tools that can facilitate the transformation of digital raw materials into new knowledge.

Digital libraries vary widely in design and topical focus. They may focus on archival materials, academic scholarship, or serve as a central search portal for electronic books. They may also aggregate resources on a specific topic or provide researchers very specialized information like multimedia resources (see the end of the chapter for a list of examples of different types of digital libraries). Digital librarians do work with digital libraries, but their work does not stop at a nicely defined boundary. Instead the lines are becoming increasingly blurred between libraries, information technology, physical spaces, and virtual communities. Here are just a few examples of the prevalence of digital interactions in libraries today:

- Reference librarians frequently have one—if not several—browser windows open during a reference interview, to either help patrons use digital resources or locate appropriate print resources. Increasingly, reference interviews transpire through digital media: chat, e-mail, or even text message.
- Similarly, instruction librarians' presentations, and the content thereof, are often produced or delivered in a digital format.

- Selectors and collection development librarians not only spend increasing portions of their budgets on electronic resources, they frequently research and purchase those materials online.
- Catalogers have worked on computers for decades, and even now debate adopting new metadata standards to better reflect an increasingly digital world of information.
- Subject specialists would be hard-pressed to truly earn that title without familiarity with the electronic resources in their field.
- Libraries themselves often represent patrons' best means of accessing the Internet, which requires further, practical expertise on the part of librarians.

These elements are not limited to any one type of library, but can be found in academic, special, public, and school libraries alike. With the work of librarians so pervaded by the digital, what sets a digital librarian apart from his or her peers? Luckily, there are some signs you can look for that will help you determine if you're a digital librarian. For example, you're probably a digital librarian if all or part of your job description simply wouldn't have existed prior to the digital information explosion of recent decades. It's also pretty telling when you're expected to be an expert in multiple areas of digital work, rather than only the one or two that happen to interact with the main part of your job description.

It's not particularly relevant if you need a computer to do your work—the truth is that many librarians find themselves with little to do if their Internet connectivity goes down (unless they've got a smartphone, of course.) What's more notable is if you find yourself taking point on digital projects: when it comes time to plan, design, implement, and manage the kinds of digital services we've discussed thus far, digital librarians tend to be on call. Within the library, your position may also be situated in the primary location where conversion of analog materials to digital, processing of born digital materials, or management of digital initiatives takes place. This doesn't mean you're all techie, per se; the amount of programming or coding ability possessed by digital librarians can vary. But a passing familiarity with those concerns goes a long way, and you will likely have to study such matters in library school. If this sounds like you, you might be a digital librarian. And if it sounds like what you want to be doing, then the chapter you're reading should help you get a better understanding of your future job.

If digital librarians take point on digital projects, and digital projects are now a ubiquitous part of library functions, that means digital librarians will often find themselves in positions of leadership, even if it might not be obvious from their job title. Digital librarians are increasingly the people charged with pulling organizations into the future (or, arguably, the present). This might be limited to a working group or department, or it might affect an entire library, or even library system. Digital librarians will often be called upon to research and plan new services and systems. This can involve focusing on creating new workflows and infrastructures to support these new offerings, or all too often, grafting these new duties onto their existing job description. That job description may contain all or some of what we've described here; it might be explicit about such duties, or leave them somewhat implicit and vague. It may be topped with a variety of titles, some of which say more about the specifics of the duties than others: digital projects librarian, digital initiatives librarian, digital collections coordinator, metadata librarian, digital archivist, digital preservationist, emerging technologies librarian, scholarly communications librarian, digital resources librarian . . . the list goes on and on.

What these positions have in common is that they revolve around technological means of sharing and storing information that didn't exist until relatively recently. They're the ones working to create communities whose members may or may not ever physically step into the library. They're the ones defining the word *librarian* for a generation of young patrons who grew up believing that all the world's knowledge was one Google search away.

Survey Says—Favorite Aspects of the Job

We asked the other chapter authors just what it was about being a digital librarian that they found most rewarding. Here are a few of their answers:

- Every day brings a new challenge
- Building respect, collaboration, and synergy with IT professionals
- Creativity and experimentation with technology is encouraged
- Collaboration and communication with diverse stakeholders
- Providing seamless online access to valuable content
- Problem-solving to get collections online
- Always learning, troubleshooting, adapting, and evolving

THE WORK OF THE DIGITAL LIBRARIAN: FUSING TRADITIONAL ROLES WITH TECHNOLOGY

You probably started thinking about library work with some vision of what you might do every day in your newly chosen career. Did this nascent vision include tasks like evaluating competing technology tools, gaining buy-in from diverse groups for large-scale library initiatives, conceptualizing and creating value-added online services and publications, or leading colleagues to embrace future-oriented user services? If so, congratulations—you are a visionary librarian and we can't wait to meet and work with you!

But if these weren't the things that immediately came to mind, never fear. Many of us share your experience. Many of us approached this field because we just plain enjoy being around the world of information (maybe you even have a strong fondness for actual, *print* books). In addition, some of us live for the challenge of seeking out answers, or relish ferreting out a hidden fact. You might be the creative type that likes to play around "making stuff" with all sorts of online tools and toys. Some of us get a thrill out of sorting chaos into order and great satisfaction from providing structure to the nearly limitless amount of information being produced. Or perhaps you are drawn to the service aspects of librarianship and feel compelled to serve others and build communities. You will be happy to hear that these aspects of the profession are alive and well, and more important than ever. The digital library has not done away with them; rather, these type of roles have expanded into fascinating new places: digital, virtual, learning, mobile, cloud, social, and personal are just some of the myriad spaces where digital librarians are pioneering new solutions. Challenges are an accepted part of the game, as additional spaces emerge and are defined only by what can be imagined.

In short, the traditional roles of librarianship remain at the core of the profession, with physical spaces and face-to-face interactions continuing to provide value to users. As a profession, we are all striving to take these shared goals out of the library and beyond it, to where users currently are—and where they want to be in the future, reinventing them along the way. In today's information ecosystem, digital librarians are often the ones keeping an eye on the horizon and helping to define the course to take. Let's begin by taking a moment to consider a few of our profession's fundamental information roles, and consider how technology and digital communication have redefined what the view looks like through the eyes, and from the desk, of today's digital librarian.

Traditionally, the definition of library science has reflected roles that librarians take in relationship to information. The *Online Dictionary of Library and Information*

Science defines library science in part as "the professional knowledge and skill with which recorded information is selected, acquired, organized, stored, maintained, retrieved, and disseminated to meet the needs of a specific clientele, usually taught at a professional library school" (Reitz, 2010). This definition still serves, but out in the real world the jargon associated with these tasks has most definitely changed (like hemlines and automobile colors, library initiatives experience an ebb and flow of trendiness). At the time of this writing, you can't walk through a library conference without hearing certain terms repeated over and over. One-stop, aggregated searching is referred to as "web-scale discovery." "Disruptive technology" is just another way of talking about innovation. "Transliteracy" is a term coined to cover new forms of multimedia communication initiatives; while models from the corporate world like LEAN and "value stream management" are applied to departments and "customers" in our libraries. Translating trends and seeking out the familiar information concept within them, as well as the "librarian skill set" behind them, is all in a day's work for a digital librarian. How? The digital librarian hones in on the information principle at hand (e.g., organization, dissemination, evaluation, etc.), identifies the problems or challenges that technology presents (e.g., retrieving relevant search results, delivering content to online users, or providing online tools to help users easily sort through a large amount of information to get to what they really want), and works to brainstorm innovative solutions.

And as you do that work, you will see that Ranganathan's underlying principles of librarianship that we alluded to back at the start of this chapter—and that were more recently updated for the Web by Alireza Noruzi (2004) and for media by Carol Simpson (2008)—stand the test of time. The sensibility stays constant, with the execution evolving over time. So what does this evolution look like on the ground? Here are just a few examples of how the familiar roles of the print world librarian are being adapted to meet new and emerging needs of the profession. Every one of these "digital challenges" can be mapped to a previous tenet of librarianship. It is the vision and the creativity of librarians like you—librarians who have taken up this new role—that has defined new structures and workflows in the field of digital librarianship.

Selection (Collection Development/Management) has evolved to include selection for what should be digitized and how it should be presented online.

Acquisition (Materials Ordering and Receiving) still exists, but deals more and more with born digital items or the processing of collections for digital conversion.

Organization (Cataloging/Technical Services) and its traditions of managing information have morphed into the vibrant new field of metadata, with emerging standards that better meet the needs of authority control and access in the online environment.

Storage, Maintenance, and Dissemination (Systems and Library Technology), including the housing, shelving, maintenance, and circulation of materials, has moved past the stacks, self-check station, and electronic document delivery to more and more instant, full-text access. Sometimes this on-demand, online, global access is provided via subscription. Other times, the information is free to anyone with an Internet connection and working software to view it, and is made possible through digitization initiatives. Librarians have become key participants in the development and deployment of these systems. They may conceptualize a system and build it in-house, or purchase a vendor-provided system. Either way, digital librarians are critical partners in successful information provision via technology systems.

Evaluation and Assessment are natural extensions of collection maintenance, and take the work beyond periodic weeding of print materials to a larger realm of continuous improvement and ongoing assessment. More and more often this involves the upkeep and refreshing of a website or upgrades and enhancements to software packages.

Beyond traditional reference (Public Services—including the online public), the digital librarian is poised to provide all sorts of innovative user services such as social media, mobile interactions, and creation of digital publishing products that contain value-added packaging (learning objects attached to digitized primary materials, new features like user tagging for a scholarly communications repository, etc.).

As digital content grows exponentially, conservation of books and printed materials (Preservation and Conservation/Special Collection and Archives) has evolved into the challenging world of digital preservation. Data migration, format and technology obsolescence, and many other preservation problems present critical issues for the sustained access and stewardship of digital collections.

All this change and evolution has left some libraries (and not a few administrators) struggling to play catch-up to refresh strategic plans, define new positions, and hire qualified staff. Pity the new graduate sifting through an RSS feed of job ads, trying to decipher just what is expected of the incumbent in these positions. Question the search committee doing the hiring, and you may receive more than one answer. Checking with the supervisor can be enlightening, but use caution, because the vision of the dean or director may go in a totally different direction. Often, it will be up to you (yes, the librarian who just arrived on site) to define the role and, whatever it is, make it work!

Digital librarian positions can be found in all varieties of cultural heritage institutions (museums, libraries, historical societies, government, etc.). Within the organization chart, they may fall under an umbrella emphasizing the "digital" part, say in the technology division. Or they may fall under the content owners in the library and be positioned in archives and special collections. Sometimes intellectual control is the focus, and digital librarians are found within technical services. Other times, digital librarians are firmly situated in user or public services departments. Basically, pick an organization chart, close your eyes and point—the position could be in almost any functional area.

There isn't one blueprint for the digital librarian seeking employment (see chapter 3 for a more detailed discussion of the job market), so one of the most important competencies a candidate brings to the interview is a demonstrated ability to keep up on trends in the field, know the jargon, and intelligently define expectations. It will be up to you to determine what success looks like to the people paying your salary. Above all, remember to exhibit a sense of adventure, be an active participant in defining your role, and don't get too comfortable, because the only thing that is certain in this profession is that it's certain to change.

RIDING THE CURRENT: DIGITAL LIBRARIANS AND TECHNOLOGY

Discussing technology in the context of digital librarianship is almost as difficult as defining digital librarians in the first place, and not for dissimilar reasons. Technology is, as we've mentioned, a fundamental part of defining what a digital librarian is; it's even baked into the term itself. But as Lankes (2011) notes, technology is moving fast enough that anything we write about it can become outdated very quickly. The programs and applications you use today can—and often will—be replaced or updated beyond recognition just as you start to get comfortable with them.

But that turbocharged obsolescence should not be denied, or seen as a bug to be worked around. It defines digital librarian skill sets far more than any given technology could. What's vital to being a digital librarian is your *attitude* toward technology, rather than your mastery of any given one. So that's what we're going to discuss here. But, being realists, we'll also discuss several areas of technology that you'll want to have a handle on for any job interviews or discussions with your boss that may happen within a year or so of publication.

Bill LeFurgy wrote an excellent blog post on this topic for *The Signal*, the digital preservation blog of the Library of Congress, entitled "What Skills Does a Digital Archivist or Librarian Need?" We recommend reading it in its entirety, but here's one key passage:

> Archives and libraries depend ever more on technology-driven systems to accomplish their mission, and those systems are ever evolving. Staff with an eagerness to help refine how things are done are especially prized. Deep technical expertise is optional here. The most important thing is a basic understanding of how the different system parts—both automated and manual—contribute to doing the job at hand. (LeFurgy, 2011)

You should be looking for and trying to develop this in yourself in order to be an effective digital librarian. As we said earlier, the digital pervades every aspect of library work. In addition to looking for new things we can do for our patrons, we also need to look at how we can do what we're doing better. Technology helps with that; you need to choose the right tech, and implement it.

Of course, determining which technologies are the right ones will also fall into your job description; at the very least, you'll be called on to make recommendations, either on your own or as part of a committee. Even without the obsolescence issue, we'd be out of line in calling out specific technologies here, because while we can talk about the work to some extent, we can't talk about your communities. To quote Lankes again, "The mission of librarians is to improve society through facilitating knowledge creation in their communities" (2011). That statement forms the backbone to his book *The Atlas of New Librarianship*, and while you might quibble with some elements, the dedication to community is one that you should take to heart. You need to look to the constituencies you serve to determine the best technologies to implement at your library. And while we're not going to try to dictate the specific technologies you need to look at, there are some areas that you're likely going to need to know about if you're pursuing these jobs in the next few years.

The Care and Feeding of Digital Objects

As Google continues its knock-down, drag-out fight with publishers over the digitization of millions of library-held books and Amazon tries to sell folks on their Kindle Lending Library, libraries are trying to figure out how to handle digital objects, and turning to digital librarians to come up with a plan. There's so much going on in this area that we're going to resort to bullet points and let the folks writing the rest of this book flesh out the details.

Electronic journals: They keep getting more expensive, the publishers keep bundling more and more together to make sure you have to buy a ton of them, and if you stop paying you generally don't get to keep anything. Plus, especially in an academic setting, your patrons will *expect* you to provide them. Which is unsurprising, because as anyone who's tried to do a literature review in the last two decades can tell you, they actually *are* that useful.

E-books: No one knows how e-books and libraries are going to work together in the years to come. You've got publishers testing libraries' reactions to desperate measures to preserve a revenue stream, e-reader producers vying for library business, and libraries finding few allies when it comes to taking advantage of the ways in which e-books remove the physical limitations of hard copy. And it's going to fall to you to ensure that when a patron wants to read about the romantic adventures of vampires and werewolves on a screen instead of a page, they can do so without a hassle.

Digital collections and repositories: If you aren't already engaged in the conversion of physical collections to digital (and all the project management, metadata knowledge, and technical expertise that entails), chances are good that someday, someone will bring you a big batch of digital objects that have been created or inherited by your library and tell you to "do something" with it. It might be a collection of digital images or documents; it might be accessible online or it might be living on a dark server in a basement; it might represent the scholarly output of a university or it might be scanned letters from a donor who died in 1953. But if it says "digital librarian" on your business card, you're probably the one who's going to figure out how best to deal with it.

Digital preservation: Finally, once you have this stuff, you're going to need to figure out how to keep it safe. (Assuming you *do* actually have it; for electronic journals and books you probably won't have a copy you keep on a server locally; this doesn't absolve you of responsibility for its safety, it just means you'll have to make sure whoever you're licensing it from is doing the job right.) There are many tools out there for handling this issue, but many of them will involve working with vendors or setting up partnerships with other institutions to ensure that if something happens to the aforementioned basement server, all those digital objects aren't lost forever. See chapter 12 for further discussion of these issues.

Social Media

This one's been on librarians' minds for quite a while now, and while former giants of the field have fallen (MySpace, Friendster), others have managed to not just survive but also thrive long after their foretold deaths (Twitter, Facebook). We've even seen new contenders like Google+ arrive and make major inroads. While initial studies indicated that patrons weren't interested in the library invading social media spaces like Facebook (De Rosa et al., 2007), more recent insights—from members of the patron groups themselves—have indicated a possible change in attitude (Gagliardi, 2011). And that's not even touching on the importance of social media to modern library networking, especially among those librarians who deal with digital projects. The authors have witnessed Twitter handles scrawled onto conference badges and business cards, and hashtags have become important parts of conference branding and discussion. And that's not even getting to those archaic forms of social media like blogs, which have been reported dead for years and yet still somehow not only persist, but seem to be a major avenue for modern librarians to communicate their thoughts to their peers.

Of course, there are also many collaborative technologies that skirt the edge of social media, allowing librarians and their patrons to work together on written documents, images, and multimedia works. We discuss collaboration more elsewhere in this chapter, but we'd be remiss if we wrote about social media and failed to acknowledge how many of the collaborative tools you'll want to be familiar with—for yourself, your colleagues, and your patrons—are now a part of the larger social media and networking world. As we're increasingly called on to work with colleagues far removed geographically, tools like Google Docs and Dropbox become more and more a part of our day-to-day work. In short: try to keep abreast of the big players in social media, dip your toes in yourself, and be ready to use them to discuss library issues and communicate with your patrons and peers.

Mobile Apps

Recent reports from the Pew Internet & American Life Project (Smith, 2011) indicate that a third of American adults now own a smartphone, and two-thirds of *those* folks use that phone to access the Internet or e-mail every day. As we noted above, that's far from universal, but it's still too large a constituency to ignore; some even speculate that smartphone adoption may someday bridge the oft-discussed digital divide (Hood, 2011). What this means for you is that in many job situations, you're going to be expected to have some handle on mobile technologies: what's out there, what tends to see use, and how your library can incorporate it. Or, to put those elements together in a more pragmatic way, you need to be able to figure out how to incorporate your library into how your patrons use mobile tech.

Again, this is about knowing your community, and being flexible. Throwing QR codes—those small, square bar codes which you may have seen folks scanning with their smartphones—onto your stacks won't do any good unless you know what information your patrons want to be able to get out of their mobile device while they're standing in your stacks. Having librarians ready and waiting for texted reference questions only works if patrons know about that service and actually find it helpful. And looking beyond the question of what to offer, there's the issue of *how* to offer it. Do you build an app? For which platforms? Maybe just create a mobile version of your website? Or is it easier to just make sure your website works on mobile devices? You may not be the one writing the apps or coding the websites, but you should be prepared to talk about mobile delivery.

Assessment

Assessment is another term that's getting a lot of attention in libraries these days, and not without cause. The notion that we should be analyzing how well we do the things we do is a strong one as budgets, payrolls, and hours are cut in many libraries. This enters the digital librarian's purview in two ways: (1) using digital tools to assess library services, and (2) the assessment of digital services. In the first case, you may be called upon to help librarians decide which tools will best allow them to assess their impact on patrons without unduly undermining their ability to work. You'll need to advise them on whether to use web-based tools, something installed only on certain computers, or maybe even a mobile app. (Be careful of recommendations which assume that everyone at your library owns a smartphone unless you're also recommending that your library *buy everybody a smartphone.*)

And when you're doing your own digital projects, you'll be called upon to assess their impact as well. Many licensed products will come with their own assessment modules; you'll need to be able to analyze them and see if they'll do a good enough job, and often find ways to supplement them. If you're building something in-house, then you'll have the freedom to create your own assessment modules, but also the responsibility to do so. There are also tools available that you can apply to many digital products, such as Google Analytics and Survey Monkey. But despite the ability to grab information on hits and views and unique visits, even web-based projects should be evaluated by opening up a conversation directly with their users. We may know the site received lots of page views, but just because a user got to the information doesn't mean that it had an impact on their research, and stats don't say much about how information is being used. We can (and should) be asking if we are providing the right digital information to users such that they can use it in a meaningful way. There are digital tools that can help with this goal. Don't eschew them just because their results are harder to throw into a graph. In the end, it all comes down to communicating the value of libraries, and as a digital librarian you will have lots of evidence of value. Just don't assume people see it, be ready to craft a message, and don't hesitate to advocate for it.

FINDING YOUR INNER LEADER: A FEW THOUGHTS ABOUT COLLABORATION

So, technology is cool. It is! And with a well-developed sense of curiosity and the help of some social networks, user groups, technical software documentation, and a sandbox to play in, many of the skills required to implement digital projects can be learned on the job. But that won't get you all the way. In the library world, there is nothing more valuable (and nothing more difficult to teach) than the interpersonal skills that contribute to successful collaboration. Digital librarians absolutely must cultivate these skills and seek to continuously develop and hone them, if they are to be effective in their positions.

Most digital librarians are in the middle of a maelstrom of activity: scanning, software management, content selection, web design, publicity, outreach, usability testing, technical troubleshooting, committee service appointments . . . oh, and presenting and publishing to boot, if you have a job in an academic library and want to keep it. So, to stay sane and keep the projects moving, the savvy digital librarian has to develop and cultivate an individual toolbox equipped with technical proficiencies, problem-solving skills, all that theory you learned in library school, and the practical ability to "learn everything that you are supposed to know as soon as someone identifies that you are one who should know it" (i.e., copyright law, how to use the new content management system, managing the student workers and volunteers scanning the collections, designing press materials, and so forth).

What is often overlooked is that these are *not* the skills that are fundamental to collaboration. What really matters when running an effective team is leadership and all the "soft skills" that go along with it. It doesn't help to have a fantastic digital librarian who can program in ten languages or knows fifteen metadata standards, because if the local museum whose collections you are digitizing ends up feeling marginalized and bulldozed after a huge political gaffe during a grant project, you've blown a huge opportunity. Navigating the hidden pitfalls of group dynamics, sensing the best messaging to use in the right situation, and using the powers of gentle persuasion to keep a project within a timeline without creating enemies, are all skills they don't teach in library school and have rarely figured out how to package for on-the-job training. You just have to dive in and figure it out. This is not to say we haven't all made our mistakes along the way. We have, and we're happy to share our stories. Regardless, it is essential that digital librarians figure out a healthy way to learn from their mistakes so that they can build a reputation as a dependable, trustworthy, and competent colleague; a colleague that excels in the areas of collaboration and leadership.

It's true that there are probably colleagues in our organizations that don't have a clue how much value digital librarians bring to the table when it comes to group decision-making and gaining consensus. Often, we are thought of as "behind the scenes" or "techie" or "that person that scans all that cool stuff we put online." Sadly, even some of our more forward-thinking colleagues may just frown and shrug when asked what a digital librarian "does." But we owe it to ourselves to promote ourselves and our specialized skills. We get stuff done, often on a tight timeline and across departmental, campus, or regional boundaries. We manage diverse staff personalities and translate complex technical concepts. We see the big picture and handle the details. As a by-product of these skills, we can be some of the best people in the library to have on a committee (so learn to say "no" or risk becoming overcommitted!). Digital librarians work in a hybrid world that, to many, is the future of librarianship. So don't be afraid to embrace the future and straddle the boundaries. It isn't always easy being a pioneer, but the view can be pretty rewarding.

FUTURE DIRECTIONS

One of the most rewarding aspects of this type of work is that you get to spend time imagining what might be coming next. Sometimes you feel as if your job isn't really all that far from a juicy science fiction novel and you actually get *paid* to ponder the role libraries will have in this future. Granted, libraries aren't the fastest-moving organisms, but as a digital librarian, you will be one of the people who are expected to be conversant with future trends and you should always have a mental list at the ready. You never know when a donor or administrator might ask, "So what's on the horizon that I should care about?" Knock their socks off, digital librarian!

Here are just a few trends to be excited about in the future:

- Digital curation and preservation
- User-generated content and greater interactivity
- New metadata standards and schemas to leverage data
- Mass digitization and aggregation of content
- New interfaces (3D, surface computing, mobile devices)
- The semantic web

What are some of the trends that excite you? If you can conceptualize it, communicate it, and commit to its value, than you have what it takes to join the ranks of digital librarians everywhere who are building a dynamic future for our profession.

FINAL THOUGHTS

We've tried to give you the basics in this chapter. We hope we've placed digital librarianship into the proper context relative to the profession as a whole, given you some food for thought about what digital librarianship actually looks like, and touched on two areas that help define this type of work (technology and leadership). We hope we may have piqued your interest with some examples

Survey Says—Future Trends

We've surveyed the authors of this book and asked them, "What future opportunities in digital librarianship are *you* most excited about?" Here are some of their responses:

- Digital librarianship and digital curation merging and blending
- Ways that technology is initiating change in the field of librarianship
- Collaboration and development of partnerships to move initiatives forward
- Working with linked data; semantic web technologies
- Improving user experiences in the digital environment
- Improved scanners and software for digitization activities
- Innovative delivery of digital content
- Increased access to rich, unique digital research content

of future directions and augmented these lofty ideas with insights from some of today's digital librarians.

The world is changing, and we leave you with some thoughts about navigating this future, from Lankes (2011): "Librarians have not only an opportunity, but an obligation to find their center and the means to continue a centuries-long mission to use knowledge to better understand the past, make a better today, and invent an ideal future." If you can connect to the traditions of librarianship, bring energy to the digital initiatives of today's libraries, and aren't afraid of embracing (and creating) tomorrow's information services, then digital librarianship may be for you.

REFERENCES

De Rosa et al., 2007. *Sharing, Privacy and Trust in Our Networked World: A Report to the OCLC Membership*. Dublin, OH: Online Computer Library Center. www.oclc.org/reports/sharing/.

Gagliardi, Kelsey. 2011. "How to Use Social Media to Engage Students". Project paper, University of California at Santa Barbara. https://docs.google.com/document/d/1dvxlOmQUm9j20r8tuf1oRMlfq-1P5-DszvJC0u9Agug/edit?hl=en_US.

Hood, Lucy. 2011. "Smartphones Are Bridging the Digital Divide: Minorities Are Accessing the Internet Through Cheap, Prepaid Wireless Data Plans." *Wall Street*

Journal Online, August 29. http://online.wsj.com/article/SB10001424053111903327904576526732908837822.html.

Kolowich, Steve. 2011. "What Students Don't Know." *News Blog. Inside Higher Ed*, August 22. www.insidehighered.com/news/2011/08/22/erial_study_of_student_research_habits_at_illinois_university_libraries_reveals_alarmingly_poor_information_literacy_and_skills.

Lankes, R. David. 2011. *The Atlas of New Librarianship*. Cambridge, MA: MIT Press.

LeFurgy, Bill. 2011. "What Skills Does a Digital Archivist or Librarian Need?" *The Signal: Digital Preservation* (blog). July 13. http://blogs.loc.gov/digitalpreservation/2011/07/what-skills-does-a-digital-archivist-or-librarian-need/.

Noruzi, Alireza. 2004. "Application of Ranganathan's Laws to the Web." *Webology* 1, no. 2. www.webology.org/2004/v1n2/a8.html.

Ranganathan, S. R. 1931. *The Five Laws of Library Science*. London: Edward Goldston. http://babel.hathitrust.org/cgi/pt?id=uc1.b99721.

Reitz, J. M. 2010. *Online Dictionary for Library and Information Science*. "Library Science." ABC-CLIO. Last modified March 9. www.abc-clio.com/ODLIS/odlis_l.aspx.

Simpson, Carol. 2008. "Five Laws." *Library Media Connection* 26, no. 7: 6.

Smith, Aaron. 2011. *Smartphone Adoption and Usage*. Washington, DC: Pew Research Center. www.pewinternet.org/Reports/2011/Smartphones.aspx.

EXAMPLES OF DIGITAL LIBRARIES

World Digital Library: www.wdl.org/en/

Internet Archive: www.archive.org

Mountain West Digital Library: http://mwdl.org/

California Digital Library: www.cdlib.org/

Nevada Digital Collections Portal: http://omeka.library.unlv.edu/omeka/

eCommons@Cornell: http://ecommons.cornell.edu/

DigitalCommons@ILR: http://digitalcommons.ilr.cornell.edu/

Civil Rights Digital Library: http://crdl.usg.edu/?Welcome

International Children's Digital Library: http://en.childrenslibrary.org

Project Gutenberg: www.gutenberg.org/

Western Soundscape Archive: http://westernsoundscape.org/

Chapter Two

Getting the Most Out of Library School

Micah Vandegrift and Annie Pho

If you're reading this, you've either made it to library school or you're considering applying. For those who have already begun, you're probably wondering why no one has mentioned much about books yet. There may be some chatter about the differences between information and data, literacy (or if you're at a progressive LIS program, transliteracy), and the elusive skill set that somehow surrounds cataloging and metadata. The actual work and definition of librarianship is expanding as quickly as the Internet itself, which has come to define much of our lives, and the profession increasingly interfaces and connects with digital topics. From public libraries to archives, the skills necessary to serve today's and tomorrow's patrons are becoming intermeshed with an expansive level of digital knowledge. The world of digital libraries matters to students of all stripes, and we're here to offer some advice on developing a digital skill set as a student.

In this chapter, we offer some practical tips on how to approach graduate school in library and information science as a nascent digital librarian. These strategies include creating your own specialty within your program, connecting with others through online and traditional venues, constantly surveying the job landscape, putting in work through part-time jobs, practicums, and internships, and engaging with related fields outside of librarianship. We'll discuss everything from choosing relevant coursework and finding places and methods to connect with colleagues and professionals, to crafting an Internet curation strategy that can effectively give you a head start on becoming an indispensable digital expert.

CREATE YOUR OWN SPECIALTY

Digital libraries require a professional skill set that is becoming increasingly necessary in the field of librarianship overall, and as such more library schools are starting to offer digitally focused coursework. Some schools offer a digital libraries specialization or graduate certificate, which can enrich and expand your basic library and information science degree. The best-case scenario for growing into digital librarianship is to follow a prescribed digital libraries track. However, perhaps your school is lagging in this area, or the course offerings are slim, with no digital specialization. Unfortunately (and this is a basic Library School 101 tip), *your program may not offer classes that will teach you everything that you need or want to know.*

A fundamental concept for the developing digital librarian, and a good professional practice overall, is Do It Yourself (DIY), meaning take the initiative. Are you finding yourself in a program that has less than stellar digital options? Not satisfied with basic HTML and CSS? The first order of business for getting the most out of library school is to create your own specialty. This can be as extensive as teaching yourself hand-coding in your downtime or as simple as reading articles from *D-Lib Magazine* (an essential digital libraries resource) to expand your understanding of digital projects. But it is imperative as an LIS student that you dig deep and get out of the degree what you went into it for, with or without the coursework or certificate.

The field of librarianship is truly interdisciplinary and can include many different areas of study, like linguistics, sociology, education, and computer science. As a result, the courses that are offered as part of the degree have to cover a lot of different bases. You might be wondering why you are required to take a management class, or why you are studying collection development and reference when a lot of resources are moving online. However, many of these subjects tie in nicely to digital libraries, and many "traditional" library skills still apply. For instance, the main job functions of a digital librarian might entail managing digital projects and initiatives, managing technology (i.e., website creation, digitization and conversion of analog materials), processing information (metadata creation, information retrieval), collection development, and other duties, which might be a combination of roles ranging from reference to instruction (Choi and Rasmussen, 2006). Tailoring the program to your own interests can be a great way to synthesize a range of skills from a variety of disciplines into a coherent track.

Approaching your curriculum with the DIY mentality allows for creativity and professional exploration, which can greatly enhance your comprehension of a subject. A practical tip on how to create your own digital specialty is to cheat off someone else's paper (figuratively, of course). Take a look at a school that has a well-established and interesting digital program and use that as a base for your self-directed program. You can and should take any class that relates to digital media, especially classes that seem progressive (like digital curation) or particularly interesting to you. Related topics to search for in a course catalog might include information architecture, markup or programming languages (XML, HTML, CSS, PHP), database design, digital humanities, human/computer interaction, metadata, information technology, digital media (working with audio/visual materials), scholarly communication, the semantic web, or digital preservation. Like it or not you only have about two years of coursework, and spending time crafting your schedule to meet your interests and professional needs will go a long way. True to the interdisciplinary nature of the field, it may be an option to do coursework in related departments—communications, media, business, computer science, and even traditional disciplines like English, history, and art history are worth exploring for developing a well-rounded, DIY library degree program. Some schools even offer dual-degree programs, allowing you to get your MLS in addition to another master's degree in one of these traditional disciplines. Don't worry too much if you can't take a class directly on any of these given subjects, because the information is out there. The key is to develop a familiarity with the ideas and topics associated with and related to digital librarianship, and pursue some independent study to get comfortable with them.

It is ideal to take a holistic approach when building a digital specialty where none exists, aiming for classes that cover a range of skills and provide a sound understanding of what libraries do with information—the why and how. Praxis and theory will be your best friends in library school, and balancing them between digital and non-digital projects will be a constant consideration. For instance, the very idea of a digital collection can spur philosophical consideration. When you get behind the theory of it, one function of a digital librarian is to take an object that exists in real space (like a text) and convert it into a completely different format (a digital scan) that separates the object from its original context. Without that context the object can lose its meaning, so it's important as a digital librarian-in-training that you understand the theory of representing information and objects and everything else that goes with it. Developing a theoretical knowledge of information objects, which one can and should get out of any library science program, will be valuable in application to digital work. This cognitive skill goes beyond learning how to code or doing digital reference, although those are excellent skills to have too, and is a good example of one tool in the digital librarian's skill set. The most

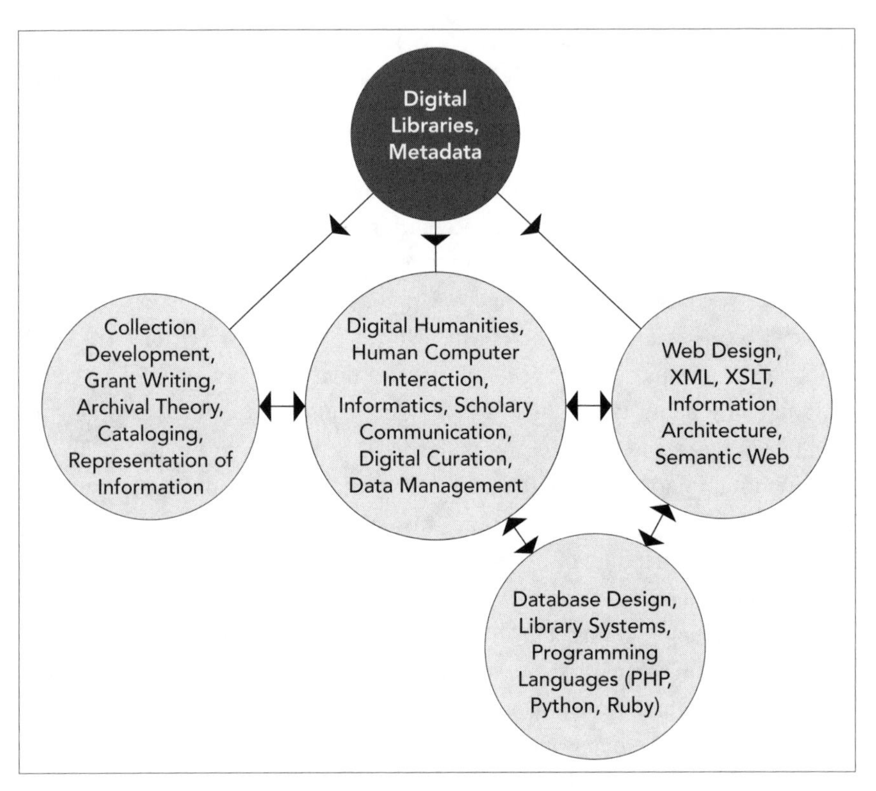

FIGURE 2.1
Recommended Coursework

important thing to remember while in school is that this is the time for you to truly create your own specialty and explore all the corners of librarianship through the digital lens.

Figure 2.1 illustrates some related topics that a digital librarian-in-training should explore. Some schools offer courses or workshops in these areas; however, you can always study them on your own.

CONNECT DEEP AND WIDE

After building your own path through the MLS degree, another skill that will play a major role in your development as a digital librarian is networking. Not

Anecdotal Evidence—Micah

I entered my MLS program knowing that I wasn't particularly a "book person," and that I was generally interested in archives/special collections/museum studies. There were a few loosely defined "tracks" that students could follow, but none of those struck my fancy. So, coming from an interdisciplinary humanities background, I decided to make up my own track. After taking a digital media concepts and production course my first semester, I knew my future would be digitally inclined and geared the rest of my studies to be as technologically focused as the curriculum would allow. I signed up for coursework in information architecture, information technology, and digital libraries.

Outside of the classroom I started to blog, explored new digital tools, developed an online portfolio, interned at a public library web applications department and with a major technology blog, started engaging in ongoing conversations in digital humanities circles, and more. The bulk of the work that has prepared me best for digital librarianship was what I did to supplement my courses. Creating my own specialty and path through the MLS program allowed me to learn what I wanted to, and that made the experience all the more enjoyable and valuable.

system administration, computer science-type networking, but the "get-out-and-meet-and-chat-with-people" type of networking. Students often have the unique opportunity to do a lot of this in the classroom with peers, which is a great way to begin. However, developing contacts outside your school and program, especially in the digital library world, is an excellent way to get your face (or digital avatar) recognized as an up-and-coming colleague. It's crucial as a student that you start making connections with people working in the field. This will go a long way toward keeping you in the loop with new trends and ideas, and also potential job prospects—which is what this is really all about, right?

Networking In Real Life

As important as it is to connect with people outside of your immediate peer group, there is a lot of potential for developing your networking skills by working in your local community. To borrow a colloquial phrase, "think globally, act locally."

There is a good possibility the information institutions in your area are either exploring new digital directions, or have considered it and don't know where to start. In fact, securing an internship, practicum, or volunteer opportunity has a twofold return: first, you get to meet people and network, and second, you gain valuable work experience that is fundamental to getting started in a career. A wise way of approaching volunteer and internship options is with the ultimate goal of strengthening your own digital skill set, while assisting your local library, archive, or museum with a project. This could be as simple as walking into the local historical society and asking if they are digitizing records or documents, or heading to the library and offering to teach Facebook 101. Developing good relationships with directors or supervisors, while getting a chance to work with digital content, is a networking must-do.

Take a look at some of the projects that are happening in your area. If there is a faculty member in your program whose interest lies in digital libraries, talk to them about how to get more involved or ask about what types of resources to look into. Librarians are a pretty friendly group of people who are usually more than willing to talk to a student about what they do. More often than not, libraries are understaffed and need help with projects, which is quite beneficial for a library school student. That could provide you a chance to get in there and get some hands-on experience, which is always the best way to learn, all while making the acquaintance of hiring managers, other professionals, and possible future coworkers.

As an extension of networking in your immediate areas of influence (the classroom, your local community), there are plenty of options for developing contacts, mentors, and colleagues by utilizing existing professional organizational structures. You may have heard of the gigantic organization that is the American Library Association. Attending a conference like the ALA Annual or one organized by your state library association, while guaranteed to be overwhelming to a newbie, can be one of the absolute best ways to develop some networking chops. We highly recommend looking into the ALA New Members Round Table, and the ALA Student to Staff program, both of which are designed to help ease you into the professional conference circuit. Fortunately, ALA is broken down into several major divisions and it's likely you can find a more manageable group to connect with by joining one such as LITA, the Library and Information Technology Association. Within LITA, the Digital Libraries Technology Interest Group is a good place to start connecting with like-minded folks. Getting out there, smiling and chatting with fellow classmates, internship coordinators, and conference attendees is a critical step to making good use of easy opportunities to grow into librarianship, digital or otherwise.

Networking Online

As a student with interests in the digital world, it is probably a given that you will be online for a large percentage of your time in school. If you're not plugged into the virtual digital library community at this point in your academic career, it's not too late. You can learn a lot just by interacting with other professionals and students who have similar interests, and the bigger your network, the more you have to gain from it. Meaning, get used to hanging around on the Internet because it will be your best friend: digital work is done 99 percent online. You must be comfortable and competent in that space. The good news? Collegiality in online social networks, especially when you get connected to the right communities, is overwhelmingly positive and helpful at its core. Potentially some of the best and most valuable connections you can make will be online, with other digitally minded information professionals. Beginning to reach out in those spaces early is an easy way to explore the field of digital librarianship, while at the same time gaining some professional colleagues.

Aside from official venues for connecting online, like ALA-based websites, this book wouldn't be worth its two cents if we failed to mention the myriad informal networks that can be of incredible value to LIS students. Social media have a reputation for being time wasters, but there are ways to utilize them to make networking less awkward. Some social media tools, like Twitter or LinkedIn, are better geared for professional networking than others. We're not really here to tell you how to manage your online life, but it's good to be aware that the Internet is a wonderful, easy, and free way to begin to connect to digital librarians who may have your dream job, and learn about their work. Here are a few suggestions you may want to look into:

Twitter: An easy way to get a head start on Twitter is to find a good list (a group of people someone else has taken the time to organize around a particular topic or theme) and follow it. Suggestions: Dan Cohen's Digital Humanities list, Kate Theimer's Archivists on Twitter list, and Micah Vandegrift's (your humble author!) Library, Archive, Museum list.

LinkedIn: A social media network that is designated for professional networking—what could be better? There are some excellent library-related discussion groups here that you can join. The LIS Career Options group, led and sponsored by Kim Dority, an information professions consultant, is very useful for exploring alternative career options.

Blogs: Utilizing blogs via RSS is another easy way to keep a finger on the pulse of the field and start to connect with digital librarians online. The blog of the National Digital Information Infrastructure and Preservation Program, the digital preservation branch of the Library of Congress, is highly recommended.

Electronic discussion lists/Google Groups: While a discussion list (a subscription to an e-mail list) may seem kind of old fashioned in the age of "real-time, always on" communication tools, they still serve a purpose for disseminating calls for papers, conference announcements, and enlightening conversation. Subscribing to a library-related Google Group is another good way to keep up with specific communities or topics of interest. Two suggestions: the Digital Public Library of America discussion list is especially active as it is developing, and the Linked Open Data in Libraries, Archives and Museums Google Group explores a growing area of interest for digital librarians.

Anecdotal Evidence—Annie

My foray into digital libraries was truly accidental, beginning with a discussion I had with an acquaintance who had recently become a volunteer coordinator at the Internet Archive. When I told her that I wanted to go into library science, she informed me that she had just put an ad out calling for scanning volunteers. I had previously worked in libraries as a circulation assistant and as a cataloging assistant, and knew nothing about the Internet Archive or what a scanning volunteer would do. But I was intrigued and decided to follow up on it. My time volunteering there taught me a lot about digital libraries, and gave me experience that helped me secure a part-time job working with digital collections once I enrolled in library school.

When I first started my program, I didn't really understand the power of networking. After attending my first ALA conference, I completely understood how much leveraging social media to make connections with librarians and information professionals mattered. It made the transition from interacting with people's avatars online to talking to them in real life so much easier. Networking through social media is free and can be a low-pressure way to make those connections. You never know what you can learn just by chatting with someone, and I've found out about so many great opportunities that way. Building connections with people is absolutely important for your success in the field.

See the end of this chapter for more resources worth exploring, both online and off.

The bottom line is, you've got to spend some time connecting with people in the field if you want to get up to date or ahead of the curve in the profession. Pull from the things that you've been studying that interest you. Scope out the names of people who are doing cool stuff. Are they presenting at a conference? Go if you can and chat them up! Have a question about digital libraries? Tweet your question! You're going to learn a lot just by talking to people who are out there doing the work. Who knows, maybe shadowing someone at his or her job can lead to something more. *Most importantly, connecting means putting yourself out there.* Be eager and interested, and professionals and colleagues will be happy to have you around, help you along, and offer support when you need it. Professional connections are a two-way street. Provide value to others, and they will reciprocate.

SURVEY THE LANDSCAPE EARLY AND OFTEN

If you are a library school student or just someone interested in digital librarianship, you may find all this information to be overwhelming. So far, you've probably had a lot of new things thrown at you, from job names or titles, duties, acronyms, names of organizations, theories, concepts, and more. In this section we'd like to introduce a simple idea that should help quell the fire hose of information that you are likely to contend with: utilize web tools to organize incoming information, and check on them often. Staying abreast of new developments in digital technologies (library- and non-library-related) will help you keep your finger on the pulse of the field, which is especially important for a student who will need to articulate this knowledge in coursework and job interviews. Fortunately, there are many constantly evolving tricks, like harnessing RSS feeds and Twitter, to assist you in staying "in the know." None of these suggestions are particularly new, but their value cannot be overestimated, and taking the time to put your personal digital information curation strategy into place will help keep you on the cutting edge of digital librarianship.

Strategies for Managing Information Overload

We are living in the "Information Age," and there is no lack of knowledge out there available to anyone with an Internet connection. The first step to separate the information wheat from the chaff is to find a niche, like digital librarianship. Utilize your coursework, professional or social networks, and supervisors or professors for suggestions or recommendations on blogs and websites of interest. Once you have a list of sites to follow, you can make sure you're getting the latest updates by using an RSS feed to pipe all the updates right to your feed reader of choice. If you have a Google account, you have an RSS reader, and there are many other free ones out there as well. Having an RSS reader set up with good incoming information related to the topic you are interested in, in this case digital libraries, means at any time you can look in on your RSS feeds and have a bird's-eye view of current events, new ideas, and general discussions.

Another tool you can use to track what you read on the Web is a bookmarking site like Delicious, Diigo, or Pinboard. The utility of sites like these, often constructed on folksonomies or social "tagging" systems, is that not only are you able to save and organize things you discover on the Web, but you can explore tags to see what others are reading and saving. Keeping track of links to articles of interest is a good way to utilize web 2.0 tools for the goal of developing a skill and staying current in the field. If you haven't already done so, the other tool you might consider taking up is blogging. Blogs are a great way to organize your thoughts and reflect on the things you've been reading and learning, much like an online diary. Digesting ideas in an open, online digital space like a blog will also prove to future employers that you are engaged and interested.

The main reason to keep up with articles and blog your own ideas and thoughts is that in doing so, you can get the edge on your library school peers and perhaps even be reading the same articles as your professors. This makes the classroom experience richer for you and your classmates and allows you to come into the discussion with examples from the real world, thus encouraging relevant and interesting conversations. This carries over into job interviews as well. Being knowledgeable about current trends and having real-life examples to discuss can make your answers to interview questions more authoritative, showing employers that you have been critically thinking about these issues. This can really set you apart from other candidates who are just reciting what their professors have told them—so start reading early!

Sizing Up the Job Market

Job announcements today are the hiring baseline of tomorrow, so do yourself a favor and search for these ads early in your academic career. It's good to have basic knowledge of some of the skills that libraries are looking for in a future digital librarian. That's why you're in school, right? The best way to gauge that is to take a look at job descriptions. After you've done some research into what area of digital librarianship most interests you, go to one of the numerous library job websites and find a position that sounds like your dream job. Aim high! Disregard the fact that some of those are asking for years of experience. What you're looking for in these job ads are the qualifications and skills that employers want you to have. This is the best way to really plan your coursework while in school.

Check out some of the resources listed in chapter 3 for position openings. Go through and highlight the exact knowledge, skills, and abilities that the listed employers are looking for. Look for things like software competencies, programming languages, or digital media experience. Identify what skills you want to learn or brush up on, then seek out ways to develop those skills, in school or wherever you can. Even if you can't take a class on a given topic, get creative and find ways to incorporate some of these emerging technology skills into your other coursework or internships. Maybe there's a local library that doesn't have a mobile website, or needs help with their current social media efforts. And there is always the need to develop and keep up your own digital presence, which could be a great training ground. You don't have to be an expert on every emerging trend, but it will help you to at least know about them.

Being aware of what's going on means you'll be ready to hit the ground running when you graduate. Technology is in constant flux, and what you learn in a digital libraries class may not be exactly what your job asks you to do. The most important skill that you need is the ability to learn and be flexible (Tennant, 2004). This state of constant learning is useful in the digital library world and applicable to many other career experiences as well. As a profession, librarianship continually strives to move forward and seek the best ways to serve patrons. Digital librarians who set the tools in place to keep libraries at the forefront of information access will be in demand.

PUT IN WORK

There's no doubt about it: getting hands-on experience is vital to the learning process and necessary *before* entering the job market. Remember when we mentioned that praxis and theory are going to be deeply intertwined in your education? Here is the part where you're going to have to step outside of the classroom and get your hands dirty. It is imperative that you have real-life experience and skills on your resume when you graduate in order to get a job. It may come as a surprise to some that librarianship is very competitive, so you want to stand out from the crowd. Realistically, you will be going up against other people who may have years of work experience. This doesn't mean that fresh graduates don't get jobs, but it does exemplify why getting experience and developing your skills is crucial during your time in school.

Many students opt to engage in internships, practicums, part-time jobs, or volunteering while they're in school to help beef up their resumes (in many MLS programs a practicum may be required for graduation, and this is a good thing). Hopefully, through engaging with your classmates, connecting with other professionals in the field, and keeping track of current events, you will hear about excellent opportunities. Your school may also partner with local organizations that will host student interns or volunteers. Another way to find opportunities is to follow the money. Have you read about a library or museum that got a large grant for a digitization project? E-mail the person who is in charge of the project to see how you can get involved. Be on the lookout for projects that you'd be interested in. It's entirely possible that you could be an integral part of making that project happen.

Do anything you can to get experience, but keep in mind that many times these opportunities are unpaid. Unfortunately, this is another hard library school truth: almost everyone has to do some unpaid work to get the chance to develop the skills they want. It's good to have a professional attitude with any sort of project that you approach. Making a good impression at your internship or volunteer job can sometimes lead to a paid position or provide you with an excellent reference. The library world tends to be well connected, so there's a chance you can build a positive reputation for yourself this way. Mold the experience so that you get the most out of it. Let's say you want to work with digital content management software or you are interested in metadata. Be up-front with the site supervisor and tell him or her what you're really looking for; that way you can work on projects that are interesting to you and ultimately help you get the skills you want. Especially if you're giving your precious free time and not getting paid, you want to truly tailor your experiences to meet your expectations.

There are plenty of other ways to put in work; it doesn't necessarily have to be through an official internship at a library. Do Lifehacker's Night School to learn coding (Dachis, 2011). Grab some data from an open data repository and start to experiment with it. If you want to get more comfortable with HTML and CSS, try creating your own website from scratch. Practice making metadata records in

XML. It's pretty fun to learn by doing, even if it's not for anyone but yourself. Even if certain skills take a while to sink in, don't worry. Just having a basic knowledge will help you once you're on the job.

Conferences, webinars and other professional gatherings are other places that can help you develop your digital library skill set. Going to a conference does a couple of things for you. The presentations and panels can be highly informative and give you ideas that you can bring back to your schoolwork or job. You also get to be among your "tribe," people who have similar interests, experience, and knowledge you can draw from. Now you have a reason to all be in the same room and talk to each other. Informal gatherings like unconferences, info-camps, or workshops serve this purpose too; in fact, they might be even better places for you to gain skills. The informal nature of these events shifts the power from the presenters to the people, putting everyone on even ground. One of the best aspects of these types of events is that anyone can plan one, even you! Check out the InfoCamp Starter Kit (Elkington et al., 2011) as an example. Really, any place that lets you play in the sandbox and have a conversation with your peers is going to foster a productive learning environment. The key here is that you are being active in your learning.

Content management systems (CMS) are also something that you will want to become familiar with as you develop your hands-on experience. CONTENTdm, Omeka, Greenstone, Digitool, Fedora Commons, DSpace—do these names sound familiar? If not, they should as you start looking around and working with digital collections that utilize these tools. The above-mentioned are commonly used CMS's in libraries, archives, and special collections as well as some museums and other cultural heritage institutions. Your digital libraries class might have you use one, your school's library may use another. It's good to try out as many as you can to see the differences and figure out which you prefer. That way you can impress future employers with some existing knowledge of systems they are already utilizing or thinking about adopting.

Put everything you've been studying into practice. The skills that you learn in the classroom are the skills that you will develop out in the working world. The best way to cement them is to put them to use! We really can't stress enough how important this is to your degree, regardless of what type of librarian you want to be. Every skill that you learn and master along the way can be a great selling point on your resume and eventually get you where you want to be. There's a lot of fun and satisfaction in seeing your hard work actualize into something real that you can link to online or show to your peers.

Anecdotal Evidence—Annie

One of my first digital undertakings as a library school student was working on a project to digitize one of the oldest African American newspapers in the country. It was a big endeavor and took a couple months of hard work to finish. Once it was done and had gone online, my department received a grateful e-mail from someone who was able to find out where her great-grandmother was buried as a result of looking at these digitized newspapers. Moments like that illustrate how digital collections can positively impact our communities.

LOOK/THINK/ENGAGE OUTSIDE THE LIBRARY

Here's a concept that might throw you for a loop: the work of digital librarianship doesn't have to happen in a library. While many LIS students begin school under the assumption that they will eventually work in an information-based institution of some sort, it is becoming truer these days that libraries, museums and archives are not the end-all, be-all of potential workplaces. LIS education is slowly warming up to this idea, and progressive-thinking instructors are encouraging students to explore beyond the library echo chamber. All kinds of industries are looking for people with skills in information organization, digital asset management, knowledge management, and information architecture. With that in mind, developing a sense of what is happening in the wider world of digital/tech culture is a useful consideration while in school.

The media scholar Henry Jenkins writes about the concept of "convergence culture," investigating the way contemporary forms of media seem to be growing into one another in new and different ways (Jenkins, 2006). This idea flows directly into the ways that digital work is being done now. Digitization projects conducted in archives are suddenly of interest to start-up companies in Silicon Valley, analysis of government data sets is taking place in journalistic newsrooms, and the creation of databases and digital asset management systems is being done in university digital humanities centers by English professors, computer scientists, and information technologists. As the world contends with an onslaught of technology tools and information overload, the digital librarian has the unique opportunity to become a curator of digital culture. It only becomes a matter of being in the right place at the right time, with the right skills.

For example, Marshall Kirkpatrick, lead blogger of the tech blog *ReadWriteWeb.com,* published an article discussing the exponential rise of job postings seeking "data scientists" (2011). While a student in library school might not think of themselves as a data scientist, it is clear that the job market is leaning toward digital skills, including (and especially) working with data. Having an open mind to alternative positions in LIS-related fields is a must as all kinds of companies and institutions adapt to new social and economic needs in regards to data and information (or turning data into information—which is Library School 101).

Aside from assessing how digital library skills align with the tech world, it's important also to consider leveraging your skills as a consultant. Believe it or not, there are still plenty of small businesses, government offices, and individuals who are not digitally inclined, and by utilizing your training in instruction and information gathering, combined with tech skills and software competencies, you could potentially develop a clientele and go into business for yourself. Taking on some side jobs could allow you to grow your skills and bring that experience to bear in whatever career setting you end up in. As digital technology connects us in new and different ways, the role that librarians play will change and expand across a variety of jobs, workplaces, and fields. Digital librarians should be at the forefront of creating tools to meet people's needs, instead of adopting and fitting needs to existing tools. And that will arise from a healthy dose of curiosity, courage to try new things, and a solid understanding of the basics of how information works—all of which can and should be part of your path to completing the degree.

FINAL THOUGHTS

As a student it is important to develop a basic understanding of digital objects and how they are handled. Ask yourself what you want to be an expert in, and what it is that you want to know the most about. Pursuing a do-it-yourself mentality, experimenting with digital tools, collecting information, and learning about the wide range of topics surrounding digital libraries will give you an edge over your peers (and perhaps the librarian working in the field who hasn't kept up with emerging trends and tools). Take the initiative to try new things, especially experimenting with how tech tools can work in the library environment. Learning to investigate and experiment with digital projects will make the difference on the job market, and in your future career.

Approaching a graduate degree in library and information studies as a practice in your own self-motivation and will to learn is fundamental to establishing your worth as a librarian-to-be. However, it is important also to accept that even in the two years you attend graduate school, there will be many things you will not have exposure to or time to learn. Just keep in mind that most students aim to develop a basic skill set and have an understanding of the tools of the trade. Don't get too caught up on specific job titles—being comfortable and confident with digital content is what digital information professionals can gather around. Use your time in school to discover your interests, meet new people, and develop your skills. You'd be surprised at how the things you do in school that genuinely interest you can translate into standout bullet points on your resume. More importantly, being open-minded and committed to lifelong learning is the key to becoming a good (and ever better) digital librarian.

REFERENCES

Choi, Youngok, and Edie Rasmussen. 2006. "What Is Needed to Educate Future Digital Librarians: A Study of Current Practice and Staffing Patterns in Academic and Research Libraries." *D-Lib Magazine* 12, no. 9. www.dlib.org/dlib/september06/choi/09choi.html.

Dachis, Adam. 2011. "Learn to Code: The Full Beginner's Guide." *Lifehacker.* Last modified January 31. http://lifehacker.com/5744113/learn-to-code-the-full-beginners-guide.

Elkington, Rachel, Aaron Louie, Kristen Shuyler, and Andy Szydlowski. 2011. "InfoCamp Starter Kit." *InfoCamp*. Last modified August 22. http://wiki.infocamp.org/index.php?title=InfoCamp_Starter_Kit.

Jenkins, Henry. 2006. *Convergence Culture: Where Old and New Media Collide*. New York: New York University Press.

Kirkpatrick, Marshall. 2011. "Jobs for Data Scientists Explode Across the Market." *ReadWriteWeb* (blog). July 20. www.readwriteweb.com/archives/jobs_for_data_scientists_explode_across_the_market.php.

Tennant, Roy. 2004. "Organization and Staffing." in *Managing the Digital Library*, 150. New York: Reed.

RECOMMENDED RESOURCES

Code4Lib Journal: http://code4lib.org

Digital Studies: www.digitalstudies.org/ojs/index.php/digital_studies

D-Lib Magazine: www.dlib.org

Digital Library Federation: www.diglib.org

DiRTwiki: http://digitalresearchtools.pbworks.com/w/page/17801672/FrontPage

GradHacker: http://gradhacker.org

Hack Library School: http://hacklibschool.wordpress.com

Journal of Digital Information: http://journals.tdl.org/jodi

ProfHacker: http://chronicle.com/blogs/profhacker

Chapter Three

Landing Your First Job

Elyssa M. Sanner, Catherine P. Wagner, and Krista E. Clumpner

By now you've decided that digital librarianship is a career you'd like to pursue. You may have just discovered that digital technology is your passion, have applied to a library school, be nearly done with your schooling, or attained the experience necessary to be involved with digital projects within libraries. But how do you go about *getting* your first job in digital librarianship? We hope that you will find the answers to that question within this chapter, where we'll give you guidelines for using the resources of today to find your dream job of tomorrow. We'll cover where to find job postings, how to craft an impressive application package, how to survive an interview, and we will discuss the validity of certain myths currently floating around the library community. Above all else, please remember that we are not prescribing the perfect way to find a job as a digital librarian, but describing how it often occurs. As librarians, we are adept at finding information, so search out the positions that interest you and forge your own unique path.

WHERE TO START

The Internet is a primary resource for researching digital librarianship opportunities. With so many online resources available, knowing where to start and how to filter specifically for these positions is key to finding the right one. There are several types of resources described in this section that you will want to monitor on a regular basis.

Job Boards and Aggregators

The best place to start searching for open positions is online job boards and job aggregators. Job boards are websites where positions are posted directly, and aggregators are search engines that pool job postings from various resources on the Web. Common aggregators such as Monster.com or Craigslist are a place to start; however, you are searching for a specialized career within a professional field, so you will want to be aware of resources catering specifically to librarians. One source to consider is websites for temporary and contract placement firms such as LAC Group (http://lac-group.com) and Trak (www.trakcompanies.com), companies that specialize in the information professions.

Other places to search are the career sections of websites for professional organizations such as the American Library Association, Library and Information Technology Association (LITA), American Society for Information Science & Technology (ASIS&T), Special Libraries Association (SLA), Association of Colleges and Research Libraries, Society of American Archivists, and Institute of Electrical and Electronics Engineers (IEEE). Most LIS programs also update physical or virtual job boards, and monitoring the online boards of multiple library schools can be a good strategy.

As mentioned in chapter 1, a "digital services librarian" is a "media and digital technology librarian" is a "digital resources librarian." A keyword search for "digital" and "librarian" on various job boards should return postings with these

Author's Note—Cathy

I found my first position as librarian at the Puget Sound Regional Council through my school's faculty adviser for the student chapter of SLA, who posted the open position on the student officers' e-mail list. The position was advertised as a digital librarian responsible for intranet maintenance, collection development, and maintenance of a primarily digital collection. I was monitoring several e-mail discussion lists to learn about job opportunities, and saw the job posting on other lists as well.

I decided to apply when I learned from my faculty adviser that the hiring committee was inclined to hire a new graduate. I asked my boss about the hiring process shortly after starting. She said that they hadn't advertised very much, only posting to a few local electronic discussion lists and contacting the SLA faculty advisor at my school. The position was only advertised for about two weeks and received over one hundred applications.

titles. However, some institutions may use different terms altogether. The title of a position with very similar roles and responsibilities could be "electronic services and emerging technologies librarian." In online employment search engines, a broader use of terms relevant to digital librarianship will return a larger array of results, although less refinement will also return job postings that may not be relevant to your search. Read through several types of employment postings to learn common titles and qualifications specific to digital librarianship to help you refine your search terms.

E-Mail Discussion Lists

Subscribing to e-mail lists for professional organizations such as LITA, ASIS&T, IEEE, and SLA is a great way to find out about digital librarian jobs. While most lists are generally devoted to discussions about professional standards and practices, some will be rich resources for finding out about open positions. There are numerous benefits to membership in professional organizations, and signing up for e-mail lists is a cost-free way to follow the conversation and connect to the network of professionals sharing information online.

The Social Web

Digital librarians are often responsible for managing the social networking services utilized by their libraries, and should be well versed in the services available as well as the direction these services are headed. Valuable networks that were once built through face-to-face contact can be developed online through social websites such as LinkedIn.com, which provide a space to represent your professional self and connect with other professionals. Following organizations you are interested in on social media spaces, as well as taking part in discussions with current digital librarians, will benefit you in the long run by helping you build your network.

The importance of networking was touched on in chapter 2, so we won't rehash the subject here. But it does bear stating that your network will be immensely important for navigating your employment search. Conferences, meetings of local chapters of professional organizations, and university events are opportunities to make connections with professionals. Volunteer with these organizations to gain experience and find mentors to tap for advice. Ask professionals if you can meet them for an informational interview. Most professionals would find your interest in their career flattering. Informational interviews are best set up through connections in your personal network. You may know someone who knows someone who has your dream job and is probably happy to talk to you about it.

PUTTING YOUR BEST FOOT FORWARD

When you find a job opening you're interested in, make sure that your experience and skills closely match the required qualifications. Although there may be exceptions in less traditional settings, applying for positions for which you don't meet the minimum qualifications is usually a waste of time for all involved, so stick to positions for which you're truly eligible. Once you've located such a job, it's time to begin preparing your application package. This will probably consist of a cover letter, resume or curriculum vitae, and list of references, with the possible addition of academic transcripts and/or an online portfolio. This package is the first impression that a hiring manager will have of you, so it is imperative that it be error-free. Keep the following objectives in mind when preparing your materials: to get noticed, to be chosen for an interview, and to ultimately get the job.

In order for your application package to get noticed, there are two steps that you must take. First, follow the directions given in the job posting. Correctly following all directions in the job posting shows that you can read, interpret, and deliver what is asked of you, all desirable qualities in an employee. This will also help get your application past the weeding stage. Job applications are often first received by the human resources department and reviewed for completion. An error-free package will survive the first weeding stage and be passed up the line for further review. A second step is to use the eyes and advice of trusted friends, family, and colleagues. Find people you trust and ask them to review your application for completeness and correctness. If you're a library school student, take advantage of human resources managers or other librarians at your school who are willing to offer their advice. In the end, the presentation and content of the application package are your responsibility, so read the job posting carefully before, during, and after you write your application materials.

Job postings usually specify the submission of professional references along with your cover letter and resume. When considering who to use as a reference, choose carefully. Approach those individuals who have a detailed knowledge of your work ethic, qualifications, skills, and potential. And remember to ask each one if they are willing to serve as your reference! It does not reflect well on you to have unprepared references, so once an individual has agreed to be your reference keep him or her apprised of the jobs to which you've applied. It is also helpful to provide your references with a current resume in case they are contacted by a prospective employer without your knowledge. If you have a heads-up that a reference might receive a call, provide them with a copy of the relevant job posting and coordinating cover letter so he or she will be able to speak intelligently about you, your work history, and your application package.

YOUR ONLINE PRESENCE

In our increasingly connected society, your online presence is becoming just as important as your physical one. There is a high probability that once you make it onto the selection list, the hiring manager is going to search online for information about you before you meet in person. Will you be proud of what they find? While embracing social media to develop a network of professional connections is important, you should also be concerned about the representation your online presence creates. We suggest you keep the personal separate from the professional. For personal pages, lock down the privacy settings or "clean up" the content. Having to first overcome a negative impression will put you a step behind in the interview process. You should be prepared to explain any online content that cannot be cleaned up if an interviewer asks about it. A truthful explanation can sometimes do wonders to repair a first impression setback.

Creating an Online Portfolio or Blog

It is smart to create an online portfolio to show a prospective employer that you are comfortable using web technology and provide examples of projects you have worked on. In fact, in today's environment, some managers may wonder why a potential digital librarian wouldn't have one. You may have the skills to develop a website from scratch; however, if you want the same benefit with less effort, there are many free programs available that you can use to create a personalized site. You may want to look at examples of what other librarians have put online. Your resume, professional goals, and representations of your best work should be included.

Many librarians these days, digital and otherwise, are also blogging about the profession and their work. A professional blog can be an excellent tool for displaying your knowledge to employers. Write about projects you have undertaken or trends that interest you. In combination with an online portfolio, this can be an excellent addition to your application package.

WRITING AN EYE-CATCHING COVER LETTER

For ideas about cover letters, we advise that you read style guides and search for examples online. The "Open Cover Letters" website posts real cover letters that worked for librarians (http://opencoverletters.com). A search through the career section of your library website can also yield a breadth of advice on format and content. The advice tends to center on three very important elements: brevity, relevance, and specificity. Keep the letter concise; about one to one-and-a-half pages single-spaced. The letter should describe why you are a great candidate, why you are applying, and why you want to work for the organization. Try to avoid simply restating information in your resume, but expand on your experiences and skills. This is the place to include more detail about a specific project you worked on which relates to the position you are applying for. Remember, this is an opportunity to highlight details about yourself that can make you stand out from other applicants.

It is also advisable to research the organization before writing a cover letter. Each cover letter should be specifically tailored to the position you are applying for, and adding information about the organization shows your level of interest. If you dream of being a digital librarian in a public library and grew up attending story time at the branch you are now applying to, it would be acceptable to mention this. Try to strike a balance between laying it on too thick and sharing details that will make you stand out and endear you to an employer.

CRAFTING AN IMPRESSIVE RESUME

Not only does your resume need to present you in a positive light, clearly showing how your experience matches the desired qualifications, but it should also look visually appealing. Microsoft Word offers many options for formatting your resume, and there are numerous books available to provide inspiration, such as Susan Britton Whitcom's *Resume Magic* (2006). Keep the formatting simple. Clean lines, an easy-to-read font, and a logical organization of information on the page are the best approach. When submitting a resume online, we recommend converting it to pdf format to ensure consistent formatting.

Consider creating several versions of your resume based on the types of positions or industries you are targeting. An application for an academic library will call for highlighting skills that may not be as applicable in a corporate environment. If your background is general and you are open to a variety of industries, it is best to keep versions of your resume tweaked to highlight skills that best match each industry. Each application should be tailored to speak to individual organizations and best match your skills with the qualifications listed in the job posting. The elements of your application package may be your only chance to introduce yourself to your future employer. Craft these materials well because they will be your key to getting to the next step in the process: the interview.

GENERAL INTERVIEW ADVICE

Preparing for an interview can be difficult, especially if you are a new graduate with no experience applying for professional jobs. This section attempts to provide some advice that will help you prepare for and ace the in-person interview. For example, how you dress can set you apart in a positive or negative way from other applicants. In most organizations, it is safest to wear a solid, dark-colored two-piece suit—remember, you are the one being interviewed, not your clothing. Always wear comfortable shoes, as it is likely that you will walk around the building or campus during the day. Also, bring a notepad of some kind with you. You can use it to keep a list of questions for the committee and take notes during the interview.

When preparing for the interview itself, investigate the job posting, library, larger institution (if applicable), related news articles, and any other piece of information that might inform you about the library's work culture and expectations of their employees. Write out and rehearse your answers to commonly asked interview questions. Consider how you can relate your previous experience to the requirements of the position, as your interviewers will want to hear how your background has prepared you for this particular job. Don't assume you can "wing it," as this approach may backfire if you become nervous or are given a question you are unprepared for. Prepare questions for your interviewers based on your discussion with them, because asking thoughtful questions is a good way to learn more about the workplace and stand out to the committee. And above all else: practice, practice, practice!

On the interview day, make an effort to be friendly and approachable. From the custodian to the receptionist to the library director or dean, how you treat people *will* get back to the hiring manager or search committee members. Be mentally present throughout the interview, whether it is three hours long or an entire day. If your face doesn't hurt from smiling after the interview, you might not have appeared engaged enough! Finally, always send handwritten or e-mailed thank-you's to each committee member or individual involved with the hiring process within a week of the interview.

HIRING PRACTICES OF VARIOUS ENVIRONMENTS

This section describes the hiring practices of public, academic, corporate, and other library settings in broad generalities. We do not intend for this discussion to apply to every library in existence, so please use it as a jumping-off point to discover exactly how the hiring process works in your ideal environment.

Public Libraries

You might have to get creative in finding a digital librarian position within a public library—as services funded by taxpayer dollars, public libraries are often run on tight budgets and can't always fund a position solely for digital services. Public libraries are often less likely to collect rare or unique materials that warrant digitization, so if you are interested in this type of work you should consider focusing on larger or urban libraries with more extensive resources. However, because public libraries serve the community and respond to its service demands, they can be quick to adopt new technologies and practices. This may result in the need for positions related to web and electronic resources, or a temporary grant-funded position for a specific digitization project. Being flexible and having the ability to wear several hats will go far in this environment.

The hiring process in this type of library is decidedly less formal than in other library environments. It often moves along quickly, as being short-staffed can lead to serious problems in the public library's ability to deliver services. The library director and department head are typically the only participants in the search for a new public librarian. In "Considering Attitude and Values in Hiring Public Librarians," Towey argues that hiring a public librarian with a warm, sensitive nature is just as important as hiring a librarian who has earned a library degree (2004, 260). So when considering pursuing a job in a public library, make sure that you love serving the people who frequent public libraries!

Academic Libraries

Most academic libraries have similar hiring processes, as they are part of academic institutions that are governed by state and federal personnel laws (rules may vary for private institutions). The search for a new librarian at an academic library can take anywhere from six to twelve months, from the time the position fulfillment request is approved to the day the new employee begins his or her job. This may seem like a surprising length of time, but in academic settings, many activities are conducted by committee. A search committee of librarians will be formed to handle the application and interview portions of the process. These individuals fit this responsibility into their already busy schedules, so finding the time to meet often proves challenging and contributes to the lengthy timeline. The committee will often work from a detailed schedule with deadlines for deciding on candidates to interview and when to recommend an individual for hire.

When applying for an academic position, your application will likely go through the institution's online job database, which is run by the human resources department, before being passed on to the search committee. The search committee will then review each of the remaining applications and choose the candidates whose qualifications most closely match the job description. Since academic institutions must follow federal and state hiring laws while facing increasingly large pools of applicants, they will use a strict hiring protocol using such tools as checklists and ratings to streamline the process. Keep in mind that often only one or two of the committee members will work directly with the person hired, and the rest may be unfamiliar with many aspects of the position. It is important to customize your cover letter with the same language used in the job posting so that someone from a different department can readily see that you possess the necessary skills for the job.

Academic libraries usually conduct phone (and increasingly, video chat) interviews before inviting their top two or three candidates to campus for an in-person interview. This is the second step in the weeding process, and your chance to expand and elaborate upon the information in your application materials. Phone and video interviews can be awkward for all involved, so the committee members will understand that you may be nervous. The fact that you were chosen for a phone interview means the committee was impressed with your application, so be confident! At the same time, being thoroughly prepared will help you combat any nervousness and present yourself to the committee in a positive light.

After evaluating phone interviews, the search committee will invite its top candidates for an on-site interview. This typically involves multiple meetings over the course of one to two days. A presentation is frequently part of the interview schedule. The search committee should give you a topic; this will often pertain to a problem that you would face in a digital librarian position at that institution or invite an explanation of your personal philosophy of digital librarianship. Create a simple but clean visual presentation to illustrate your response to the topic, and don't be afraid to interject some humor and personality into your presentation. And again, practicing your presentation and being thoroughly prepared will go a long way towards moving you up on the search committee's list. Things such as speaking too softly or ending your 20-minute presentation in 10 minutes will probably not impress them.

You will generally have to wait for a response while the committee interviews other candidates, a process that can take over four weeks after your interview date. Don't get discouraged during the wait, but use the time to objectively analyze your interview experience in order to improve your next one.

Corporate Libraries

Many large corporations turn to information professionals to manage the content their employees rely on to do their jobs. These libraries tend to be specialized collections; many are primarily digital and are often closed to the public. Your role in such a library will likely include maintaining digital collections, social media, and journal subscriptions, managing the company intranet or external websites, providing reference services for organization staff, taking the lead on digitization projects, and various other library administration tasks.

Corporate libraries can be found in such organizations as law firms, architectural firms, clothing design companies, newspapers, magazines, and television stations. Tech companies also hire information professionals for digital projects utilizing theories of librarianship, though these positions may not necessarily be situated within a library. Companies such as Serials Solutions, OCLC, LexusNexus, and ProQuest are for-profit corporations that serve the library community and hire librarians with digital technology skills. Organizations with a long corporate history, large staff, and unwieldy amounts of information to manage often rely on information professionals to organize and provide access to materials. These positions may incorporate elements of public relations as corporations shift into social media outlets for marketing and advertising purposes.

In the corporate environment, the "library" may be a physical space or entirely virtual. Your purpose is to provide access to information. These settings are unlike traditional libraries because you are a corporate employee, conforming to a corporate culture and managing classified proprietary information that is generally unavailable to the public. You will probably not receive a stream of constant visitors. You will perform functions very close to those of the information technology department. It is up to you to explain your role to staff and management if there is not already a well-developed library presence.

When applying for corporate library jobs, you should research the organization to gain a better understanding of the culture. If you know someone who works with the company, ask them to give you an honest assessment of the work environment. The interview will most likely include a high-level executive, a human resources (HR) representative, the library manager (or the entire library staff), information technology staff, and a mid-level manager or two that work often with library staff. If all of these people are not in a room with you at once, be prepared to meet them through the course of the interview. You will work closely with all of these people, and all will probably have some say in the final hiring decision. The hiring process in most corporate environments moves much faster than in an academic library environment. Hiring managers may also have a little more leeway in selecting a candidate they "like" and think will be a good fit for the environment rather than strictly hiring someone who meets the minimum job qualifications.

Federal Libraries

The federal government sector is worth checking into when looking for digital librarian positions. Positions will be advertised on agency websites, through discussion lists, and traditional employment resources, but all applications must be processed through the USAJobs website (www.usajobs.gov). It is advisable to set up a profile there and become familiar with the application process.

Each posting will clearly detail the requirements for applying. Read the posting carefully. If a form is required but you do not include it, your application will be disqualified from consideration for the position. You will usually be required to fill out a Knowledge, Skills, and Abilities (KSA) form. Many agencies have switched to a multiple-choice format for these questions, but some still require essays (although there are plans to eliminate the use of these altogether). You should be able to review the questions via a link found in the job posting. For positions that require essays, we recommend you review the questions and write your responses in a separate document before beginning the application. There are many online resources for advice on crafting a KSA, and some commercial vendors will help with applications for a fee.

All federal government applications go through a centralized human resources department. The HR person will create a list of candidates based on a scoring system. Experience is scaled based on hours worked to ensure you have the appropriate amount of experience to qualify for the level applied for. A current "Fed" who runs the Careers-in-Federal-Libraries Google Group recommends putting the total number of hours worked in each position on your resume to help the human resources department properly credit experience. Without knowing if you worked full-time or part-time, the HR person will not know how to properly credit you for experience. This could be enough to eliminate you during the first step in the hiring process. The hiring process for federal jobs can require four to six weeks from the closing date of the post to the date of hire, and sometimes longer if any level of security clearance is required.

Other Library Settings

Other library settings are nonprofits, military base libraries, foreign service posts, museums, religious organizations, primary schools, or any institution with a collection of information that needs maintenance. Their hiring practices will depend on the size of the organization. A small organization may be in need of the skills of a digital librarian, but without the resources to fund a full-time position in addition to a cataloger, manager, and so on. The expectation may be that you will be a jack-of-all-trades, primarily serving in a digital librarian role but willing to wear other hats.

Some small nonprofit organizations may not offer stellar salaries and benefits, but do offer unique and rewarding experiences in a non-traditional library environment. Historical societies, museums, and charity agencies may be in need of the services of a digital librarian. With a limited budget the job ad may only go out to various message boards and rely on the viral nature of online communities to circulate the posting. These positions can be found on discussion lists for local chapters of professional organizations as well as the hiring organization's website. These postings can sometimes be picked up by professionals and passed through social media and e-mail discussion lists, as well as some employment aggregators, such as OpportunityKnocks.org which specializes in the nonprofit sector.

Small organizations will probably want you to play many roles. Large, well-funded organizations may not ask you to be more than a digital librarian but will expect you to embrace the mission and values of the organization. It is important to be aware of the differences in industry culture and to research the agency so you can be well prepared for the interview and understand what to expect as a member of that particular organization.

AFTER THE INTERVIEW

If you are offered the position, congratulations! If you accept it you may have some room for negotiating start date and salary, within a predetermined range. If you didn't receive the job offer, don't worry or obsess over it—use this opportunity as a learning experience, carefully examine what you did or didn't do well to discover areas for improvement, and contact the head of the search committee to see if he or she would be willing to share any observations or suggestions with you. It's likely that you didn't do anything wrong, but that other applicants were simply more qualified. Remember that applying for jobs is a numbers game—your odds increase with each application you submit, so don't allow yourself to get too discouraged if you don't get an interview or aren't offered a particular job. Keep applying for every job you are qualified for. It may well take some time to score that first job, but this is normal and should not be seen as a sign of failure.

Salary Expectations

Salary expectations will vary across each of these environments, and while not the primary focus of a job search, it is an important consideration when selecting positions to apply for. The range of salary for your position will depend on the resources of the organization. Corporate and federal librarians may be at the higher end of the spectrum, digital librarians in public and academic libraries are generally somewhere in the middle, and nonprofit or small organizations with limited budgets tend to pay at the lower end of the scale. Geography is a factor too, as rural or small-town libraries will generally pay less than urban ones—but keep in mind this is usually a reflection of differences in cost of living. Consider also whether a given position has the potential for advancement, or if you will eventually need to move to a different organization in order to take on a higher-paying supervisory or managerial role.

HONESTLY SPEAKING

Beyond the technical aspects of searching for a job as a digital librarian, additional factors such as time and place must also be taken into consideration. The current economic climate has constricted employment opportunities, requiring flexibility and patience in your job search.

The Graying of the Profession: Fact or Fiction?

The impending specter of the "graying of the profession" has loomed on the library horizon for several years, having been discussed as early as the 1980s, as exemplified by an editorial on the topic by John Berry in the November 1, 1986, issue of *Library Journal*. In a more current article discussing the issue, Rachel Singer Gordon describes a modern take on the situation in her article "Get Over the 'Graying' Profession Hype" (2004). Past demographic studies predicted that by 2009 more than 25 percent of professional librarians would reach retirement age, and more than 58 percent would be ready to retire by 2019 (Berry, 2002). At the time, it was believed that 40 percent of library directors would retire by 2009, causing an inevitable shift up the chain and opening up a wealth of entry-level positions for new graduates.

However, no one predicted the economic crisis of 2008 and its repercussions. Not only did professionals not retire at this rate but budgets were shrinking, so open positions were not back-filled and staff size declined. New graduates were competing with seasoned professionals for available positions, and the competition became fierce. While the market for positions in public and academic libraries is still very competitive, placements can be found with persistence. Among 2010 survey respondents, advice for future graduates was hopeful: "keep a positive and professional attitude; something will come along eventually" (Maatta 2011, 26).

A bright spot can be found in employment opportunities in private industry. According to *Library Journal*'s 2010 placement and salary survey, 9.4 percent of placements were with the private sector. This is a slight rise from 2009 responses. "Graduates from an array of LIS programs identified their new employers as companies such as Google, Wolfram Alpha, and AT&T" (Maatta 2011, 24). Graduates also took positions in sectors outside the LIS field, such as information technology or research.

The library profession will forever experience the flux that comes with generations retiring and newcomers moving in. Digital librarians of today are well versed in technology, comfortable keeping up with its advances, and ready to implement the innovations needed to keep information services relevant, pertinent, and available to all. Persistence and continued education will help current and new digital librarians stay competitive in a tight job market, but it is also important to be aware of current realities.

The Importance of Geographic Mobility

Because librarianship is competitive, it's important that you seriously consider how far you are willing or able to move for a job in this field. For your first position, be prepared to compromise. It's likely that you will either have to be very geographically mobile for a job, or willing to take a less-than-dream job (that might include a mix of duties, including digital responsibilities) in order to stay in a specific geographic area. Committing to a specific area can also lengthen your job search, particularly if you plan to remain in the same town where you attended library school, which will likely have a market saturated with other graduates.

Being geographically mobile not only means being willing to move for a job, but also includes actively looking far and wide for positions. Your first digital librarian position is an opportunity to do something that you find new and exciting, so take advantage of it! Consider looking for positions in a location where you've always wanted to live, such as a different coastline, a large city, a tiny town, or an entirely different country. At the same time, don't write off locations that seem less than desirable, as you may be more likely to get your foot in the door due to a smaller applicant pool. It is not expected in today's library world that you will spend your entire career with the first organization that hires you, and being flexible with your first job will allow you to build the skills to exert more control over your future career prospects.

Be Yourself

The most important part of the job search process is to be yourself. Embellishing your abilities, claiming to know MySQL when you don't, or significantly altering your personality during the in-person interview will only hurt you in the long run. Remember that besides investigating whether you are a good fit for the position, you're also investigating whether you will fit into the work environment. Can you get along with the individuals that you will work with most closely? Are there individuals who could serve as mentors or provide career guidance? Can you see

Author's Note—Elyssa

When it came time for me to look for my first professional job, I decided that the job itself was more important than the location. I wasn't tied to one geographic location by marriage or children, so I decided that feeling fulfilled in my professional life was more important than living in a specific place. It was frightening to think of applying to jobs all over the country, but I did and was serious about moving to those locations, because each position was related to what I really wanted to do in my career. Meeting the librarians and staff while interviewing at my current institution convinced me that I'd made the right decision. Nice, genuine people are all over the world, and can make any location feel like home. Because of this flexibility, I'm currently in my dream job!

yourself flourishing in that environment? Your interviewers are also looking to see if you fit into their workplace, so relax and be yourself.

According to one special collections librarian we spoke with, when making hiring decisions the most important question she asks herself is "Can I work with this person?"—can I see this person every day, have a conversation, spend the next several years working closely with him or her? Remember that it all boils down to people hiring people to spend an enormous amount of time together fulfilling an important role.

It is often helpful to try to view the hiring process from the perspective of the employer, which admittedly may be difficult when one is new to the profession. For one librarian's advice, we turn to an actual hiring manager at an academic library. She offers her take on the library employment landscape, from the other side of the desk.

COMMENTARY: FROM THE EMPLOYER'S PERSPECTIVE

by Krista E. Clumpner

Technology and changing standards, the move to share information digitally, the trend towards access over ownership, and the shifting economy have all had roles in the reshaping of the library job market and profession. So catalogers have become metadata specialists, acquisitions librarians have become digital resource managers, archivists are managing institutional repositories, and reference librarians have to guide people through the maze of online resources to find information.

The impact this has had on the profession is that while basic skill sets are still needed, additional skills are also required. Often librarians who have been in the profession for many years are unable or unwilling to adapt to these changes. This fact, more than the "graying" of the profession, can account for the posting of many librarian positions. Sometimes the position is a new one for the library, developed to add some of the latest skill sets to existing staff. Other times, it is a rewriting of a long-held position after a person has retired. Too often, new duties are just added to preexisting ones in a long list that can be daunting to the job seeker. If the library has been given the time to do so they may have rethought the needs of an existing position, keeping some of the previously required skills as well as adding needed new ones.

What does an employer want? What does an employer say they want? If an employer lists items as required skills then they are pretty serious that they want someone with those skills. If it is not apparent how you meet these requirements, then you have to point this out in your application. It is not the employer's job to discover your hidden talents. It is your job to make them obvious. Develop your cover letter for the specific position using the position advertisement or description. Point out how you meet the requirements and explain any additional skills or knowledge you may bring to the position, especially addressing any desirable attributes they ask for. While tailoring each letter and application takes time, it is well worth the effort. Be realistic about your knowledge and skills; the worst-case scenario is for you to stretch the truth, be offered a job, and find out after starting that it is beyond you. Remember, you will be working with these people, maybe for years, and the relationship should start with a clear understanding of what each party brings to the position. Honesty really is the best policy.

Geographic mobility is a must in today's job market. This is not only true for the job seeker but for the job filler as well. The rules of supply and demand come into play and if there are more job seekers than jobs to be filled, the job filler has the luxury of casting the net close to home to ensure a good pool of candidates. This is often true of areas with library schools within the region, while employers away from these centers need to cast their net wider to find applicants with appropriate skills. Often one productive method is to send calls for applications to the library schools themselves. This is especially true if you are posting for an entry-level position or a position requiring knowledge in relatively new areas, where the possession of a skill may outweigh the need for experience in the field. Of course all these requests will fall on deaf ears if applicants are not willing to relocate. Look far and wide and be willing to adapt to new environments.

FINAL THOUGHTS

We hope the information and advice provided in this chapter will help you feel prepared to venture out in search of your first job with confidence. In the end, we leave you with this piece of advice: the profession is constricting in areas, expanding in others, but the realm of digital librarianship is here to stay. Persistence in finding a placement, respect for the elders of the profession, and innovative enthusiasm will be important in weathering the current climate of change in the information profession and landing your first job as a digital librarian.

REFERENCES

Berry, John W. 1986. "Problems of a 'Graying' Profession." *Library Journal* 111, no. 18: 6.

———. 2002. "President's Message: Addressing the Recruitment and Diversity Crisis." *American Libraries* 33, no. 3: 7.

Gordon, Rachel Singer. 2004. "Get Over the 'Graying' Profession Hype." *Library Journal* 129, no. 1: 62.

Maatta, Stephanie L. 2011. "The Long Wait." *Library Journal* 136, no. 17 (October 15): 20–27.

Towey, Cathleen A. 2004. "Considering Attitude and Values in Hiring Public Librarians." *Public Libraries* 43, no. 5: 260–61.

Whitcom, Susan Britton. 2006. *Resume Magic: Trade Secrets of a Professional Resume Writer.* 3rd ed. Indianapolis, IN: JIST.

RECOMMENDED RESOURCES

ALA JobLIST: http://joblist.ala.org

ARL Careers Database: www.arl.org/resources/careers/positions/index.shtml

AUTOCAT Listserv: https://listserv.syr.edu/scripts/wa.exe?SUBED1=AUTOCAT&A=1

Careers-In-Federal-Libraries: http://groups.google.com/group/careers-in-federal-libraries

Conglomerated list of interview question resources: http://mrlibrarydude.wordpress.com/nailing-the-library-interview/library-interview-questions

"How to Apply to a Library Job": http://liswiki.org/wiki/HOWTO:Apply_for_a_library_job

I Need a Library Job (INALJ): http://inalj.com

Job-searching articles written by librarians, for librarians: www.liscareer.com

Jobs in Library and Information Technology: www.ala.org/lita/professional/jobs/looking

LibGig: http://publicboard.libgig.com

Library Job Postings: www.libraryjobpostings.org/special.htm

Library Jobs on the Internet: www.libraryjobpostings.org

LISJobs: www.lisjobs.com

LITA-l: www.ala.org/lita/involve/email

Metadata Librarians: http://metadatalibrarians.monarchos.com

SLA division lists: www.sla.org/content/community/lists/divisionlists5979.cfm

Chapter Four

Making a Career Shift

Michelle Czaikowski Underhill and Linda Burkey Wade

As libraries increasingly offer more content and services digitally, librarians from all areas of the field are seeing their roles shifting towards digital librarianship. If you are looking for a job in a digital library unit, find that your job duties are changing to incorporate digital tasks, or have recently made the switch from another area into digital librarianship, this chapter is for you. In it, we will discuss transferable skills from select areas of librarianship and offer tips for making the transition as smooth as possible.

Any career change requires adjustment. Learning new workflows, processes, software, scripting languages, or standards may seem a daunting task at times. Librarians coming from other areas of the field may bring different strengths, skills, perspectives, experiences, and connections to a team. This chapter will help you determine not only what knowledge and skills you have developed elsewhere that are easily transferable to a digital library unit, but the unique perspectives you might offer to a staff, team, or project.

TRANSFERABLE SKILLS FROM OTHER AREAS OF LIBRARIANSHIP

We learned in chapter 1 that various institutions define digital librarians in different ways. Duties and practices vary by institution, and may differ within an institution based on the needs of a particular project or item. For instance, how items are scanned may differ greatly. Some institutions may outsource scanning to a vendor while others may have students or volunteers scan items in-house. Another may require that only professionals with photography degrees operate imaging equipment to ensure every color is captured as precisely as possible. Because tasks vary by institution, no single list describes all the duties of digital librarians, just as no single list describes all the duties of access, reference, or technical services librarians. Therefore, this chapter is not intended to offer a comprehensive list of all transferable skills between digital library positions and other areas of librarianship, but provide a general idea of possible transferable skills that you may adapt to your experience and needs.

Some knowledge and skills readily found in a number of other areas of librarianship are easily transferable to digital librarianship. In particular, managerial, supervisory, and project management duties are required of many library professionals regardless of their area of focus. Strong communication and collaboration skills are necessary for all professional librarians when working with external organizations, peers, different departments within an institution, and patrons. In the following sections we will list other transferable knowledge and skill sets from the areas of technical services, special collections and archives, reference and instruction, access services, and library systems.

Technical Services

Technical services librarians are often equipped with specialized expertise and have a broad range of duties. These may include copy cataloging, original cataloging (especially for specialized materials), acquisitions, and more. A number of institutions place digital librarian positions in the library's technical services unit. If you work in technical services, your position may already incorporate digital librarian duties or you may work closely with digital librarians.

Commonly transferable skills include a working knowledge of controlled vocabularies and metadata schemas, knowledge of licensing agreements, budgeting, working with integrated library systems, knowledge of foreign languages, the ability to troubleshoot hardware and software, working with vendors, and conducting quality control checks.

Many libraries use MARC, Library of Congress Subject Headings, Library of Congress name authority files, and the Getty Art and Architecture Thesaurus when developing metadata for digital collections. Naturally, these same standards and vocabularies are routinely utilized by catalogers. In turn, a number of metadata librarian positions require candidates to have cataloging experience. If you are proficient in these areas, you may easily capitalize on this skill set.

If you work as an acquisitions librarian, you may communicate with vendors to negotiate pricing or subscription agreements for your institution and manage multiple budgets. You may also join and coordinate with library consortia to obtain better pricing on subscriptions, software, or other agreements. This experience relates to digital librarianship when it comes to working with vendors to acquire subscriptions or software and when working with department or project budgets. Experience with consortial agreements is also transferable if your institution obtains access to databases or digital asset management systems through a consortium.

Acquisitions librarians communicate with subject specialists and catalogers as items or subscriptions are ordered, received, and sent for appropriate processing. Digital librarians act similarly as items may be selected with the assistance of subject specialists for specific collections. They may also work with cataloging staff to have digital items added to the library's catalog and other systems, or for assistance with metadata creation. Quality control checks may be an integral part of your current or previous position in a technical services unit. They are required in many digital library units for varying reasons as well, from checking metadata records to running checksums on digital resources to ensure no data is lost or changed in files over time (for more on this topic, see chapter 12 on digital preservation). Quality controls are also used to check for color and size consistency of images.

Additionally, knowledge of foreign languages is often considered a plus for librarians working in technical services, particularly for catalogers. Though not required for many digital librarian positions, this ability may also be helpful in digitizing or creating metadata and access tools for items in other languages.

Finally, change is inherent to technical services—standards are revised and updated, new formats are added to collections, systems and databases that staff use on a daily basis change or are updated. The same is true for digital libraries. Asset management systems are upgraded, metadata decisions change, interfaces need updating, and workflows are revised. Your ability to be flexible when changes arise is a readily transferable skill for those making the switch to digital librarianship.

Special Collections and Archives

If you are a special collections, archives, or rare books professional, you are likely well versed in a variety of library duties. You may run a distinct library of related or rare items and thus have experience in almost every traditional task required of the library profession, including reference, access, acquisitions, cataloging, and preservation.

A review of the Association of College and Research Libraries' "Guidelines: Competencies for Special Collections Professionals" identifies a number of skills and knowledge sets that are transferable to digital librarian positions (Rare Books and Manuscripts Section, 2008). These consist of collection development, knowledge of library systems and metadata schemas, website creation, supervisory skills, grant writing and management, preservation of digital and physical items, creating finding aids or access tools, project management, instruction, outreach, and marketing.

Particular expertise that you, as a special collections librarian, might bring to a digital library staff is specialized knowledge of conservation and preservation practices for fragile items under consideration for digitization. How items are digitized or handled may vary based on an item's condition or unique features. Simple conservation repairs may be required for some materials while others may be removed from the digitization queue if it is decided that the handling necessary for digitization would severely damage the material. Digital librarians need to be able to determine whether an item is too fragile to digitize or is in need of repair.

As a rare book or special collections librarian, you may be able to easily identify physical characteristics of books or other materials that warrant special attention in the digital version. For instance, there may be particular weaves for clothbound books or subtle differences between editions or printings of specific titles that are of interest to particular scholars who will use the digitized versions. Perhaps it is important to digitally capture the spine of some materials but not others.

You may already market items in special collections and connect them with larger collections at your institution. For instance, perhaps you select and highlight items for special exhibits that tie in with university themes or programs. Digital librarians do the same as they create online exhibits and pathfinders by linking digitized items with other library or institutional resources available on the Web. Selecting items for an exhibit, whether physical or digital, and making decisions about how to organize and display them are transferable skills.

You may also manage collections with materials requiring different levels of access due to privacy concerns, copyright, and donor agreements, and thus have an understanding of laws related to archives and records management. These factors will need to be addressed should the same collection of items be considered for digitization. Legal counsel may need to be consulted in these instances as well to determine what materials may be lawfully distributed online.

Reference and Instruction

If you are a reference and instruction librarian, you have a great deal of interaction with a library's patrons and may contribute valuable insight into how users view or interact with digital library resources. You may also be able to recommend items for digitization based on repeat reference inquiries and usage statistics from non-circulating collections. Other transferable skills from reference and library instruction positions include knowledge of integrated library systems, knowledge of databases and how patrons and staff interact with them, information-seeking behaviors of patrons, copyright law, web and/or interface design, hardware and software troubleshooting, instruction, usability/user experience assessment, supervisory experience, and strong communication and presentation skills.

Often, when working closely with patrons or faculty and receiving their feedback on a regular basis, reference librarians develop a sense of the materials that are used and those that are underutilized. Additionally, they can discern what resources are intuitive and what are deemed frustrating to use. In answering patron inquiries regarding databases or other online tools, they may see patterns regarding which features or interfaces result in patron frustration. Many are subject specialists who have created finding aids and other access tools such as pathfinders or online exhibits. All of these factors and experiences may be used to enhance the user experience as it applies to digital collections. Therefore these skills will help you make sure digital collections are presented in ways that are intuitive and useful for patrons.

Communication skills apply to all areas of digital librarianship, as questions may come through a variety of channels. Special training in the reference interview process is already required of reference librarians so they can accurately determine patron needs in order to assist them. The reference interview is likewise a useful tool to accurately determine information needs when assisting patrons and staff with digital collections. At academic institutions in particular, reference and instruction librarians generally have well-established relationships with faculty and staff, and this familiarity can be helpful for pursuing collaborative projects and keeping channels of communication open with potential digital content providers.

Instruction librarians develop targeted training workshops for specific user groups or classes. A core competency for instruction librarians is knowledge of curricula and the ability to incorporate information literacy into training (ACRL Board, 2007). Naturally, this enables you to carefully design presentations and promotional materials to address specific user needs. Taking instruction to another level, many teaching librarians also consider that attendees of bibliographic instruction classes or workshops bring with them different learning styles and abilities. As a digital librarian, you may design presentations about digital collections for targeted user groups or subject areas when developing tutorials.

Access Services

In many libraries, the circulation desk is the first staffed desk you see after security. For this reason, access services librarians are often asked questions about everything from where bathrooms are located to how to best navigate online resources. They see firsthand how users interact with digital collections, and this alone can provide valuable insight on user interfaces and functionality. In academic libraries, access services units generally include circulation, course reserves, interlibrary loan, and photocopy or reproduction services. If you work in such a setting you may already be involved in some digitization activities, for example electronic course reserves or filling patron reproduction and interlibrary loan requests. These experiences may provide you with recommendations for items to digitize based on use and demand.

A general knowledge of copyright is required of both access services and digital librarians. Copyright restrictions apply to interlibrary loan, reserves, and reproductions just as it must be considered when selecting items for inclusion in digital collections. Other skills that are transferable include customer service, and the ability to troubleshoot technology and to keep up with new trends. Patrons may frequently ask for assistance with a variety of library equipment, websites, and services that are constantly evolving. Digital librarians need to remain aware of how common websites and online tools function to ensure the digital collections behave in ways that are recognizable to patrons.

Systems

Systems librarianship became its own niche when library automation systems became common and integrated library systems (ILS) began being hosted locally. Today systems librarians manage much more than a library's ILS. As a systems librarian, you may also manage proxy servers, discovery or federated search tools, web servers, and content management or digital asset management systems. Digital librarians may also work with web servers and administer content or digital asset management systems. As a systems librarian you may head a department that provides infrastructure to digital library and technical services units and other technology-dependent library areas.

Some duties of digital librarians are similar to those of systems librarians, but with a different focus or approach. In general, digital librarians manage specific digital collections, databases, content and digital asset management systems, or websites and interfaces. Systems librarians may manage multiple library servers, systems, and the tools that permit them to interact with one another. Both systems and digital librarians may track and report statistics on websites and web-based services to library administration. As a systems librarian, you may work directly with end users to assist them in authenticating their library accounts to use remote library services. Digital librarians may also work directly with end users to assist them in using digital collections or subscription databases. Systems librarians may serve as front-line technical support for library staff and, in some cases, library users. Digital librarians may assist staff in using content and digital asset management systems or subscription-based online materials. The communication skills necessary to work with these different groups are the same, even though the material covered is slightly different.

Easily transferable skills include website development, use of relational databases, web server administration, and application of programming and scripting languages. Digital librarians may also manage websites and web resources, create or manage databases, and track usage statistics. Ongoing education is inherent in systems librarian positions in order to keep up with library technology trends and make recommendations to your institutions concerning library systems and software. Digital librarians are called on to do the same for products and services that relate to the resources they manage. Project management is required of both systems and digital librarians, and so it is also a highly transferable skill. The ability to troubleshoot hardware and software that comes from providing technical support can be an added benefit to a digital library team; experience in helping peers and users with hardware and other software can transfer to assisting them with digital library resources, tools, and services.

Systems librarians have been called on to configure and maintain proxy servers and federated search and discovery tools. Such tools are often acquired specifically to improve and streamline access to the electronic resources managed by various digital librarians. With the creation of simpler access points, usability often increases, which in turn increases usage. A digital librarian who has experience configuring proxy servers and federated search and discovery tools can make effective recommendations for tools that best serve a library's users, as well as facilitating communication between library units about these matters.

JOB-HUNTING FOR CAREER CHANGERS

Librarianship has become more and more specialized over the past few decades, and digital librarianship is but one of those specializations. Many library schools have developed academic tracks to train digital librarians, so some graduates step into those positions right out of library school. However, coming from another area in libraries may offer you an advantage if you carefully consider how your specific experience could lead to new ideas or improvements for a library's digital resources. Chapter 3 has extensive information about landing your first job as a digital librarian. Below are three additional tips specifically for those changing careers from other areas of librarianship.

Accentuate the similarities. Show that your experience is both similar to and applicable to a digital librarian's. Identify transferable skills you bring to the table and match them to the required and preferred qualifications of the digital librarian positions to which you are applying.

Formulate a plan for improving the skills that digital librarian positions require. Identify the skills you need to strengthen and be ready to discuss this with potential employers. What discussion lists, classes, or books are available on those topics? Show potential employers that you recognize there are areas you need to improve and that you are already taking initiative to improve in those areas.

Accentuate the differences. Illustrate that your experience brings unique perspectives and, possibly, new approaches to a position or team. What skills might you offer that differ from other digital librarians or team members? Are you an expert trainer? Perhaps you would be the only team member with a background in cataloging. Think creatively about how your experience might benefit the creation of digital resources or a library's online presence.

Be prepared to explain why you want to switch to a digital librarian position. If you have already taken classes, joined digital library discussion lists or associations, or read books (like this one) to improve necessary stills, you may want to mention that as well. This will show that you have taken action toward career change beyond simply submitting resumes and that your interest is in digital libraries, specifically.

■ CASE STUDY ■

Transitioning from Interlibrary Loan to Digitization

by Linda Burkey Wade

My story is an example of a successful career shift to digital services from interlibrary loan (ILL), which was facilitated by a willingness to experiment with new technologies that made it easier for customers to communicate with staff. My first pioneering change was a simple online request form made with HTML and PHP; this was a welcome change for ILL staff that had previously spent hours trying to decipher written requests. However, some customers and staff would protest using the new form without even trying it out (this was the most resistance to change I had seen by library consumers in my entire career, with the exception of the library's removal of the card catalog). Years later, I created a blog allowing customers to follow interlibrary loan's migration to the ILLiad resource-sharing management software, and the customers loved it. This time staff protested the switch to ILLiad; however, patrons were ready for this change because they wanted a system enabling them to see the progression of their requests via ILL.

Because I had proven myself as someone who was comfortable adopting digital technology, in 2009 I was asked to create a new digitization unit at my library. You might think it would be easy to leave one department behind for another—after all, I did volunteer to take on this new unit, and had devoted considerable time to helping customers embrace technology use in my previous position. While I had some background in image manipulation stemming from my first master's degree in instructional technology, the new unit needed policies, workflow, quality control standards, production standards, and preservation procedures as well. Stepping outside my comfort zone to meet these needs was not easy, but my experience in interlibrary loan proved to be helpful in taking on this new role.

New Responsibilities and Challenges

The digitization unit was a newly established functional unit, and one of my first tasks associated with this was space planning. All of the scanners were to be placed in an area designated for digitization, requiring me to redesign the layout of the area. I needed to plan for equipment the library currently owned as well as that which had not yet been purchased, with the addition of shelving and locked compartments to provide security for materials undergoing scanning. I was assigned to be on the libraries' digitization committee and asked to create policies and procedures and establish imaging standards for all new digital collections. Additionally, I lost half of my staff during the transition and was left with only three student assistants.

The first few months were frustrating, as I was unable to hire the much-needed student assistants who now do the unit's scanning. I had to justify every hiring or supply request to my supervisor before getting approval to move forward. Much of my time was spent researching what other digitization units were doing and identifying resources for further educating myself. During the establishment of the unit many of my educational requests were turned down, forcing me to rely on the state digital librarian and any materials I could order via ILL or access for free via the Internet.

Furthermore, I had to establish a new equipment list. More research was involved, which produced an elaborate budget. By the time the unit began digitizing there was no funding for needed items, so I had to use my creativity to utilize the scanners and software we already owned. Many new procedures were created by trial and error, based on my experience in ILL. Finally, six months later and with four student assistants, we set out to digitize our first and biggest collection, the university yearbook. During the production of this first collection I was creating benchmarks and quality standards and establishing production ideals.

Transferable Skills

Fortunately, my time in ILL had given me the workflow analysis skills I needed to continue my success as a unit coordinator. Skills that helped me transition from interlibrary loan to digitization included copyright knowledge, budgeting, website design and management, supervising and training staff, workflow analysis, project management, systems administration, data and request searching, and troubleshooting hardware and software. I took with me my customer service mindset for providing good patron assistance. Quality and production control analysis also aided me in creating this new unit from scratch. The ability to remain flexible and communicate effectively transferred to my new digital duties as well.

Challenges

Initially, my most important task was to create a workflow and practice the new digitization process. This was quite different from my main charge in ILL, which had been searching for and physically sending materials out to patrons. I knew I could not make this transition all on my own and that I had a great group of people with hands-on experience working with me, so I relied heavily on their help. Keeping the lines of communication open with both staff and supervisors is essential. The digitization staff and I instituted regular brainstorming and work sessions during which we would discuss various ideas for solving the new unit's issues, which included deciding on new policies and procedures and meeting the production demands of my supervisor. My employees were happy that they got to provide input, and I felt as if I did not have to solve every problem on my own.

The biggest challenge I faced was leaving a set of known ILL processes and procedures behind to create new ones. Once I established workflows, procedures still needed to be adjusted for individual yearbook volumes as each presented different issues (to this day, workflow procedures are constantly in a state of flux and are evaluated and established for each new collection the unit digitizes). This process was quite time-consuming and I began to think I would never see the collection make it online. This uncertainty was difficult for the student assistants as well. The students who transferred with me from ILL were apprehensive about working in the new digitization unit. An overarching problem I faced was keeping them motivated and their "eyes on the prize," especially when the administration seemed unwilling to address their concerns. Supervising staff or assistants during a time of transition can be difficult, as one needs to provide encouragement to them as well as oneself.

Dealing with Change

An important thing to anticipate when transitioning to a new professional position is the emotional toll that such a change can have. Although taking on the role of head of digitization was a positive career opportunity, on a psychological level the adjustment was more difficult than I had anticipated. After eagerly taking on leadership of the new digitization unit, I did not understand why I felt emotions such as loss, anger, and regret. However, according to Bakken (2006) and Bridges (2004) this type of reaction is common for those experiencing workplace changes, and typically cycles through predictable stages: the "ending," the "neutral zone," and the "new beginning" phases (Bridges, 2004, 105). When transitioning to a new role as a digital librarian (or in any career change), it can be helpful to understand these cycles and how best to deal with them.

The Ending Phase

It is only now that I understand the feelings I experienced when eagerly taking on leadership of the new digitization unit. During the "ending" phase I felt loss, regret, grief, and anger. This was due to the library administration's slowness to act, uncertainty about the new unit's role in the library, and my own sense of isolation—I missed the daily routine that included in-person public service. No one told me all these feelings were normal reactions that should not be denied or trivialized. Strategies I employed for dealing with these emotions included acknowledging them and trying to stay positive and confident in my abilities. While you may be tempted to underestimate yourself, remember your past triumphs and utilize similar techniques to forge ahead in your new position. When I was panicking and thought the new unit would never have a routine or produce a product, I reminded myself of the past successes that had gotten me to that point.

The Neutral Zone Phase

The "neutral zone" phase may include questioning, confusion, uncertainty, and a sense of discovery (Jeffreys, 1995). This becomes your opportunity to learn and develop ideas based on your best skills and to define your own path. Find out about best practices and research what others are doing to help you effectively present your ideas for change. Be prepared if management does not always take you up on your ideas, as they can be slow to embrace change too. Chances are you are going to become the "go-to" person in your new field, so embrace every opportunity to enhance your authority. For instance, if you are digitizing images, become the expert on file management and preservation. In my role as head of digitization I was asked to write a grant. I read that grant forwards and backwards until I knew every procedure, requirement, and guideline, and this helped me to communicate effectively and build confidence in my knowledge on the part of staff and supervisors.

The New Beginnings Phase

Finally we transition into the "new beginnings" phase, where we are energized and excited and can visualize the future. When we can visualize the future, it is under control. Often, it takes a while to "see" where you are headed and how you're going to get there, but once you have this insight it will give you the momentum to move forward in your new role as a digital librarian.

You can continue to grow in your new role by constantly looking for learning opportunities. In addition to taking advantage of free online tutorials, workshops, and classes, check with other colleagues in your area who are willing to share resources and information about digitization. A good resource for this may be your state digital librarian. Mine provided me with numerous helpful online resources and reading materials related to digital imaging standards and procedures. Investigate whether your organization belongs to any statewide library organizations or consortia that offer free or low-cost training sessions for members.

■ ■ ■

FINAL THOUGHTS

Though a relative "new kid on the block," the digital librarian will find his or her role firmly rooted in traditional areas of librarianship. Professionals in more established specializations such as cataloging, reference, and archives may feel that digital project work is beyond their purview, but we hope this chapter will show you that this is not the case. If your job duties are shifting toward the digital (whether intentionally or not), look to your already-established skills as a springboard and have confidence in your ability to learn new ones. Remember that change often does not happen smoothly, and have patience with yourself as you grow into your new role. No one becomes a digital librarian overnight, but those who capitalize on their existing strengths and approach the challenge with curiosity and persistence will have a definite head start.

REFERENCES

Association of College and Research Libraries (ACRL) Board. 2007. "Association of College and Research Libraries Standards for Proficiencies for Instruction Librarians and Coordinators." ACRL website. www.ala.org/acrl/standards/profstandards.cfm.

Bakken, Elizebeth. 2006. "Dealing with Workplace Change". Cytec's Corporate Medical Resources. http://cytecmedicalresources.net/wrkplchange/index.htm.

Bridges, William. 2004. *Transitions: Coping with Life Changes*. 2nd rev. ed. Cambridge, MA: De Capo.

Jeffreys, J. Shep. 1995. *Coping with Workplace Change: Dealing With Loss and Grief*. Menlo Park, CA: Crisp.

Rare Books and Manuscripts Section. 2008. "Guidelines: Competencies For Special Collections Professionals." Association of College and Research Libraries website. www.ala.org/acrl/standards/comp4specollect.

RECOMMENDED RESOURCES

Choi, Youngok, and Rasmussen, Edie. 2009. "What Qualifications and Skills Are Important for Digital Librarian Positions in Academic Libraries? A Job Advertisement Analysis." *Journal of Academic Librarianship* 35, no. 5: 457–67.

Dixon, Diana. 2011. "From Manuscripts to Metadata: The Changing Face of Local Studies Librarianship." *Australasian Public Libraries and Information Services* 24, no. 2 (June): 74–81.

Han, Myung-Ja, and Hswe, Patricia. 2010. "The Evolving Role of the Metadata Librarian." *Library Resources & Technical Services* 54, no. 3 (July).

Ohaji, Isaac Kenechukwu. 2010. "The Changing Professional Image of Librarians: Focusing on the Job Positions of Digital Librarians in Academic Libraries in the United States of America." Master's thesis, Oslo University College. http://hdl.handle.net/10642/429.

Sutton, Sarah W. 2011. "Identifying Core Competencies for Electronic Resources Librarians in the Twenty-First Century Library: A Dissertation." PhD dissertation, Texas Woman's University. http://repositories.tdl.org/tamucc-ir/handle/1969.6/33.

Thompson, Susan M. 2009. *Core Technology Competencies for Librarians and Library Staff: A LITA Guide*. New York: Neal-Schuman.

Whitlatch, Jo Bell, et al. 2003. "Professional Competencies for Reference and User Services Librarians." *Reference and User Services Quarterly* 42, no. 4: 290–95.

Chapter Five

Furthering Your Career

Roy Tennant

If you're reading this book, you probably already understand that simply performing your day job to the best of your abilities is not enough to be both a well-rounded professional and a hot employment prospect. To advance in your career, either at a single institution or through a succession of increasingly responsible positions at a variety of institutions, it's necessary to demonstrate professional engagement. This means writing, speaking, participating in professional associations—really a selection of activities from the range I will outline in this chapter. You will also discover that by doing these things you have moved from having a job to building a career—and believe me, there is a world of difference there.

There are many ways you can build a successful and meaningful career in digital librarianship. Some of the methods I describe here may resonate with you and provide a natural path to success, while others will seem foreign and uninteresting. It will be the rare individual who will employ all of the strategies in this chapter, as it is very difficult to find the time to do everything listed here. Only you can decide which strategies you wish to employ, and doing so effectively will require knowing yourself well. Part of knowing yourself well is trying things out and seeing how they work for you. Therefore, don't hesitate to try things out even if at first they don't seem to be a good fit. We don't always know what is best for us, and pushing our individual boundaries can be a good thing.

Most particularly, don't allow any fears or uncertainties to prevent you from exploring new professional options. When I first began speaking publicly, I was terrified. It took years of enduring butterflies in my stomach, a constricted throat, and a variety of other physical and mental effects of fear before I eventually gained the confidence necessary to be calm in front of an audience. Had I not conquered my fear I would have missed what has been a very rewarding part of my career.

Also, managing your career is a constant activity. You should always be considering adjustments to your strategies and selected career path. New technologies can offer new opportunities for building your career and as you gain more experience you may find some strategies not so useful while others become more important. Check in with yourself periodically and consider whether any adjustments of your tactics would be beneficial. For example, my career began before the advent of blogs, Twitter, Facebook, and all the many ways that I now use to help build an audience that is prepared to buy my next book or attend my next talk.

MENTORS AND FELLOW TRAVELERS

No one makes it alone. I know this as well as anyone, having been blessed with several major mentors and many helpful colleagues. Mentors and peers are sources of support, advice, and many different kinds of assistance for creating a successful career. It's quite likely you will have several mentors over the course of your career.

Mentors can be acquired through either formal or informal relationships. Professional associations or your place of employment may be sources for establishing a formal mentor-mentee relationship with a more experienced librarian. With a formal mentor, you will likely follow guidelines on how and when you interact. Regular meetings may be established when you can discuss your career objectives, share challenges, and receive advice. Obviously, at particular times you may need to call upon your mentor for things that will happen outside of your usual mentoring calendar, such as to write a letter of recommendation or be a job reference. But mostly a formal mentoring relationship establishes certain expectations of both the mentor and mentee that are often managed through guidelines, schedules, and evaluations.

Informal mentor relationships can be initiated either by a librarian who wishes to help the career of an individual or set of individuals, or by the person wanting a mentor. Either way, it's best to establish such a relationship with someone who shares your professional interests. Find someone who has been successful in the particular library specialty you enjoy and ask if they would consider being your mentor. In the latter part of my career, I have sought out individuals whose careers I wish to advance in my own specialty of library technology. At any major conference I attend (e.g., ALA, Internet Librarian, etc.) I host a dinner with the group and also schedule individual meetings. Throughout the year we communicate and I have provided most of them with job references, letters of recommendation, and advice.

Thanks to technology, your mentor can be anywhere. With e-mail, video-conferencing via Skype, Google+, or other platforms, not to mention the good old telephone, mentors can provide advice and assistance from afar. Online chat is another way you can use technology to stay connected. As a digital librarian, you should be comfortable using these technologies to establish and maintain a mentor relationship.

Peers can also be an excellent source of advice, assistance, and a shoulder to cry on. They can provide leads for jobs or other opportunities. Seek out friendships with people in remote but similar organizations and roles, as these are likely to be the most effective relationships. Peers at the same institution will not likely be as free to provide an unbiased perspective, as they are embedded in the same environment along with the same people you are. With all the methods available today to communicate virtually, these relationships can be cemented through text chat, video chat, social networking sites, and telephone as well as the occasional meal or drink at a conference.

As a digital librarian, I have found the Code4Lib IRC channel (chat room) to be a particularly good way to be collectively mentored. That is, by virtually hanging out with colleagues who are also doing digital library work you can both help and be helped by people facing some of the same challenges. These interactions are strengthened even further if you can travel to the Code4Lib annual conference and meet them in person.

PARTICIPATION IN FORMAL PROFESSIONAL ORGANIZATIONS

One path to professional success is through steady and increasingly responsible participation in one or more professional organizations. Most librarians will find a professional home in the American Library Association or the Special Libraries Association, or a specialized professional association such as the American Association of Law Librarians or the Medical Library Association. State associations are also potential avenues of professional involvement. The most obvious ALA division for digital librarians is the Library and Information Technology Association (LITA), but other divisions are not without technology programming, since technology cuts across all areas of librarianship.

The level of your participation may vary depending on the particular association you choose to engage with. It can be easier to aspire to the highest office in a smaller association than a larger one. In most associations, however, there are many ways to lead. A lot can be accomplished by leading a small group with a specific goal. For example, one of the first professional committees on which I served was a committee of the Machine Assisted Reference Service section of ALA's Reference and User Services Association. This was in the early days of the Internet (pre-Web, if you can believe it), and we set out to write a guide to libraries on the Internet. The end result was the publication *Library Resources on the Internet: Strategies for Selection and Use*. Although it is now outdated, at the time it was the only resource available on the topic.

Another factor affecting your ability to participate in professional associations is the level to which your employer supports such work. Participating in a professional association often means travel to conferences that may or may not be reimbursed by your organization. At the least it might require release time that an organization may not afford you. Academic librarians are more often likely to be supported, even at a paltry level, for association work than public librarians, as the former are often evaluated on their participation in professional associations. For those without access to internal travel assistance there may be options for external funding. For example, the Code4Lib Conference often offers scholarships for digital librarians of underrepresented ethnic groups to enable conference attendance. LITA also offers similar scholarships. Your state library association may also be a source of travel grant support (for example, the Washington Library Association offers travel grants of $500 for its members through an application process).

As with any of the methods of advancing one's career discussed in this chapter, association work may not be the path you choose to take. Being effective within the political structure of a professional society is a skill that you may not have or wish to cultivate. After serving on a couple of ALA committees I soon realized I was not cut out for such work and decided to take my career in a different direction. On the other hand, I have good friends who both excel at and enjoy leading in that context. My advice is to figure out where you fall on this spectrum sooner rather than later, as you can flounder ineffectually for years if you don't fully understand your desires and abilities.

PARTICIPATION IN INFORMAL PROFESSIONAL ORGANIZATIONS

I've mentioned Code4Lib as a group that I have found very helpful in my career as a digital librarian. Code4Lib represents a clear departure from standard professional organizations, in that it lacks all of the typical accoutrements of a professional organization—bylaws, officers, and so on. But therein also lies its unique strengths as a path to professional advancement. In the Code4Lib world, those who step up, lead. That is, if you want to do something as a part of the group, just do it. You don't need to (and won't) be appointed or elected. The *Code4Lib Journal* was launched by a group of individuals who volunteered to do it. Anyone was (and still is) welcome to help out. Similarly, at the annual conference, master of ceremonies duties are passed around to whomever cares to do it.

Another example of an informal professional organization is The Library Society of the World (http://thelsw.org/). This is a loose-knit group of mostly young professionals who do not feel well served by traditional library organizations like the American Library Association. As with Code4Lib, you lead simply by stepping up and doing something.

Keep in mind, however, that your place of employment may not accord activities with these informal professional groups the same weight in your performance review as they do activities with formal professional organizations.

WRITING

As someone who has built his career on the foundation of writing, I understand the potential impact of writing on all aspects of one's professional life. In my case, writing established a professional identity that I then enhanced by public speaking and other professional activities. Although this may not be a path you choose to pursue, everyone should consider it given its potential to enhance your professional reputation (or, to be honest, also potentially to damage it).

If you work in an academic library, publishing in peer-reviewed journals may be an expectation of your employment, and in particular your advancement. Publishing books in the field is also considered part of your professional portfolio of work when you are reviewed for tenure or promotion. However, writing a blog or contributing articles for magazines will not be afforded the same consideration. This doesn't mean you shouldn't write for those venues, only that you cannot expect such writing to be given the same weight in your performance review as publication in a peer-reviewed journal. Having a well-regarded blog or a magazine column can still provide professional benefits—such as creating a professional identity that can lead to speaking engagements and other opportunities.

The variety of writing venues is diverse and offers different challenges and rewards. It's quite possible you will discover that you love to write a blog but abhor writing books. More typically, you will either discover you enjoy writing or you don't. If you enjoy it, you will likely write in a variety of venues. My first major foray into writing was a magazine article. This was followed with a book, coauthored with two colleagues. From there came a monthly column and eventually a blog. So over time I have experienced a wide variety of publishing venues, each with its own particular challenges and opportunities.

Magazines

Magazine writing is one of the easiest ways to break into formal publishing in the library profession. A more relaxed writing style is expected and encouraged and your piece may be edited but not peer-reviewed. This also means that it will be published more rapidly after you submit it. I have written both one-off articles and a monthly column for *Library Journal* for a decade. A monthly column is not for everyone, as you must come up with a new topic on a regular basis and have enough to say about it to be credible, but if you think you would enjoy it, it can be a great way to get your name in front of your peers on a regular basis. One method to prepare for writing a column is to start a blog. Use the blog to write lengthier-than-usual posts that are both informative and easy to read (see the section below on blogging for additional advice). This experience can help you decide whether a column is the right venue for you.

As a digital librarian, you should pay particular attention to magazines such as *D-Lib* (www.dlib.org) and *Ariadne* (www.ariadne.ac.uk/), as those are two sources that serve the digital library community. Also, since they are published online instead of in print, they tend to have shorter publishing time frames.

Journals

Writing for professional journals is usually a requirement for academic librarians, as they are often held to the same or similar standards as faculty. Academic advancement typically requires publishing in peer-reviewed journals, which tend to seek research articles rather than opinion or explicative pieces. The publishing timeline is also elongated due to the requirements of the peer review process. Therefore, topics that have a limited shelf life are not good choices for this type of publication. Your best path into the peer-reviewed literature is to perform research. The typical library research piece involves a survey and an analysis of the results of the survey, but that is not the only path by any means. Try to find a topic that intrigues you and think about how you could research the topic in a way that will significantly add to the literature on that issue.

The e-journal of note for digital librarians is *First Monday* (http://firstmonday .org/), which is a top-notch peer-reviewed journal of significant impact in the digital library space. And again, since it is published electronically it tends to have a shorter time-to-market than print journals.

Blogs

The good thing about blogs is that it is trivial to start one. That is also the bad thing about blogs. Since it is so easy to start a blog, many have, and yet not everyone keeps up with writing on a regular basis. Also, since there are so many from which readers can choose it can be difficult to gather an audience. If you choose to blog professionally, keep a few things in mind:

Pick your professional angle and stick with it. I don't mean that you must select a particular subspecialty of librarianship, but your blog should not be where you talk about what you made for dinner or where you went on vacation, unless you can turn that into something useful for your librarian readers.

Cultivate your own voice. There are many, many library bloggers out there. Have something useful to say in a unique way or you may find yourself writing a blog that few read. This is particularly important if you are seeking to make your reputation on your blog alone. An example of a library blogger who accomplished this is Meredith Farkas, who became known for insightful, well-written pieces that quickly garnered a large audience. Her *Information Wants to be Free* blog (http://meredith.wolfwater .com/wordpress/) afforded opportunities for additional writing (her book *Social Software in Libraries* is a seminal book on this topic for librarians) and speaking opportunities.

Be consistent or shut it down. You don't have to blog on a regular schedule, but you can't let weeks—or months!—go by with no posts. If someone encounters your blog and the most recent post is from four months ago, they are very unlikely to add it to their RSS reader.

Be considerate and constructive or don't bother. Rants will not win you followers. You can be assertive, and back up your claims with facts, but being shrill will not help you. Argue the point, not the person who promulgated it, if you have an axe to grind.

Books

Writing a book is a huge commitment, although some types of books are less work than others. I have published three kinds of books—written from scratch alone or with colleagues, edited collections, and a collated and updated collection of magazine columns. Each was a different experience and required different things from me to complete them. The key consideration for taking on a book project is whether you have the time to devote to it. If you write a book from scratch (that is, without previous material you can use), it will take months if not years to complete. Even an edited collection can easily take a year between communicating with the authors, providing them guidance and editing, making sure they meet their deadlines, working with the publisher, and all of the other jobs that go into creating a book. If writing or editing a book intrigues you, I suggest talking to a few published authors about their experiences.

Choosing how to publish is also a consideration. You can self-publish via a service like Lulu.com or Amazon, or you can take the traditional path and partner with a publisher in the field, such as Neal-Schuman, Information Today, ALA, or many others. If you choose to self-publish you retain complete control and garner all of the profit, if there is any, but you are also then responsible for all of the marketing. Traditional print publishers have well-established methods of advertising to the library market such as book catalogs and booths at professional conferences. I've used both strategies, and each has its challenges and rewards. However, if you are just starting off I recommend going with a traditional publisher. Having the support, advice, and marketing assistance can be essential for new authors.

Writing a book on a technical topic presents both challenges and opportunities. A major opportunity is that new technologies are coming along all the time, so there are new chances to become an expert in that technology and write a book on it. A major challenge is that technical topics change rapidly, which means either working hard to keep your book up-to-date or allowing it to fall into obsolescence and stop selling. If you wish to write a book, don't wait for a publisher to come to you—write up a proposal and shop it around to library publishers. For example, the publisher Neal-Schuman, which caters to the library community, has some rather specific instructions on how to propose a book (see the references at the end of this chapter).

Social Software (e.g., Twitter, Facebook, Google+)

It might be difficult to consider iterations of no more than 140 characters (Twitter's limit) to be "writing," but writing well at that length is challenging and therefore more likely to be appreciated by readers. With Facebook, Google+, and other social networking sites the 140-character limit of Twitter does not apply, but succinctness is still appreciated. Make sure that what you write presents your professional persona to its best advantage. The best contributions are likely to be pointers to good articles or blog posts that have to do with digital librarianship. Go ahead and be yourself, but keep in mind that some kinds of humor, such as sarcasm, can be difficult for your readers to interpret appropriately. Social software is particularly useful to establish the kind of network of friends you should develop to help you throughout your career. I've found that watching someone's posts come across in Facebook or Twitter or Google+, and responding to them, breaks the ice and makes me more likely to seek them out at conferences to meet in person. Then you can use these same networks to keep in touch throughout the year, thus cementing new friendships.

If writing interests you, I suggest getting Walt Crawford's book *First Have Something to Say: Writing for the Library Profession*. Walt has been writing in the library field for decades, and he distills what he has learned about writing and publishing in this book. He includes advice on how to retain your personal voice in your writing and speaking, how to build confidence and avoid writer's block, and even how to deal with contracts and copyright. Perhaps especially helpful to someone new to writing for publication are his insights on working with editors and publishers.

SPEAKING

Public speaking is not for everyone, but if you feel like you have any interest in it at all you should try it out. Doing so will likely require conquering your fear, as speaking in front of an audience is one of the most widely held anxieties. Here are some tips to help you get started.

Know your audience. Knowing your audience isn't a matter of identifying one type of individual who represents the whole, but rather the general categories of attendees and roughly how many of each group you can expect. That is, most library groups of any size will have a mix of job classifications, if not a diversity of organization types. Try to get a sense of what your audience should be told related to what you wish to tell them. One evening I arrived at a speaking engagement with a set of presentation slides prepared for my talk the next morning. I met with the organizers and we talked about what they wanted to accomplish the next day and who would be in attendance. I promptly threw out what I had planned to speak about and started from scratch. The next morning I gave a talk specifically tailored to their needs but grounded in my expertise and opinions. Admittedly I should have performed my homework before arriving ill-prepared, but from their perspective there was no difference in the result.

Know your venue and setup. Find out what the room is like where you will be speaking. Will you be at a podium on a stage, or will you have the option of having a wireless lavalier microphone and the ability to roam the floor? How much control do you have over lighting? Where are the controls and who can adjust them when you want them adjusted? I always make it a habit to show up ahead of time with enough time to discover all of this and more and to work out any problems encountered. I also make it a habit to meet the audiovisual technician if there is one, shake his or her hand, and find out how I can contact them if they will not be there the entire time. The audiovisual technician is sometimes the only thing standing between a successful talk and an utter disaster. Treat them with the respect they deserve.

Know your tools. Computers, projectors, microphones (standard, wireless lavalier, etc.), electronic pointers, and so on are all tools of the speaker's trade. Get to know all these tools well enough to not make a fool of yourself in front of an audience. I can't begin to count all of the times I've seen a speaker fumble with their computer or some other piece of technology, and witnessing that does not build an audience's confidence in your abilities—particularly when you are speaking about technical topics.

Know your topic. You might think this goes without saying, but it bears repeating. Good speakers know their topic well enough that they can be compelling without the use of props—primarily Microsoft PowerPoint these days, but potentially many other tools. Being comfortable with your topic will allow you to be comfortable in front of your audience—especially when things go wrong. The flip side to this is to not be afraid to admit your ignorance. It is much better to be honest about the limits of your knowledge than to make things up. You may think your audience expects you to know everything—to be the expert on the topic—but they also know that you are human. You are more likely to be admired for being honest about your failings than you are for saying something plausible but wrong.

For more advice on speaking, including what you need to know about getting paid to speak, see my *Library Journal* blog post, "Speaking from a Speaker's Point of View" (Tennant, 2008).

CONTINUING EDUCATION

Continuing education is a vital part of any professional career. Most professions cannot be practiced over time without renewing skills and knowledge, but this is even more important for digital librarians given the pace of technological change. Thankfully, there are many methods to acquire new knowledge and skills these days that do not require travel. Many library schools offer virtual courses and degree programs. A variety of sources from professional associations to regional networks provide online webinars and workshops. Some of these are free and others are available for a small cost. Many of the divisions of the American Library Association offer online courses (www.classes.ala.org) on an ongoing basis throughout the year. Online courses offer the flexibility to participate when it is convenient. Many of these are open to librarians anywhere. If your employer pays your expenses for attending a professional conference such as the ALA Annual Conference, you may be able to persuade them to also support attending one or more of the preconferences that are offered in conjunction with that meeting. Pre-conference sessions can be a good way to explore a new topic, although they are not typically a good way to pick up new skills because they tend to be general overviews more than hands-on workshops.

For a digital librarian, picking new things up as you go along cannot be overemphasized. If you have an assignment that offers an opportunity to learn a new skill while completing it, jump at the chance to flex your mental muscles.

This may be the perfect time to learn about regular expressions or how to compile software from source code. A good digital librarian will be able to pick up a new skill by using cheat sheets or step-by-step descriptions found on the Internet, or a good reference book. This too is continuing education, and the finest kind, as you reinforce what you learn by using it then and there to solve a problem.

KEEPING CURRENT

Current awareness is an essential ongoing activity for any successful professional, but it is of particular importance for any profession grounded in technology, as is digital librarianship. There are many strategies for keeping up-to-date, and what one person finds efficient and effective may not work for another. My own strategies are in frequent flux, as new methods come along and supplant others. For example, I now find myself consuming very little RSS. If a blog post is not noted in my Twitter, Facebook, or Google+ feeds I am likely to miss it. I am using my friends as a filter—if something isn't good enough to be noted by the people I follow, it likely isn't going to be of use to me. Sure, I may overlook some useful things, but that is also likely true of *any* filtering strategy.

Cultivate your own current awareness strategy by trying out various tools and publications until you find a mix that works for you. Then, check in periodically on other ways of keeping up, as there are new methods cropping up all the time. Here are some specific tools, sites, and publications you should consider:

Steven Bell has a wonderful resource center for library current awareness resources called *Keeping Up:* (http://stevenbell.info/keepup/librarianship.htm).

LISNews is a current awareness/library news blog that sustains a near-constant feed of happenings in or related to libraries: (http://lisnews.org/).

Current Cites is a monthly current awareness newsletter for librarians that has been published every month since August 1990. It includes 8–12 brief citations and informative summaries of items selected by a team of reviewers: (http://currentcites.org/).

Whatever you choose to monitor and read, you must set aside time each day or week to do this. Keeping current is necessary to do your job well, and part of being a professional; for a digital librarian it is essential.

GENERAL ADVICE

Be opportunistic. Every now and then someone has asked me about my goals. Often phrased as "where do you want to be in five (or ten) years?" this question always left me puzzled. I really don't know, I would think at the time. Eventually I came to realize that I didn't want a future so limited and dreary that I could imagine it. What fostered this revelation was looking back at where I had come from and where I was "today"—whenever today was. How I had arrived was not by staking out a long-term process to achieve a specific goal, but by grabbing my career by the throat and beating my chances out of it. Part of this is being opportunistic. This means watching for opportunities, recognizing them when they arrive, and seizing them if they are right for you. This is particularly important for digital librarians, as envisioning where you might be in 5 or 10 years is in some ways laughable. Who could have predicted, for example, that Google would come along or that they would choose to digitize entire libraries of content? I sure didn't.

Create your own opportunities. The "Digital Libraries" column I wrote for *Library Journal* for ten years was my idea. I pitched it to the editors and luckily they agreed. If I had sat around waiting for someone to offer me such an opportunity I would still be waiting. The point is to actively think about how you wish to advance your career and execute on that plan with energy and imagination. Perhaps you don't want to write a monthly column—that's fine, but what *do* you want to do? Figure that out and make it real. This may mean garnering advice and assistance from colleagues, mentors, and friends along the way.

Don't hang your professional hat on too small of a peg. One path to professional fame is to become an expert on a particular topic. This usually means picking something fairly specific, which has its dangers. If you become known for being an expert in one small area, what happens when that area is no longer of any importance? How do you move on? An example of someone who has mastered an important topic well is Marshall Breeding. Through long and effective effort he has built a reputation as being the "go to" person on all things relating to the library automation business. His Library Technology Guides website (http://librarytechnology.org/) has a wealth of information on this business community and how it has changed over the years. His chart of the history of library automation is a prime example of the service his site offers, but you will also find an excellent directory of libraries, a constantly updated archive of press releases from library automation companies, and more. From this work he has become a highly sought-after speaker who often travels far and wide to speak about the library automation landscape. Since the topic in which he selected to specialize will never go away, neither will the importance we accord Marshall's contribution as long as he keeps doing what he's doing.

Complacency presages retirement. Complacency has no place in a profession. As a professional, you must continue to learn and grow. Once you stop doing that you are only treading water and should likely get out of the way so someone else who remains engaged can take your place. If you are feeling complacent, then that is probably a sign you need to shake things up. Are there new challenges you can volunteer for? New things you would like to learn that would take your library to the next level? Maybe it's time to learn the next hot programming language, or become experienced with a new platform like the iPad. There are so many options for reigniting your interest in the digital world, you may just need to take a good look around.

Evolving is what successful species do. Furthering your career means extending and enhancing your knowledge, skills, and experience. This should be an ongoing set of tasks you perform, from keeping up with the professional literature to learning a new skill. Doing this well will require investing some of your own time in professional development, but this is no different than what is expected from any other professional.

Find a friend, be a friend. As I said earlier in this chapter, no one makes it alone. Find fellow travelers you can lean on and that you can support in your turn. Seek out a mentor and later be one for someone else. You will find that the rewards far exceed your efforts.

FINAL THOUGHTS

There are many ways you can further your career. Although I have tried to identify many methods in this chapter, I know that there are strategies I have not highlighted (bribery, for example). So you should remain vigilant for additional opportunities you can exploit or create as you build a successful career in librarianship. If you are reading this book, then clearly you are already well on your way.

REFERENCES

Crawford, Walt. 2003. *First Have Something to Say: Writing for the Library Profession.* Chicago: American Library Association.

Neal-Schuman Publishers. *How to Propose Your Book.* http://neal-schuman.com/how-to-propose-your-book.

Tennant, Roy. 2008. "Speaking From a Speaker's Point of View," *Digital Libraries* (blog). *Library Journal.* May 29. www.thedigitalshift.com/2008/05/roy-tennant-digital-libraries/speaking-from-a-speakers-point-of-view/.

PART 2

Practicing Your Career

Chapter Six

Understanding Key Technology Concepts

Matt Zimmerman

As the rest of this book illustrates, being a digital librarian is not just about technology—but technology, of course, is a big part of the digital librarian's life. The amount you need to know really depends on your role. If you are at a large library you may have a team of technologists with whom you work, and you will only need to know enough to be able to converse with other digital librarians and technologists. If you are at a smaller institution, you may do a lot of the technical work yourself and will need to get your hands dirty and learn the nuts and bolts of certain web technologies. The following chapter serves as an overview of the key technologies you will encounter as a digital librarian.

Not all library technology involves the World Wide Web; there are still stand-alone programs and locally installed clients that do not require the use of a web browser. Since 1991, however, when Tim Berners-Lee launched the Web, library technology has become more and more web-based. Twenty years after its birth, the Web makes up such a large portion of library technology that this chapter will focus largely on the technologies that make the Web work. It will introduce you to the "three-tier architecture" that is at the heart of all websites (HTML, databases, and programming) as well as XML, digital imaging, and content management systems. It is rare that anyone would ever become an expert in all of these areas, so choose the approach that is best for you. If you just need an overview, reading this chapter will suffice, but if you wish to pursue any of these technologies in depth, consult the list of resources at the end of the chapter to get started.

THREE-TIER WEB ARCHITECTURE

All modern websites use what is called a "three-tier architecture." Depending on who you speak to, there are different names for these tiers, but a common delineation is to refer to the "presentation" layer, the "data" layer, and the "application" layer. Web development uses the three-tiered approach to create a division of labor and allows technologists to become experts in interface design (presentation), database design (data), or programming (application). It also allows one part of a web application to be improved or changed without having to touch the other parts. At a large institution there will usually be different people doing interface design, database design, and programming. At a small library, however, you or someone else might have to take on responsibility for all three. The following sections explore each layer in more detail, and finally explain how they all work together.

Presentation Layer

In web development, the presentation layer refers to web pages written in HTML and viewed in a web browser. This is the part of the web application that the end user sees and interacts with, such as a search screen for your library's institutional repository.

HTML

Hypertext Markup Language (HTML) is the basis of the World Wide Web. Even without the data and application layers, you can still create a website solely with HTML. It is a relatively simple set of tag pairs (each tag enclosed in brackets) that is used to describe the structure of a text document. Each tag pair, or "element," has a start tag such as <H1> and an end tag such as </H1>—the difference being the "/" included in the end tag. The easiest way to see real-life HTML is to view the HTML source code of a web page the next time you are using your web browser (in Internet Explorer you can do this by choosing the "View" menu and then choosing "Source"; in Firefox choose the "Tools" menu, "Web Developer," and "View Source").

In order to ensure that no single organization has a monopoly on how browsers should interpret HTML the standard is maintained by the World Wide Web Consortium (www.w3c.org), often referred to as the W3C. Web browsers, such as Internet Explorer, Firefox, and Chrome are supposed to be developed to conform to the W3C standard so that HTML displays the same regardless of the web browser

A Note about the Word *Server*

Discussions about the World Wide Web can become muddled because of the two meanings of the word *server*. The first meaning is that of a physical computer connected to the Internet, usually housed in some sort of machine room at your institution. But the word *server* can also be used to describe a piece of software that runs on one of these physical machines to perform a certain service, such as e-mail server software or web server software. For the rest of this section, when the word *server* is used, it refers to software, not hardware.

being used. The current standard is HTML 4.01, with HTML 5 still in "working draft" status.

How Does a Web Server Work?

HTML works very simply. Right now you could create a simple HTML file, name it something like "test.html," and save it to the desktop of your computer. You could then open it up and view it with the web browser of your choice. The beauty of the World Wide Web, of course, is using the Internet to allow the whole world to see your web page. That is where web servers come in.

Web servers are very simple; one might even say "dumb." They do one thing; they do it very well; and they do it over and over. This is easier to explain by example. Let's say you are sitting at your computer and you want to visit the Library of Congress's website. You enter www.loc.gov/ into the address bar of your web browser. Your browser then sends a request to www.loc.gov/ for the main website page, most likely a file named "index.html" (when you enter an address like www.loc.gov/ without a particular file name the web server assumes you are looking for "index.html"). When the web server named www.loc.gov/ gets your request it says "Ok. This person would like a copy of 'index.html'" and sends it back to your browser. You now see the main Library of Congress web page in your web browser. At this point you could disconnect your computer from the Internet and you would still see that page because it has been sent from the Library of Congress server to your local computer for viewing. Every time you click on a link or enter a URL, you are simply retrieving HTML pages from a web server. For this reason, unless you are going to become a web server administrator, the primary thing you need to learn if you want to create a website or web pages is HTML.

CSS

When HTML was first developed in 1991, there were no choices about how to display the text on the computer screen. HTML was viewed in monochromatic web browsers with no bolding or italicizing of texts and no choice of fonts. When graphical web browsers were developed (around 1993), the HTML standard began to include "inline" formatting, that is, formatting commands that could be included directly in the HTML. A typical example of this is the <FONT></FONT> element. If you wanted to set the size, font, and text color of a particular paragraph you could use the following code:

```
<P>
<FONT size="5" face="arial" color="red">Welcome to my web page.</FONT>
</P>
```

You might see the limitation to this immediately. If you had ten, 20, or even 100 HTML pages that made up your website and you decided to change the font face, size, and color of the text, you would have go through every page and make changes. This isn't practical.

Cascading Style Sheets (CSS) solve this problem. CSS is a styling language that allows you to separate your web pages' formatting from content. Instead of including your formatting information within the HTML, with CSS you include the styling information in a separate file that is referenced by the HTML. For example, in your HTML you would enclose all of your top-level headers in an <H1></H1> element and then define the style for H1 in a CSS file like this: H1 {color:blue; font-family:"Times New Roman"; font-size:40px;} This would make all of your first-level headers blue, Times New Roman and 40 pixels high. If you decided to change the color of your headings you would only have to make the change in one place.

This approach has many advantages. First, you can link hundreds, even thousands of web pages to one CSS file. If you have a large website, with many pages, you only need to change the CSS file in order to affect the whole website. Second, you can have more than one CSS file per website. Perhaps you want to style the pages differently for your mobile site. You only need to create a second CSS file and use the same original content.

Hand Coding vs. WYSIWYG

Many people ask the question "What software do I need to start developing HTML?" The good news is that you can start with the simplest of text editors (Notepad on Microsoft Windows Systems or TextEdit on Apple Macintosh). There

Why "Cascading"?

Even though the most effective way to use CSS is to include the styles in a separate file from your HTML, you can also include the style sheet within your HTML and even do inline styles within an HTML element. Cascading refers to the order of precedence followed in using these styles. Highest priority is given to inline styles, followed by a style sheet embedded in HTML, followed by the external style sheet. This allows you to declare general styles for your whole website in the external style sheet and then include styles within HTML pages where you would like to ignore these general rules.

are also many free text editors available for download that offer additional features to help with writing HTML, such as color coding to differentiate tags from content, syntax checking for mistakes in your HTML, and automatic indenting so that tags are "nested." Examples of free and low-cost text editors are Notepad++ for Windows and Komodo Edit for both Windows and Macintosh.

The editors mentioned above are all tools for "hand coding" HTML, that is, viewing and editing the actual HTML code. Another option is to use a WYSIWYG (What You See Is What You Get) editor. With a WYSIWYG editor, instead of editing the actual HTML code you simply type, format, and lay out the page the way you would in a program like Microsoft Word, and the program generates the HTML code for you. The most popular WYSIWYG editor is Dreamweaver. There are, however, advantages and disadvantages to this approach. Advantages are that you can get started quickly, you don't have to learn HTML, and you can develop pages right away. The disadvantages are that often WYSIWYG editors create "bad" or non-standard HTML that may work in one browser but not in another, and WYSIWYG editors cost much more than simple text editors. Also, since you are not learning HTML code, you won't be able to hand-code small changes to the HTML if needed.

The best approach is to start learning HTML with a simple text editor. As you progress and perhaps develop more complex sites you may decide a WYSIWYG editor is for you, but it is better to know how HTML code works first.

Data Layer

The data layer refers to the database of information behind the scenes that the user is trying to access; for instance, the title, author, subject, and other information about the objects in a digital repository.

Databases

Computer databases have been around much longer than the World Wide Web—since the mid-1960s in fact. A database is loosely defined as an organized collection of data. Typically, when we use the word *database* we are referring to a Database Management System (DBMS), such as Access, Oracle, or MySQL. Though database management requires a higher level of technical skill than HTML, there are two key concepts that will help you get started.

Relational Model

It is easiest to conceptualize a database as a table composed of rows and columns. Each row is an item in the database and each column is a unit of information about that item. For instance, if each row in the table represented a book, the columns might represent title, author, year of publication, publisher name, and so on, as shown in table 6.1.

TABLE 6.1
Example of a simple database table

First_Name	Last_Name	Title	Publisher	Year
William	Faulkner	The Sound and the Fury	Viking	1990
Joseph	Heller	Catch 22	Black Swan	1991
Toni	Morrison	Beloved	Knopf	1987
Thomas	Pynchon	Gravity's Rainbow	Viking	1973
Virginia	Woolf	To the Lighthouse	Harcourt, Brace	1927

With a large database, having only one table starts to become a problem. What if there is more than one author for a book? And for information that could be repeated often in a database (such as an author or publisher name), how do you ensure it is always spelled the same? What if one bit of information, like a publisher's name, changes? You would have to go back and change every instance of it.

The relational database model solves this, much like CSS solves the styling problem in HTML. In the relational model, multiple tables are created to separate information into discrete parts. For instance, in our *books* database example we would have one table for books and a separate table for authors.

In table 6.2, you see that instead of repeating the authors' or publishers' name in the *books* table, it is simply listed once in the *authors* table and then referenced multiple times in the *books* table. If, for some reason, the spelling of this author's name ever changed we would only have to change it in one place. You can even

TABLE 6.2
Example of tables in a relational database

Books Table

Author_ID	Title	Publisher	Year
1	The Sound and the Fury	Viking	1990
1	Absalom, Absalom!	Chatto and Windus	1969
2	Catch 22	Black Swan	1991
3	Beloved	Knopf	1987
3	Song of Solomon	Knopf	1977
4	Gravity's Rainbow	Viking	1973
5	To the Lighthouse	Harcourt, Brace	1927

Authors Table

ID	First_Name	Last_Name
1	William	Faulkner
2	Joseph	Heller
3	Toni	Morrison
4	Thomas	Pynchon
5	Virginia	Woolf

solve the problem of multiple authors in the relational model by creating what are called linking tables.

In table 6.3 we have a unique ID for each book and author. A third table links these together. For instance, book 2 is related to both authors 1 and 2.

SQL

You might be wondering how useful these tables are by themselves, and the answer is not very. To extract information from a database, you need a special language.

Which Database Software Should I Use?

Typically you will not get to choose which DBMS to use. Often your system administrator or institution will already have chosen one. Large institutions tend to use Oracle. Midsize institutions often use Microsoft SQL server. Many nonprofits use MySQL since it is free. All have their advantages and disadvantages, and your choice, if you have one, will depend on your needs and budget, but if you are just starting out, using a free database for learning purposes is a good choice.

TABLE 6.3
Example of linked tables in a relational database

Books Table

ID	Title	Publisher	Year
1	Conversations with Toni Morrison	University of Mississippi	1994
2	Toni Morrison's "Song of Solomon": A Casebook	Oxford University	2003

Authors Table

ID	First_Name	Last_Name
1	Jan	Furman
2	Danielle Kathleen	Taylor-Guthrie
3	Toni	Morrison

Linking Table

Author_ID	Books_ID
2	1
3	1
2	2
1	2

Luckily, all relational database management systems use some form of Structured Query Language (SQL). There are sometimes slight differences between how SQL is used in Access, Oracle, or MySQL, but for the most part they are the same. Some more good news is that SQL is easy to learn, assuming you understand the structure of the database you are trying to query. The SQL to retrieve all of the titles from a table called *books* where the publication date is 1983 would be "SELECT title FROM books WHERE date=1983". That's it!

Application Layer

The application layer is the computer programming that allows the presentation layer and data layer to communicate with each other using a programming language. There are different names for this layer. Some call it the "programming layer"; others call it the "business logic" layer or "middleware." Whatever you decide to call it, this is the part of the three-tier architecture that allows your web pages to talk to the database. It enables you to create web pages where users can search your catalog and have results returned, or display custom information based on choices they make—in short, to make your web page dynamic. Without the application layer, you would just have static web pages and databases that no one could access.

Shortly after HTML was developed, programmers realized it would be useful to connect their web pages to database back ends for richer, interactive websites. The first programming language that was used to do this (and is still used today) was called Perl. Other languages were developed soon after, many of which you may have heard of, such as PHP, ASP, JSP, and Cold Fusion.

How Does the Application Layer Work?

To use one of these programming languages you must have that language's "application server" installed. Typically it will run on the same physical machine as your web server because the web server and application server work together. Here is a very simple example of how the web server, application server, and database work together. You have a web form written in HTML where a user can enter information to search your institutional repository's collection of electronic theses and dissertations. The user enters information (such as an author's name) and hits the "search" or "submit" button on the web page. At this point the information from the form is passed on to the application layer, which creates an SQL query and submits the search to the database. The application layer waits for a reply from the database and, when received, outputs the results in HTML. You can see why many call this layer "middleware." Whichever programming language you choose, it is the middleman between your web pages and database, passing information back and forth.

What Programming Language Should I Learn?

Depending on your role, you might not have to learn one of these languages, but it is good to at least be familiar with them. As with databases, you may not have a choice of what programming language to use as your system administrator or institution may have already made this decision. Often, if you are using Microsoft's SQL server as your database you will use ASP as your programming language, since it is also a Microsoft product. Most organizations that use MySQL as their database management system opt to use PHP. In actuality, most of these programming languages are the same. Some experts will argue that one has better security features, or claim that another runs faster. The good news is, if you learn one you can quickly learn another since for the most part they use the same syntax.

Many people choose to start with the PHP/MySQL combination since both the MySQL database and PHP application server are free to download. You can even download them to your desktop computer. If you don't have a system at work to learn on, often the easiest thing to do is purchase web hosting through a company like www.godaddy.com or www.bluehost.com. For a small fee each month you have a system on which you can learn and practice MySQL, PHP, and HTML. If you are a student in library school, your program may also provide free network server space that you can use for the same purpose.

Do you need to become proficient in all three layers? As with many questions, the answer is "it depends." At a larger institution you may have dedicated staff that handles these technical aspects. If you are at a small library you may be the one doing all the technical work. Regardless, it is good to understand the three-tier concept and that every web application involves HTML pages, a database, and middleware to connect them.

XML

XML (eXtensible Markup Language) as a concept is very simple, but its uses are varied. XML is simply a set of rules for encoding text. XML "looks" like HTML in that it uses tag sets enclosed in angle brackets (like <tag></tag>), but the difference is you can name those tag sets anything you want, as opposed to being limited to the defined set of tags in HTML. If you want to call an element "<author> </author>" in XML, you can. Or you can create an element called "<speaker> </speaker>". You can do whatever you want when creating an XML document as long as it follows these rules:

- There is one "root" element. There must be one tag that encloses the whole document.
- All elements must have a beginning and end tag.
- Tags are case sensitive.
- Elements must be "nested" and cannot overlap.

If all of these rules are followed, then your XML document is considered well-formed, which simply means it is following the rules of XML.

Uses of XML

So what is the point of XML if you can name the tags whatever you choose? XML allows people to have a simple, text-based, nonproprietary way of exchanging information. Take RSS for example. If you have ever subscribed to an RSS feed, you know that you simply enter a URL into your RSS reader and instantly get news from the site to which you subscribe, no matter what RSS reader you are using. This is because RSS is an agreed-upon XML standard. If you are going to create your own RSS feeds for others to use, or if you are going to develop an RSS reader, you must comply with the set elements agreed upon in the RSS XML standard. Since XML documents are simply text files, any application can create them, and any application can read them.

A more complex example is the Text Encoding Initiative (TEI). TEI is an agreed-upon set of XML elements used for marking up literary and linguistic texts, and is often used in the field of digital humanities (which has significant overlap with digital libraries). If you have access to TEI-encoded files, and you know the standard, you can write any sort of application to work with these XML files (language analysis, HTML creation, etc.) Likewise, if you create TEI-encoded files, others can use them for different purposes. Two other XML standards used in libraries are METS (Metadata Encoding and Transmission Standard) and EAD (Encoded Archival Description).

The short of it is, an XML document by itself is a simple text document. But when you have a group of people who have agreed upon a certain set of elements, it becomes a powerful tool for information exchange.

CONTENT MANAGEMENT SYSTEMS

After reading the previous sections of this chapter, you might begin to wonder if you really can handle designing databases and user interfaces as well as writing computer code. The good news is, there is a way around this, and that is to use a content management system (CMS). Content management systems allow you to create and manage your website through a web interface that involves little, if any, programming, layout, or databases design. It still uses HTML, a data layer, and a programming language to create dynamic sites, but most of the work has been done already for you or is done behind the scenes. As the name implies, a CMS also allows you to distribute content creation throughout your organization. Certain people can create content (articles, subject guides, etc.) using simple web forms. That content can then be reviewed in the system by editors and made "live" online.

There are a wide range of CMS software packages available, from commercial products that cost hundreds of thousands of dollars a year to open source and free

Commercial Systems vs. Open Source Systems

There is often an assumption that libraries should choose open source systems (whether a CMS, database, or programming language) because the cost ("free") fits into library budgets, but this assumption can be wrong. Even though there are fewer up-front costs with an open source system, there are still costs involved. Open source systems often require more configuration work during setup and sometimes a full-time staff member to handle long-term upkeep and maintenance. When choosing a system, be sure to consider not only the initial cost of the system, but what the setup and long-term maintenance costs will be.

systems. There are some popular choices used for general websites such as Joomla! and Drupal as well as systems designed specifically for digital libraries such as CONTENTdm, Greenstone, DSpace, and Fedora.

Your choice of a CMS will depend on your needs and budget, and since each one uses a particular database and programming language you will need to have them installed on your server before you can use the CMS. For instance, Drupal uses PHP and MySQL, so you would need both of those applications installed on your server to use Drupal.

So if a CMS does all the work for you, why would you *not* use one? Here are a few drawbacks to consider:

- Most content management systems take some work to install and get up and running.
- Most content management systems have a steep learning curve.
- The convenience of a CMS also limits some of your freedom in designing the look of your site.

DIGITAL IMAGING

In addition to understanding web programming, databases, HTML, and XML, a digital librarian will need to learn a bit about digital imaging. Digital imaging is a subject that could encompass an entire book, so we will just cover the basics. A digital librarian will typically become involved with digital imaging for one of two reasons: preparing images for use on a web page or doing digital preservation of images. Preparing images for use on a web page will typically require less work and attention to detail than digital preservation.

When preparing images for use on a website, such as your library website or perhaps the welcome page for your institutional repository, your goal is ease of use for your user. You will want to create images that look good on the computer screen and are small enough that they download quickly. You will, therefore, use one of three types of image files:

JPEG (Joint Photographic Experts Group) files end with the .jpeg or .jpg extension and are called compressed files. This means they were run through some sort of compression software to decrease their size (to the kilobyte range) so they can be easily sent over the Internet.

GIF (Graphics Interchange Format) files end with the .gif extension and are compressed files. GIF files are small and can be easily displayed on web pages, but only have access to 256 colors (as opposed to the millions of colors JPEG and TIFF files use) so are only useful for simple images and logos.

PNG (Portable Network Graphics) files end with the .png extension. The PNG format is a compressed file format designed to replace the GIF format since GIF is a patented file type. PNG is intended to be used only for Internet images and not for print images or digital preservation.

When preparing files for digital preservation, the goal of the digital librarian is not ease of use for the end user, but preserving as much information about the image as possible. Though there are emerging alternatives such as JPEG 2000, the standard for digital preservation is still the TIFF file. TIFF (Tagged Image File Format) files end with the .tiff or .tif extension and are called "uncompressed" files, meaning they contain a lot of digital information and therefore are usually large in size (typically in the megabytes). They are usually used for long-term storage and preservation and are often called "master" files since they can be used to create different type of derivative files (for example, jpegs).

FINAL THOUGHTS

Though not every digital librarian needs to become a "hard-core" technologist, every digital librarian needs to know the basics about the technologies involved in their daily work. Technology changes so quickly that often digital librarians fear that their skills will become outdated. It is true that you will have to keep up on technology via blogs, discussion lists, conferences, and colleagues, but the technologies mentioned in this chapter offer solid grounding that you can grow upon. For instance, once you learn the basics of HTML you will only need to learn the changes that occur in the HTML standard every few years. The same holds true with CSS. Database design and SQL have not changed much since their inception in the 1960s, and once you learn one programming language, such as PHP, you will know the basics of programming and can learn another if needed. The rest really is practice. Like any skill, the more it is used, the more it is kept sharp.

Where you go from here depends a lot on what your needs are. This chapter covered a lot of information in a short space, and each topic offers the opportunity for much deeper study. The good news is that once you understand the basics, many digital technologies can be more or less self-taught. The resources listed at the end of the chapter can guide you in planning your own course of study. When teaching yourself new technologies, please give yourself time. Start with learning HTML and CSS, and play around with digital imaging. Next, consider adopting a CMS. If you want to get more hands-on, then learn a programming language like PHP. Once you're comfortable with that, you might take a class in database design and SQL. The important thing is to go at the pace that suits you. There is a lot to learn while jump-starting your career in digital librarianship!

RECOMMENDED RESOURCES

Adobe, "Cold Fusion Developer Center": www.adobe.com/devnet/coldfusion.html.

Castro, Elizabeth. 2006. *HTML, XHTML, and CSS*. 6th ed. Berkeley, CA: Peachpit.

Forta, Ben. 2004. *Sams Teach Yourself SQL in 10 Minutes*. 3rd ed. Indianapolis, IN: Sams.

Forta, Ben, Raymond Camden, and Charlie Arehart. 2010. *Adobe ColdFusion 9 Web Application Construction Kit, Volume 1: Getting Started*. Berkeley, CA: Peachpit.

Freeman, Eric T., Elisabeth Freeman, and Elisabeth Robson. 2005. *Head First HTML with CSS & XHTML*. Sebastopol, CA: O'Reilly.

Harold, Elliotte Rusty. 2005. *XML 1.1 Bible*. Indianapolis, IN: Wiley.

Hernandez, Michael J. 2003. *Database Design for Mere Mortals: A Hands-On Guide to Relational Database Design*. 2nd ed. Boston: Addison-Wesley.

Mitchell, Scott. 2010. *Sams Teach Yourself ASP.NET 4 in 24 Hours: Complete Starter Kit*. Indianapolis, IN: Sams.

O'Reilly Media. "XML from the Inside Out." www.xml.com/.

Valade, Janet. 2009. *PHP & MySQL for Dummies.* 4th ed. Indianapolis, IN: Wiley.

World Wide Web Consortium. "Web Design and Applications." www.w3.org/standards/webdesign/.

W3Schools. "CSS Tutorial." www.w3schools.com/css/default.asp.

W3Schools. "HTML Tutorial." www.w3schools.com/html/.

W3Schools, "PHP Tutorial": www.w3schools.com/php/default.asp.

W3Schools, "SQL Tutorial": www.w3schools.com/SQl/default.asp.

W3Schools, "ASP Tutorial": http://w3schools.com/asp/default.asp.

W3Schools, "XML Tutorial": www.w3schools.com/xml/default.asp.

Chapter Seven

Managing Digital Projects

Ione Damasco, Frances Rice, and Somaly Kim Wu

The work of digital librarians generally involves the planning and implementation of specific digital projects, such as digitizing collections for online access, developing an institutional repository, or migrating library website content to a content management system. Staff from various departments within the library or from units external to the library might be called upon to perform specific tasks related to a digital project, often under the constraints of a limited budget and a short timeline. Given these challenges, managing digital projects through the use of project management techniques can increase the likelihood of a project's successful completion. Digital librarians are often expected to function as de facto or "accidental" project managers, so familiarizing yourself with project management techniques can help you mitigate some of the challenges posed by digital projects. In this chapter we will provide a general framework for digital project management, and then demonstrate its application in two case studies exemplifying different digital project scenarios.

LITERATURE REVIEW

A survey of existing library literature reveals a need for more research and writing on the topic of project management in libraries, especially digital project management. However, many of the generalized articles and resources on project management list similar processes as key functions, and offer various methods and techniques that can be adapted for librarians. In an article in *Serials Librarian*, one librarian draws on her project management certification to discuss the integration and application of project management techniques adapted from the Project Management Institute (PMI), an association that offers products and services to help make project management successful (Marill and Lesher, 2007). The PMI, seen as the creator of global guidelines for project management, defines project management as a series of five process groups: initiating, planning, executing or monitoring, controlling, and closing (PMI, 2008). Revels (2010) provides a brief explanation of the PMI project management process for "accidental" digital project managers. In addition, *The Handbook for Digital Projects: A Management Tool for Preservation and Access,* developed by the Northeast Document Conservation Center (Sitts, 2000), devotes an entire chapter to project management. The chapter lists goal setting, effective communication among team members, and thorough documentation as elements of successful project management.

Case studies offer insight into the practical applications of different project management methods. Burich et al. write of their experiences expanding newly implemented services beyond their individual libraries to other institutions, utilizing modified project management techniques (2006). Although the projects did not initially use formal project management techniques, the process of completing each project demonstrated the practical value of such methods. As a result, the authors defined their own project management steps: project visualization, definition and planning, implementation, and completion. Another case study that focused on the digitization of a specific collection cited the value of preplanning for effective project management, noting the importance of communication through regular meetings with project participants, as well as the need for developing and documenting project standards (Symonds and May, 2009).

MANAGING DIGITAL PROJECTS IN LIBRARIES

Libraries are constantly engaged in various types of projects, which are not to be confused with daily operational tasks. Although projects may share some similarities with standard operational activities, projects by their very nature are temporary (which does not necessarily mean short), have a stated end, and culminate in the delivery of defined products within a specific amount of time. As mentioned previously, digital library projects can be conceptualized to include a wide range of activities ranging from shorter, very discrete tasks, such as the digitization of a specific physical collection, to larger undertakings, such as developing and launching an institutional repository. Digital projects can also entail adding individual collections to existing repositories or other digital resource management software. As Massis states, "the specifics of library projects fit, more often than not, into the category of significant, boundary-widening projects set outside the realm of customary organizational structure of the daily operational workflow" (Massis 2010, 527).

For the purposes of this chapter, we define project management as consisting of five phases: (1) visualizing the project, (2) planning the project, (3) executing or implementing the project, (4) controlling and monitoring the project, and (5) concluding or closing out the project. In addition to these specific project phases, projects also operate under constraints such as budget, time, resource availability (including personnel), and risks. Good project management entails a balanced approach to project tasks within the context of such constraints. Project management addresses any needs, concerns, or expectations that arise throughout the life of the project. It also guides project activities to ensure the project is successful. Whether you are managing and overseeing a formal digital program with dedicated staff, functioning as a leader for a project-based team, or flying solo as the only digital projects librarian at your institution, using the following project management strategies will help you efficiently and successfully complete a wide range of digital projects.

Phase 1: Visualize the Project

During this key phase you should be able to articulate the rationale for the project, outline a strategy for executing it, and state the desired outcomes, including any final products that should result from the project. You should also be able to identify who will function as the project manager for the duration of the project. To help you envision and clearly articulate the project, there are questions you or your project team should ask. Does your project fit the mission of the library? Is there a specific goal in your library's strategic plan that your project is designed to meet? Who are the stakeholders for this project? What is the scope? If you have a clear vision up-front you are more likely to develop a realistic plan with achievable goals, rather than creating a project that is too ambitious and beyond your resource capabilities, which can lead to a great deal of wasted time and effort. As part of your strategy, you should list the benefits of your project, as well as any potential risks or threats that could impede it, and how you anticipate mitigating those threats.

Surveying the larger library environment to see if similar projects have already taken place can help you identify existing practices to assist you and also avoid potential pitfalls. There are many institutions that have already developed long-standing, successful digital projects, including the development of detailed, online planning guidelines and checklists which you can consult to help you get your own projects off the ground (we refer you to some of these in the final section of this chapter). As part of your project vision, you should estimate your resource needs, including funding, equipment, personnel, and so on, based upon the strategy for work completion that you have outlined. Once you have clearly defined these factors, you can move forward with project planning.

Phase 2: Plan the Project

Planning activities include defining and refining the scope of a project, verifying equipment or other resource needs, defining a budget based upon actual costs, creating time frames and work schedules, identifying appropriate project personnel, and developing assessment outcomes. Planning should begin with identification of the tasks to be completed, and then listing those tasks in order. Naming those tasks will give you a better sense of how to refine the scope of your project. For example, if your project entails creating a digitized collection of materials from your special collections department, one of your tasks should include determining the copyright status of the materials you have initially identified as candidates for digitization. As a result of this, you might determine that your institution only has the right to provide online access to a small subset of those materials, which in turn would narrow the overall scope of your project.

You will also determine at this point what resources such as hardware, software, or other equipment are needed to complete the project, and create a budget based upon those resource needs. At this point, you may need to leverage your project vision by advocating for more funding for resources from your administration. If your deadline is more flexible, you might also consider applying for external grants, such as Library Services and Technology Act grants from your state library, to help you pay for hardware, software, or temporary project staffing related to your project. Grant writing can be a very time-consuming process, so you will need to adjust your planning schedule accordingly to ensure you have enough time to secure grant funding while meeting your project deadlines. Furthermore, the full grant process from application to award can take anywhere from a couple of months to almost a full year, depending upon the size of the grant, which can impact your project schedule. You might also want to consider identifying possible collaborators who can help with cost sharing. For example, your library might be considering the development of an institutional repository (IR) to preserve and provide access to the scholarly activity of your campus community, but the IR platform you wish to use costs more than your library can afford. You could promote the benefits of an IR for faculty to several academic departments at your university, who would then agree to help share the costs for the hardware (such as a server) and the software (the IR platform) for this project.

At this point, you might also want to look at outsourcing certain tasks or responsibilities for the cost-effective completion of your project. For example, if your library lacks the proper equipment and trained staff to conduct in-house scanning of images, you might want to consider outsourcing scanning activities. Perhaps your library does not have sufficient internal IT support to effectively develop and maintain an open source software product to manage your digital collections. In this instance, it might be worth investing in a software package that includes dedicated customer service and technical support to ensure ongoing maintenance of your digital collections.

Appropriate project personnel can also be identified once a task list has been created. Staff should be matched to specific tasks based upon their knowledge and skills. Whether or not a project team is formally created as part of the planning process, it is important to document project relationships that are task-oriented to ensure that clear lines of accountability are stated and understood by all staff involved. This is especially useful if you are working with project teams that consist of staff from various departments or units, as it helps clarify their roles. One method of organizing tasks, people, and responsibilities is through the use of a responsibility assignment matrix (RAM) (PMI 2008, 221). The matrix is used to visually illustrate the connection between tasks with the people involved and their level of responsibility. Responsibility levels can vary by project and range from those directly accountable (A) or those that need to be informed when tasks are complete (I), to those that perform quality control (QC). (See table 7.1.)

Tasks should be organized into workflows that demonstrate how some tasks might be grouped together, and how they will flow into one another as part of the overall project process. Along with workflows, as part of planning you should create a project schedule that defines the beginning and end of each task. The schedule should also include projected milestones along the way that can help you benchmark your progress throughout the project. Tools such as Gantt charts can help you visually depict the summary of tasks necessary for a project, as well as the

TABLE 7.1
Sample responsibility assignment matrix (RAM)

	Digital Project Manager	Scanning Technician	Archivist
Write standards for scanning	A		I
Select images for scanning		I	A
Scan images	QC	A	I

actual timeline for each task. Developing and documenting standards to accompany workflows is also an important part of the planning process. Standards function as the rules or specified guidelines for activity completion. Examples of standards for digital projects can include specifying which programming language to use for the scripting of web pages, identifying scanning specifications for digitization tasks, or creating a metadata application profile for the cataloging of a specific online collection (for more on application profiles, see chapter 9). Other guidelines might include formal documentation for file-naming, file storage, and file preservation, to ensure digital files are named consistently, are easy to locate, and are appropriately archived for long-term use. Based on their specific responsibilities throughout the project, members of the project team should be thoroughly informed of task standards to ensure accurate and consistent completion of each activity.

In addition to planning the actual work to be performed, there are other factors to be considered as part of the project planning phase. How will you ensure quality control throughout the process, as well as for the final product? What assessment methods and criteria will you use to measure the overall success of the project? What is your strategy for communication among project team members throughout the project? Without regular communication the scope of a project might be misunderstood and tasks can veer away from the initial plan. You might choose to conduct regular meetings with team members; this allows the project manager to listen to concerns, hear suggestions for changes to the scope of the project, and discuss next steps in a process.

Meetings can also bring to light omissions in the initial workflow such as additional equipment or personnel needs, or the addition of unforeseen but necessary tasks. Communication with members of a team is essential to keeping the project on track. If you are working solo, but are accountable to administrators or another set of stakeholders, communication is still very important for helping you manage their expectations. Have you built any feedback loops into the process with stakeholders to ensure the project is on track? Project milestones need to be shared with administrators and other stakeholders who would be interested in the outcomes of your project. For example, a university alumni association might be interested in a project to digitize old yearbooks and put them online for public view. Decide how you will communicate accomplishments over the course of the project, such as official reports or through periodic, informal e-mails. Either communication method provides an opportunity for non-team members to comment on projects or suggest modifications. Constant review of a project should be considered a part of the workflow. Planning is an iterative process, and requires flexibility and adaptability in case unforeseen circumstances arise.

Phase 3: Implement the Project

Implementation involves ensuring that all of the necessary project resources, including personnel, are acquired and allocated appropriately. Most of your budget expenditures will likely occur during this phase. During the implementation phase, project personnel perform the tasks defined by the workflows outlined during the planning phase to make the project a reality. As work progresses, this is the phase where problems and other unexpected disruptions can occur. However, good planning can help you avoid potentially damaging interruptions that can completely derail your project. For example, failure to develop a plan to back up archival-quality digital image files as part of a digitization project could lead to duplication of effort if the original digital image files are lost and need to be re-created. Making sure you have decided upon a long-term digital preservation strategy for those files, and including that documented decision-making in your overall project plan, can help you avoid this scenario (please refer to chapter 12 for more on the topic of digital preservation).

Phase 4: Monitor and Control the Project

The process of monitoring and controlling a project gives managers insight into its progress and highlights any tasks or areas that need additional attention, and often overlaps with the implementation phase. It also provides an opportunity to review the workflow and determine if changes should be made. For example, one of the tasks in a digitization project might require completed scans to be reviewed and approved before they advance to the next task of metadata creation. As the project manager, you learn that there are too many scanned images for only one person to review and approve within the defined timeline for that task. As a result, you quickly assign an additional person to the task, ensuring the project stays on schedule.

As you monitor a project, you can also find out if team members are adhering to defined project standards. For instance, in a website creation project, the project team may define standards stating that web pages with images must include the "alt" tag in the HTML coding for each image. As you review the pages for quality control, however, you realize this specific standard is not being applied consistently. You can remind the team of the standard, and require them to fix the errors early on in the project. Monitoring also ensures assigned tasks are being completed successfully. If team members are failing to meet deadlines or expectations, you have the opportunity to determine if the team needs additional resources to be successful, or address any misunderstanding of expectations.

During this phase, project managers ensure expenses are being controlled to fit within the project budget. Managers are also responsible for controlling other problems that might arise, facilitating major changes to the scope of the project, and ensuring the lines of communication are kept open. Project managers should also be ready to develop and execute a contingency plan in case the project does not go as expected, or in some cases, be ready to stop a project completely.

Phase 5: Close Out the Project

Once the project is concluded or completed, closeout activities will occur, including the systematic and objective assessment of the project. During this phase, you can determine the actual level of achievement against the original scope of the project. Your team should meet and discuss if objectives were met or if revisions were made to workflows, standards, or other processes during the project. Failures or mistakes that occurred during the project should be identified so recommendations can be made for how to avoid them in future projects. Often, changes in personnel can result in the loss of key information needed for ongoing project maintenance or the execution of a new idea; therefore, document all decisions made and any lessons you learned from the project. Archive all relevant project documentation so it can be referenced or used for future projects.

PROJECT MANAGEMENT IN ACTION: TWO CASE STUDIES

The following case studies illustrate the application of project management principles in two different types of digital projects that you might undertake as a digital librarian: digitizing collections for online access, and migrating websites from one platform to another. In each case, projects were developed without a formal project management framework in mind; however, the execution of each project demonstrates how project management principles often arise during the planning and implementation processes out of necessity or practicality. Both cases point to the conclusion that projects can be better organized, run more efficiently, and completed with a greater chance of success if guided by project management principles.

CASE STUDY 1

Digitizing University Archives Photographs

The University Photographs Digital Collection, part of the resources at the University of Dayton Libraries, began with a project to digitize a small collection of photographs from the University Archives collection. The project was conceived as part of a larger digitization program that was based upon strategic initiatives and goals outlined by the *University Libraries Strategic Plan, 2006–2011*. One of the specific goals within the plan states, "The Libraries will identify collections to digitize that are unique to the University of Dayton and have a national or international value." The strategic plan had already led to the creation of a Digital Projects Cross-Divisional Team, which was charged with achieving this goal. The team consisted of representatives from around the University Libraries, including the University Archives, the Information Systems and Digital Access Division (ISDA, essentially IT faculty and staff), the Marian Library (a special library), and the Information Acquisition and Organization Division (cataloging faculty), as well as a visual resource curator, which was a unique joint appointment between the University Libraries and the Department of Visual Arts. The team was chaired by the ISDA Division director. Over the course of the project, the specific individuals serving on the team occasionally changed, but the overall unit representation remained the same.

Visualization

As part of the larger digitization program planning, CONTENTdm software had already been selected and purchased to store, organize, and display digitized collections online for public access. The team decided that the first project for use with CONTENTdm would be the creation of an online collection of photographs, the physical copies of which were housed in the University Archives. These photographs chronicled the history of the University of Dayton, and depicted different aspects of campus life, including students, faculty, staff, buildings, and events. Selection for these photographs was based upon the fact that they were already deemed high-use materials. The need to limit physical handling to ensure long-term preservation also made them good candidates for digitization. Furthermore, the team was able to identify potential users of a digital collection based upon known users of the physical collection, which included faculty, students, alumni, external researchers, and other campus offices, such as Public Relations and Advancement. The team decided that a test batch of twenty images would be selected to test the workflow from beginning to end, including the final display and functionality of the images online. The project would culminate with the uploading of a much larger selection of 109 images, to be the first project made available for public access.

Planning

As part of the planning process, a subset of the larger Digital Projects Team was identified to work on the project, based upon their skills and typical job responsibilities. The visual resource curator functioned as the project manager, while a representative from the University Archives and a cataloger worked together on the project to develop metadata standards and provide cataloging for the digitized materials. The chair of the full Digital Projects Team was also informed of the group's progress along the way. As the group started to develop preliminary workflows, tasks were identified that were necessary to complete the project. The tasks included creating the collection in CONTENTdm where the images would reside, selecting the photographs to be digitized, scanning those photographs, importing the digital files into CONTENTdm and adding metadata to those images, and then checking those records for quality assurance before ultimately making the collection publicly viewable online.

The team began to develop specific documentation to accompany the scanning and cataloging tasks identified for the project. After conducting research on best practices for scanning photographs for preservation purposes, the visual resources curator developed a set of specifications including bit depth, resolution, and image size. The preservation files were saved in TIFF format. The project archivist and the cataloger worked together to research the development of data dictionaries, and created a data dictionary that defined the metadata fields to be used for the photographs collection, which mapped to Dublin Core metadata elements (these metadata practices will be covered in more depth in the following two chapters). The dictionary provided explicit instructions for creation and input of information for each field, including the use of controlled vocabularies such as the Art and Architecture Thesaurus and Library of Congress Subject Headings for consistent application of terms for subject headings and other descriptors for each photograph. The project archivist developed a document outlining file-naming instructions for each photograph, following the classification system used for physical materials held in the University Archives. The archivist also worked on copyright clearance issues for the images identified for the project, making sure the images were either in the public domain, or that permissions to digitize (where it was possible to obtain them) were on file. The visual resource curator created specific documented workflows for the process and additional training manuals to ensure the tasks were completed accurately, consistently, and efficiently.

Implementation

Scanning of photographs began in the fall of 2008. The visual resource curator trained student workers using the scanning guidelines that had been developed in the planning stage. Images were stored in folders on a shared network drive that allowed different team members to access them from various locations around the libraries. Images were minimally processed for image correction using image-editing software. The curator reviewed the processed images for quality control purposes, and then loaded them into CONTENTdm. Once loaded, the curator notified the project archivist, who provided descriptive metadata for each image. Once the archivist was done, she notified the cataloger, who completed the metadata for each image by adding appropriate LCSH terms for each record. The cataloger was also responsible for final quality control for each record, making sure all metadata information was entered correctly for each item. Finally, the cataloger uploaded the live collection online and once that was completed, reported back to the team who could then view the images as they would appear to the public through a web browser. After the initial test batch of twenty images was successfully loaded, the team followed the same workflow and by August of 2009 was able to create a collection consisting of 109 digitized photographs.

Project Monitoring and Control

As the project moved through each step, the visual resources curator functioned as the project manager and periodically followed up with the project archivist and cataloger to track the project's progress after the initial test batch. While most of the communication occurred as needed via e-mails between the curator, archivist, and cataloger, monthly face-to-face meetings also provided updates to the larger Digital Projects Team. During the implementation process, some problems with the initial file-naming structures were discovered, and the project archivist revised the initial guidelines to accommodate some necessary complexities in file naming. Another issue that was discovered through the quality control processes was inconsistent or inaccurate work being performed by student workers. Some students were naming files incorrectly, while others were not scanning the images according to the scanning specifications. These issues required intervention from both the curator and the archivist, who both spent time retraining students to ensure consistent quality from their work.

Closeout and Lessons Learned

After the first full set of 109 items was loaded online, the team decided the general workflow was appropriate for making the collection dynamic, so it continues to grow as additional photographs are digitized from the University Archives holdings. Usage statistics available from CONTENTdm and Google analytics for the collection website have demonstrated that use continues to increase for the collection. Although it was initially deemed a success, there were some issues that the team had to deal with over the course of the project that were unexpected, beyond normal input errors. Communication was an important factor to manage. Although Lotus Quickplace (an online collaborative software tool) was initially used to facilitate document sharing and archiving, the team never used it to its fullest potential, which included discussion lists and messaging. The team always seemed to default to e-mail as the preferred means of communication, despite the fact that e-mail is not a good way to archive discussions and documents. Since then, the team has abandoned Quickplace, and now uses shared folders on a network drive to house all necessary documentation. Another issue that arose was the fact that the visual resources curator was responsible for overseeing several digital projects at the same time, which proved to be difficult. However, the development of project timelines guided her progress in a more organized manner. Finally, the team struggled with clarification of roles and responsibilities, as there was some personnel turnover that occurred during the implementation phase of the project. Responsibility for the supervision of students was sometimes scattered and unclear, and at times the students seemed unsure of their instructions. Clearer reporting lines for the team and explicit delineation of responsibilities would have helped the project move along more smoothly.

Since the initial project was completed, additional collections have been digitized and put online, following the model of the University Archives photograph project. The Digital Projects Team has used the same workflow for digitization and cataloging, and has improved upon the process by creating specific timelines for each project with projected completion dates. However, the reality of working at a smaller institution has meant that deadlines have often been readjusted to accommodate interruptions in workflow from higher-priority projects. The team has also learned to accept the fact that problems will arise outside the scope of its control, particularly larger technical issues that occur at the university level. The team has proven to be flexible, and shifts projects as needed so that no work time is lost. Finally, the team has learned the importance of archiving all decisions and documentation, especially when turnover occurs. Although individuals might be responsible for specific tasks, the knowledge they have related to those tasks has to be documented and shared; otherwise, when someone has moved on to another unit or institution, other team members may waste significant time trying to figure out how or why certain processes occur.

CASE STUDY 2

Web Page Auditing and Site Migration

In the fall of 2009, the J. Murrey Atkins Library at the University of North Carolina at Charlotte embarked on a large-scale usability and web refresh project. A task force was assembled to tackle web usability and a redesign of the library's home page. Throughout the spring of 2010 the task force conducted forums, interviews and surveys to collect usability data on the library's home page. In August 2010, the Atkins Library launched a newly redesigned home page, and the changes to content and navigational structure relied entirely on usability data. In this phase only the library home page was redesigned. Supplemental pages did not undergo usability testing or redesign. The library's plan to review supplemental pages coincided with a university-wide initiative to migrate all websites to Drupal, an open-source content management system. Following the launch of the library home page, the Drupal Migration Project began in fall 2010.

Visualization

The Drupal Migration Project focused on content and platform migration of the Atkins Library website. The Atkins Library consists of five departments: Collections Development & Electronic Resources, Special Collections, Library Administration, Collections Access & Outreach Services, and Library Information Technology. In terms of web maintenance and content creation for their respective areas, the departments were fragmented. The library lacked a standard protocol for the creation, maintenance, and deletion of web content. Although the original project was envisioned as simply a migration of web content to a new platform, the scope of the project was quickly expanded, due to an initial inventory of the site which revealed over 3,000 unique web pages. This inventory uncovered pages authored by persons no longer employed at the library and pages that had not been updated in over four years. These discoveries expanded the scope of the migration project to encompass an "auditing" process. The library-wide site audit needed to focus on assessing the needs of the users to establish best practices and guidelines for development of future web content. The audit would also include a thorough review of what currently existed on the website. The purpose of this review was to identify duplications as well as relevancy, accuracy, consistency, and currency of the pages. The audit would rely on prior usability data for the development of new content. Launching the new site in Drupal would complete the project.

Planning

The auditing process was critical to the development of a virtual presence both internally and externally. The usability data gathered from previous studies helped prioritize users' needs. By assessing the needs of their users, each department

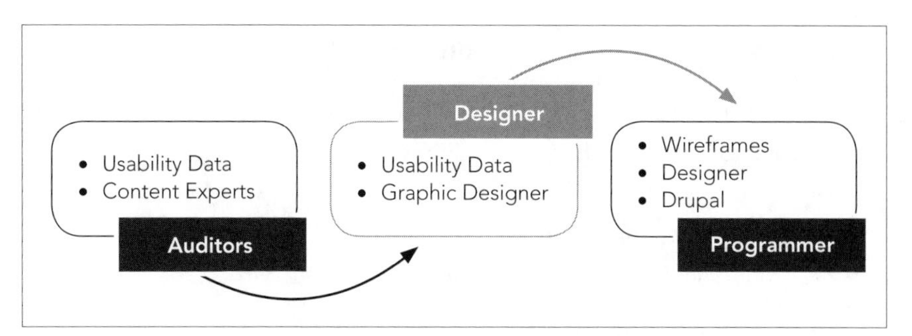

FIGURE 7.1
Workflow for website migration

could design and create content that was consistent and relevant to its constituent users. The process incorporated content experts from each department with the understanding that they could best interpret usability data and the needs of their constituents. The three-pronged process involved departmental auditors, a graphic designer, and a programmer. Figure 7.1 depicts the basic workflow. The content experts would gather and analyze usability data and work with the graphic designer to develop mock-ups. The final step would involve the web programmer programming the pages.

To coincide with the university-wide web migration project and the academic calendar, the library's migration process needed to be completed by August 2011. Working backwards from the deadline, an appropriate timeline was developed. By working backwards from a deadline, the migration project kept to the original timeline with minor deviations.

Implementation

The Drupal Migration Project relied heavily on usability data and the interpretation of that data by content experts. Having auditors represent the various departments within the library helped to establish a communication structure that was previously absent. Departmental auditors were identified early in the process. Collections Development & Electronic Resources, Special Collections, Library Administration, and Collections Access & Outreach Services were represented by an auditor. Library Information Technology had very little public content and did not require an audit at the time. The graphic designer and marketing communication specialist were also part of the auditor's group. Of the 3,000

Timeline for Drupal migration project:

September 2010

- Departments identify primary auditor
- Auditors conduct site inventory
- Identify functional needs and requirements
- Drupal sandbox created for auditor group

October–December 2010

- Information gathering and analysis of usability data
- Report findings
- Departments submit recommendations for function and content needed for their future web presence

Early December 2010

- Report findings and recommendations to graphic designer and web programmer

January–February 2011

- Review and analysis of reports by graphic designer and programmer
- Usability and testing of content structure

March–April 2011

- Migrate content
- Design wireframes (page mock-ups)
- Usability testing of wireframes
- Drupal beta site (test site) is launched

April–May 2011

- Final content migration
- Drupal production site ("live" instance of Drupal) is made available to project team
- Usability testing, tweaks, maintenance conducted

June 2011

- Preliminary launch of site to staff
- Staff training

July 2011

- Public launch

web pages, the department known as Information Commons (IC) owned fully one-third. Being the primary public services area for the library, the auditor for IC was identified as the groups' leader. During the fall of 2010 the auditors systematically inventoried their respective departments' web pages. The review process identified duplications, inaccuracies, and gaps in coverage. Working with the graphic designer, the auditors developed the architecture for the new site. Throughout the spring of 2011 auditors communicated departmental goals and priorities to the graphic designer and mock-ups were created.

As the auditors and graphic designer worked on the content, the web programmer was busy learning Drupal. At the time, Atkins lacked staff with the required expertise to migrate content, and this knowledge gap created delays in programming. Functional additions such as a single sign-on for library users were put on hold indefinitely. An unanticipated loss in staffing prevented further usability testing from being done, but there was enough data from prior studies to move forward with the intention that usability testing would continue following the launch. A Drupal sandbox (virtual testing area) was created for auditors and the graphic designer to test the site's design and navigation. Content in the Drupal sandbox was moved to a virtual machine in May.

Project Monitoring and Control

The auditors and the graphic designer met frequently at the start of the project. Auditors communicated the groups' work back to their respective departments and shared departmental requests at a biweekly meeting. Auditors prioritized "current content" and "desired new content" into various categories. The list was put into an Excel spreadsheet and auditors assigned according to functional areas. Once the initial inventory was completed the graphic designer met individually with the departmental auditors to develop templates. Templates were reviewed and tested by staff. The auditors tracked their work using Google Docs. Once templates were completed, the previously audited content was migrated to the new Drupal platform. Auditors relied on usability data and users' needs to implement changes and deny requests based on preferences. The lead auditor coordinated the work. There were minor deviations from the original timeline. Adjustments were made to the workflow to accommodate more Drupal training for auditors once migration began.

Communication was an integral part of the overall project. The three-pronged approach used for this project established communication among the content experts (auditors), graphic designer, and programmer. Auditors met biweekly to review progress. Weekly updates were given to the university librarian, and updates were provided at the monthly all-staff meeting. Staff and public users had the option of notifying their departmental auditor or sending feedback and suggestions via a virtual suggestion box. These channels, as well as the enforcement of decisions made by the project managers, ensured that goals, expectations, and progress were widely and frequently shared with the staff.

Closeout and Lessons Learned

The project concluded in August, one month behind schedule, due to a delay with the university Information and Technology Services Department. The delay impacted public users but provided staff an opportunity to become familiar with the new site. During the "soft" launch in July, staff tested the site and communicated issues to their auditors. Due to the many changes and revisions to the website that occurred in a short time frame, the auditor group provided an orientation session for staff. The lead auditor was then able to begin performing usability testing on the new site, with the library planning to put it through more testing at a future time. Further integration of third-party systems is also on the horizon. The successful launch of the newly designed library website in July 2011 concluded the Drupal Migration Project. The auditor group successfully completed an inventory of their web pages, and a system for addressing and communicating changes to specific pages was implemented.

Over the course of the Drupal Migration Project, several issues arose that underscored the need for thorough and thoughtful project planning. The earliest stages of project visualization in this case led to a considerable broadening of the scope of the original task. When a project is first envisioned, it is important to clearly define the goals, priorities, and scope of the project to make sure stakeholders and administrators are on board. Identify project requirements to ensure goals and priorities are met. During the planning stages, you should decide as a group how to proceed if goals are not met or when the project grows beyond the scope that was initially defined during visualization. If tasks arise that do not fit the scope of the current project, you might need to save them for future projects. In this case, adding certain website functions, such as a single sign-on feature for users, were put off for future implementation since it would have hindered the progress of the migration project.

Although a timeline was developed during the planning stage, the need for flexibility with timelines was evident during the implementation stage. Making a timeline available early to all stakeholders is crucial, but it is also important to emphasize that timelines must be flexible to accommodate unforeseen circumstances. Provide as much detail when possible without being frivolous. It is necessary to make clear that there is room for renegotiation, but also a need for deadlines to keep the project on track. Although e-mail communications can be useful, important information can get lost, so you should use more stable, concrete means for documenting milestones. In this case, Google spreadsheets were used since they are capable of being shared among many users. We also created rubrics to determine different levels of priority for specific project tasks. Always be ready to present your plans to administration to help you manage expectations when your plans have to change.

Another issue that arose was the need for clarifying project roles and responsibilities. The business and web services librarian served as the informal project leader, but this was never entirely clear to all involved in completing the project. The departmental auditors were leading their respective departments' audits, which may have obscured the role of the business and web services librarian as project manager to the staff in those areas. To avoid confusion over reporting, authority, or accountability, you should define roles and expectations early and restate them often. Furthermore, clarifying such roles can lead to the identification of training gaps, which you should address in order to ensure the project stays on track.

Finally, it was important to manage expectations throughout the project, especially since responsibilities were spread among several auditors. In this case, the best way to manage staff expectations was to empower the auditors to deal with those expectations for their respective departments. Auditors could identify and manage expectations that went beyond the scope of the project by referring to previously named priorities, project goals, and research data. Overall, the project team made sure it only promised outcomes that could truly be delivered.

■ ■ ■

FINAL THOUGHTS

Despite limited research on project management techniques for digital projects, these case studies demonstrate the necessity and usefulness of adopting project management processes for library projects. These scenarios also demonstrate how project management processes can be used by formal project teams, or by individual digital librarians who have responsibility for various projects. You can avoid project pitfalls if you keep these principles in mind whenever you are assigned to a project. Deliberate management of projects from beginning to end can ensure smooth, efficient, and ultimately successful project completion.

REFERENCES

Burich, Nancy J., Anne Marie Casey, Frances A. Devlin, and Lana Ivanitskaya. 2006. "Project Management and Institutional Collaboration in Libraries." *Technical Services Quarterly* 24, no. 1: 17–36.

Marill, Jennifer L., and Marcella Lesher. 2007. "Mile High to Ground Level: Getting Projects Organized and Completed." *Serials Librarian* 52, no. 3/4: 317–22.

Massis, Bruce E. 2010. "Project Management in the Library." *New Library World* 111, no. 11/12: 526–29.

Project Management Institute (PMI). 2008. *A Guide to the Project Management Body of Knowledge (PMBOK Guide)*. 4th ed. Newtown Square, PA: Project Management Institute.

Revels, Ira. 2010. "Managing Digital Projects." *American Libraries* 41, no. 4: 48–50.

Sitts, Maxine K., ed. 2000. *Handbook for Digital Projects: A Management Tool for Preservation and Access*. Andover, MA: Northeast Document Center. www.nedcc.org/resources/digitalhandbook/dman.pdf.

Symonds, Emily, and Cinda May. 2009. "Documenting Local Procedures: The Development of Standard Digitization Processes Through the Dear Comrade Project." *Journal of Library Metadata* 9, no. 3/4: 305–9.

RECOMMENDED RESOURCES

Digital Project Planning & Management Basics: www.loc.gov/catworkshop/courses/digitalprojplan/index.html

Moving Theory into Practice: Digital Imaging Tutorial (Cornell University): www.library.cornell.edu/preservation/tutorial/

Northeast Document Conservation Center: www.nedcc.org/home.php

Project Management Institute: www.pmi.org

Washington State Library Digital Best Practices: http://digitalwa.statelib.wa.gov/newsite/projectmgmt/resources.htm

Chapter Eight

Learning about Metadata

Jennifer Phillips

When trying to get your career in digital librarianship off the ground, a basic understanding of metadata—its principles, standards, and best practices—can go a long way. At first metadata may seem somewhat mystifying, like an obscure, technical branch of cataloging or an issue of concern primarily to software engineers and computer programmers. However, if we think of metadata in terms of its relationship to core principles of librarianship, it becomes more approachable. Demonstrating an understanding of metadata and how it relates to the librarian's job of assisting in the discovery, access, and use of information resources can be extremely useful when trying to get involved in digital projects.

This chapter will provide an overview of the concepts and define the terminology used in discussions of metadata. It is intended to be a high-level discussion of metadata rather than an explanation of the nuts and bolts of metadata implementation, which will be addressed in chapter 9. If you come from a technical services background or if you focused on cataloging in library school, many of the ideas here may already be familiar to you. If instead you come from a public services background, or are new to library and information science in general, this chapter will familiarize you with metadata and the issues surrounding it in a library context.

The goal of this chapter is to define metadata in a way that invites you to think about how it pertains to both the public service and technical aspects of digital library work. Another aim is to introduce you to or refresh your memory about categories of metadata and metadata standards, so that you will be able to articulate the importance of metadata for modern libraries. Metadata is not an obscure topic just for technical people. Familiarity with the basic principles of metadata is necessary for all people working in digital librarianship, and a solid foundation can help you stand out professionally.

WHAT IS METADATA?

Metadata is difficult to define briefly, because the term is used for a variety of kinds of information that describe other information. To understand metadata in a general sense, it is important to bear in mind a few key points:

- metadata is information or data that is associated with other information resources
- metadata is structured information
- metadata is used to enable a range of functions with respect to the resource it describes

While metadata is a type of information that is always about other information, it can be about any form of information. In other words, metadata can describe information resources of all types—from physical books and images to websites, audio files, data sets, and software. It can be stored in a database, separate from the resources it explains, or it can be embedded in the digital files it describes. Because it is structured, metadata can be machine-processed, and it is therefore fundamental to the way that information resources function and are used in an electronic environment. Finally, part of the definition of metadata should include its purpose, which is to support the description, discovery, use, management, and preservation of information resources.

A few familiar examples of metadata can help clarify the concept and illustrate the contexts in which some forms of metadata have been developed. Most of us have encountered data about digital files that is stored within the files, without necessarily thinking about it as metadata. For example, the Apple iTunes application for managing music files (MP3s) on a home computer displays songs according to their name, artist, album, time, track number, and genre. These categories are all elements of metadata encoded in the ID3 tag at the end of an MP3 file. This file-based metadata is displayed by iTunes and gives the user the ability to sort and search for songs according to these properties. (See figure 8.1.)

FIGURE 8.1
iTunes metadata

Another example, which also illustrates how file-based metadata can be in part system-generated and in part supplied by the user, is the properties of a Microsoft Word document. In Word, you can view characteristics of a file and information about its content. The system-generated information includes the date created, date modified, size, and file type; the metadata the user can supply includes the author, title, subject, keywords, and a description. This metadata allows for input from the user on the one hand, and on the other facilitates system-based operations such as the interaction of the file with the software application or operating system. You can organize, identify, and search for your documents based on both the values you have specified and the automatically generated properties. (See figure 8.2.)

Since the metadata associated with an MP3 or Microsoft Word file allows the user to describe, arrange, search for, and select their files, these everyday examples of metadata show how metadata supports user tasks.

Metadata has evolved from several different communities including library and information science, records management, database design, and software design. One example of metadata that many librarians are familiar with is the MARC (Machine-Readable Cataloging) record. MARC is based on a set of rules, the International Standard Bibliographic Description (ISBD), and is designed specifically for bibliographic data to meet the needs of the library community. A MARC bibliographic record is a source of information about a bibliographic resource

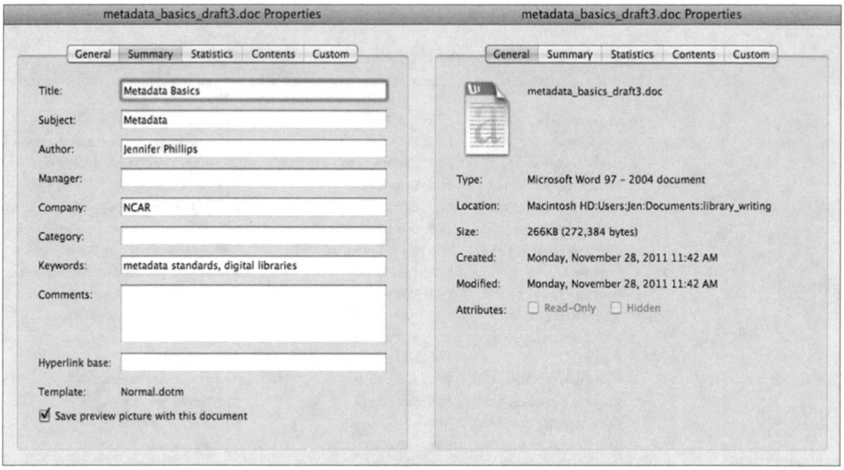

FIGURE 8.2
Microsoft Word metadata

(book, serial, sound recording, video recording, etc.), and when you look at an online library catalog you are being presented with a view of MARC records. MARC takes the information that describes the intellectual and physical characteristics of a resource and structures it in such a way that allows it to be displayed in catalogs and shared with other systems. The MARC format for bibliographic records defines the data elements—units of data with specific meaning—and the codes used for encoding bibliographic data. For example, MARC defines the data element "title and statement of responsibility" and puts it in the "245" field. Indicator and subfield codes characterize and further mark up the data contained within the field. The first indicator indicates whether there should be an added entry for the title in the library catalog, and subfield "a" distinguishes the title from the statement of responsibility in subfield "c." Personal author information goes in the "100" field, and imprint information (publication, distribution, etc.) goes in the "260." As such, the basic elements for an edition of Herman Melville's *Moby Dick* would be encoded in MARC as follows:

100	1	$aMelville, Herman,$d1819-1891.
245	10	$aMoby-Dick, or, The whale /$cHerman Melville ; foreword by Nathaniel Philbrick.
260		$aLondon :$bPenguin,$c2009.

Thus structured and encoded, bibliographic metadata can be interpreted and displayed by library system software and exchanged with other agencies, regardless of the language of the content. MARC enables the discovery, retrieval, and use of resources by making them searchable in library catalogs according to a broad set of elements, including title, statement of responsibility, publication information, physical description, information specific to medium, and subject.

WHAT IS THE PURPOSE OF METADATA?

Metadata supports the use of information resources in a digital environment. As you consider the relevance of metadata to your career as a digital librarian, it may be useful to think about how metadata reflects the core values of librarianship in general and the principles that underlie library cataloging in particular. There is a clear example of this in the case of digital libraries, where metadata can in part be seen as serving the same purpose as bibliographic records in traditional libraries. Like bibliographic records, metadata should support the generic user tasks of finding, identifying, selecting, and obtaining resources, as defined in the International Federation of Library Associations and Institutions' Functional Requirements for Bibliographic Records, or FRBR (IFLA Study Group on the Functional Requirements for Bibliographic Records 1998, 8).

A digital library normally consists of collections of digital resources that are made available online through a user interface. The users of such collections may vary. A digital library may be open-access and designed for the public, as is the case for a collection of digitized versions of unique, local resources. On the other hand, there may be use restrictions, as in the case of repositories for electronic records or subscription-based materials. Regardless of the type of digital collection and user, however, the purpose behind specific data elements can be articulated in terms of supporting user tasks.

Perhaps the most obvious purpose of metadata in this regard is its role in search and discovery. When deciding which metadata elements to employ in a given context, it is vital to consider what use elements will have from the user perspective, as well as the search functionality they will support. It seems clear that today's user will most often search by keyword. Metadata improves the results of this type of search by enabling keyword matching on metadata terms, which have been selected because of their relevance, rather than relying on the possibility of matching words from within the text. More sophisticated queries may include author/creator name and title or title keyword, and since these data elements are the backbone of most descriptive efforts, metadata supports this method of searching in particular.

Beyond being aligned with specific search criteria, metadata also enables browsing and collocation. Metadata pertaining to subject or resource type can allow for multiple resources, sometimes from different contexts, to be automatically associated with each other "on the fly." For example, to return to our earlier example of iTunes, you can use the metadata associated with your songs to arrange your music. In order to browse your music collection, you can sort by album, artist, title, or genre, and you can create automatic or "smart" playlists based on songs that match each other according to these and other metadata elements. Similarly, in digital libraries, lists of associated items and browsable collections of resources can be flexible and user-driven.

Another user task that metadata commonly serves is identification. Metadata allows for similar objects, such as different versions of the same content, to be identified. Most metadata element sets include some kind of standard number used to uniquely identify the object to which the metadata refers. Such identification numbers function in the same way that an International Standard Book Number (ISBN) does for a book: different editions or manifestations of the same work or content can be distinguished thanks to a unique identification number. As for the user task of selection, metadata can facilitate selection based on criteria such as format. Just as you can sort files on your personal computer based on their file extension and therefore file type, you can also usually limit your selection of resources in a digital collection based on format. For example, depending on your needs you might want only visual resources, or you might only be able to use the audio version of some content that is available in both textual and audio formats. The metadata associated with digital resources will allow you to sort and select according to such criteria.

Finally, metadata facilitates access. Metadata might point to a Uniform Resource Locator (URL)—the "location" where given content can be accessed via the Internet. To the extent that the location of digital files often changes on file servers, making URLs unstable, "persistent" URLs and Digital Object Identifiers (DOIs) resolve common URLs and bring the user to a file, even if its location has changed.

Metadata serves the user by supporting discovery and use. It also supports the internal structure and systems underlying digital libraries and repositories. Information architecture depends on metadata, as does the processing and presentation of digital objects, which are normally defined as the combination of an identifier, metadata, and data or content. Metadata elements such as identifiers allow for digital objects to be identified beyond their location, as well as providing a link between metadata records and the content they describe. Just as the MARC record allows for the exchange of bibliographic data between different integrated library systems, metadata can enable the exchange of information between computer systems that do not share the same system design or the same data structure. This is done based on interoperable design and crosswalks (concepts that will be discussed in the following chapter).

Metadata is also crucial for the management and preservation of digital files: without metadata concerning provenance and file history, the authenticity and integrity of files are at risk. Traditionally libraries and archives have played an important role in the long-term preservation of information resources, and thanks to metadata this role can be extended into the digital environment.

Finally, semantic web technologies such as "linked data" depend on metadata. The idea behind linked data is to create connections between data and other information on the Web that is not explicitly linked via hyperlinks. Linked data relies on using Uniform Resource Identifiers (URIs) formulated as HTTP statements (ex. http://digLibX.com#XXXXX) to identify things, and on articulating the relationship between things in terms of subject–predicate–object, or Resource Description Framework (RDF) triples. By way of example, consider if we were to assign URIs to the metadata about this book chapter. First, you could assign the URI <http://digLibX #42570> to the chapter and then articulate its attributes as illustrated in table 8.1.

TABLE 8.1
Sample URI/metadata assignments

URI	Attribute	Value
http://digLibX.com#42570	Creator	Jennifer Phillips
http://digLibX.com#42570	Topic	Metadata
http://digLibX.com#42570	Topic	Digital libraries

Because these attributes are fundamental to the description of resources, URIs have been assigned to them. It is even possible to assign URIs to the values; this is especially fruitful when the terms come from controlled vocabularies and are likely to be used in other contexts. After assigning URIs to the attributes and values, as shown in table 8.2, we would be able to articulate statements about the chapter using URIs alone.

TABLE 8.2
Sample RDF triples

Subject	Predicate	Object
http://digLibX.com#42570	http://purl.org/dc/terms/creator	http://viaf.org/42570#jenniferPhillips
http://digLibX.com#42570	http://purl.org/dc/terms/subject	http://lccn.loc.gov/sh96000740#metadata
http://digLibX.com#42570	http://purl.org/dc/terms/subject	http://lccn.loc.gov/sh95008857#digital_libraries

By expressing information about this chapter in this way, we would achieve a couple of things. Statements about the resource, such as "this resource has the creator Jennifer Phillips" and "this resource has the topic metadata," could be articulated according to web semantics, that is to say in RDF triples, which are machine-processable. By assigning URIs to the terms used to describe this chapter, connections could be established between different environments where the terms are being used. It is in this way that linked data allows users to seamlessly connect between information environments and overcome the barriers between separate "silos" of information. All of this work takes place in the space of metadata, and shows how metadata is the backbone of the semantic web.

CATEGORIES OF METADATA

When explaining metadata, it is typical to divide it into categories such as descriptive, administrative, structural, technical, and preservation. These categories can be briefly defined as follows:

- descriptive metadata is information that helps users find, identify, select, and obtain a resource
- administrative metadata helps collection managers manage digital objects, and may include provenance, processing, and rights information
- structural metadata describes relationships between parts of digital objects, many of which are comprised of multiple files
- technical metadata is format-specific and provides specifications concerning the creation and rendering of a file

- preservation metadata is any data element that supports the understanding and use of a digital object in the long term, including information about file integrity and format transformation decisions

To be clear, there are no hard and fast lines between types of metadata. Specific data elements cannot be uniquely identified with only one of the above categories; rather these categories are ways of describing metadata according to what it is intended to accomplish. When presenting your ideas about metadata or deciding what elements to employ, use these categories to articulate the functions metadata elements are intended to serve.

An example of how these categories can be used to describe the logic behind a metadata element is "file size." "File size" is a common element recorded for digital files. This could be useful descriptive information for users wanting to know how large a file is that they are trying to download. File size could also be used for administrative purposes in calculating storage needs. Finally, file size information could be part of a preservation strategy and used to verify that the right number of bytes have been retrieved from storage.

Examples from each category of metadata can help you better understand the various rationales behind metadata selection. Descriptive metadata is the type of metadata most familiar to us, because it is what is visible from the front end of digital collections and libraries. Descriptive metadata normally includes elements such as title, creator, date, subject, and resource type. Because such elements make up the public view of a resource, descriptive elements should allow the user to find and assess the relevance of a resource. Therefore, user expectation plays an important role in deciding which elements to use and how to display them. "Date," for example, could describe the date a historic photograph was taken or the date that it was digitized. Most users will expect the image date to reflect the original, although "date digitized" could be an important element to include for management or preservation purposes. Also, when specifying how descriptive metadata fields should be populated, you will want to consider the best practices employed in library and archives communities. For example, it is best for dates to be structured YYY-MM-DD according to the ISO 8601 standard for dates. This enables items to sort properly, and it allows for systems to exchange date information accurately.

Administrative metadata is information that is primarily available to collection managers and is likely to be shaped by local considerations and needs. Administrative data might include contact information for collection builders or those who have submitted electronic records. It might detail file provenance and history: when it was created and by whom, when it was transferred to a managed digital library or repository environment, and any format transformation or migration decisions. Finally, administrative metadata may speak to agreements governing the use of digital assets, such as copyright and license information for copyrighted material or use restrictions for archival materials and electronic records. Such information can help collection managers make decisions regarding the final disposition of electronic resources, whether to curate (maintain and preserve) them in perpetuity or just for the short term.

Structural and technical metadata are closely linked to the files to which they apply and are not always supplied or actively managed by librarians. Structural metadata indicates the relationship between the parts of a whole. It is used when a set of files is needed to render a complex digital object, such as a digital version of a book that includes the marked-up full text and illustrations. Structural metadata might refer to the page images that make up a digitized manuscript or to the component parts of a recorded interview that spans numerous audio files and includes a textual transcription. A clear case for the use of structural metadata is web pages. Web pages often consist of HTML text, CSS style sheets, image files, and even audiovisual files. If you wanted to take a web page offline and archive it as its component parts, structural metadata would allow you to map out the relationship between the files so that site architecture would be documented.

For librarians, structural metadata is particularly useful where there are characteristics of a whole that differ from its parts, as is the case with complex digital objects that are comprised of multiple files. For example, an oral history might be presented online as audio accompanied by the synchronous presentation of the transcribed interview. The digital object as a whole might include audio files that are sized and formatted for dissemination over the Web, a Synchronized Multimedia Integration Language (SMIL) XML document that would synchronize the audio with its transcription, high-definition master audio files, and an original interview transcript. This online presentation of the oral history has certain characteristics as do each of the constituent files, and structural metadata organizes the metadata that applies to each of the files as well as articulating the relationship between them (which files are presented, in what order, etc.). It is also worth noting that many files may have structural information embedded within them to determine such things as page order, as is the case with multi-page PDFs, Microsoft Word documents, and TIFFs.

Likewise, technical information about a file is often automatically generated and embedded in the file. Technical characteristics vary considerably by file format.

For example, an image file will contain information about dimension, resolution, color profile, and possibly the camera or scanner that generated the image; a sound file on the other hand will contain length of recording, sample rate, number of channels, and possible information about recording device. If you look at the file properties of an image or sound file, the technical details can vary widely and some of the characteristics are vital to the accurate rendering of the content. One issue with technical metadata is whether to rely in the long term on what is embedded in the file, or whether to extract the metadata and store it separately, like descriptive information. There are arguments for both approaches, and since there is no clear best practice, it pays to be aware of the issue.

Preservation metadata is difficult to define, because in many ways all metadata is preservation metadata if it contributes to the future usability of a resource. To be more precise, preservation metadata is information that is used to manage digital objects and that helps ensure objects can be used over time as digital environments (software applications and operating systems) change. Preservation metadata includes elements such as "file format," "creating application," and "checksum"—a unique value that is calculated on a file bit stream using an algorithm and can be periodically audited to make sure nothing about the file has altered. Like checksums, much preservation metadata is expected to be automatically generated by the repository in which a digital object is stored. Creating this kind of metadata manually is very labor-intensive and error-prone, and does not scale to a large digital library or repository. Regardless of whether some level of automation exists in the environment in which you are working or not, preservation metadata should be specified according to the community the digital objects are being preserved for. Records managers have different needs than software developers, and preservation metadata should speak to those who have a long-term vested interest in a given collection of objects. Finally, preservation metadata is an area where best practices have not always made their way into implementation. When considering preservation metadata, the ability to articulate the rationale behind a set of elements is ideally combined with an effort to envision possible implementation strategies.

METADATA STANDARDS AND SCHEMAS

Sometimes the array of acronyms used in metadata discussion is an obstacle to getting interested and involved in digital library projects. To someone new to the field, metadata might seem like an impenetrable alphabet soup. Before diving into the sea of metadata acronyms, it is important to understand the distinction between metadata standards, content standards, and schemas. Metadata standards define sets of data elements for a particular purpose or environment and are generally established by an authority. Content standards prescribe how data elements should be used; in other words, the acceptable values for given fields. A metadata schema describes how a given set of data elements should be encoded. Each of these categories comes into play when creating the library bibliographic record. The MARC format is a metadata standard that defines record structure and data elements to be used for bibliographic, authority, and holdings records in a library catalog. In order to populate the elements of a MARC record, content standards in the form of cataloging rules, subject thesauri, and classification schedules are used. Specifically, the contents of a MARC record are defined outside the MARC format by such standards as ISBD, Anglo-American Cataloguing Rules, Second Edition (AACR2), and the Library of Congress Subject Headings (LCSH). AACR2, for example, is a content standard that covers how to describe and provide access points for library resources. Finally, the MARC XML metadata schema supports the Extensible Markup Language (XML) encoding of MARC records; it provides the tags for marking up bibliographic, authority, and holdings MARC records.

Another example of standards and schema comes from the archival world. AACR2 is insufficient for describing archival collections, where Describing Archives: A Content Standard (DACS) is used instead. DACS is a set of rules for describing archives, personal papers, and manuscript collections, and it specifies the elements to be used at different levels in multilevel description. DACS tells you how to write a finding aid, which could be implemented in MARC or in Encoded Archival Description (EAD), the standard for encoding archival finding aids in XML. This example illustrates an important point, which is that content standards are output-neutral—they tell you how to describe something but not how to format that description.

There are a variety of metadata standards that you should be familiar with when embarking on a career in digital librarianship, but it can be difficult to get situated amidst the range of international, national, and subject-specific standards. Rather than focusing on the names of standards and the consequent list of elements, think instead about the appropriate context for implementation and how a standard might be influenced by local needs. In other words, whether you can enumerate MARC formats and field codes, or recite Dublin Core and EAD elements, is irrelevant if you cannot articulate the context in which they might be used and why one would choose one element set over another for description. "Seeing Standards:

A Visualization of the Metadata Universe" (Riley, 2009) is a poster that maps out the metadata landscape for the cultural heritage community. Its creator, Jenn Riley, evaluates 105 standards according to their strength in terms of the communities they target, the materials they are suited for, their function in metadata creation and storage, and the type of metadata they record. While somewhat daunting in terms of the number of standards she cites, this visualization might help you get situated in the universe of metadata standards.

Knowledge of the Dublin Core Metadata Element Set (DCMES) is crucial because thanks to its flexibility, extensibility, and broad application, it is relevant to most digital libraries in some way. It may be the metadata schema employed by a local system, or local metadata may be designed to be converted to Dublin Core when exchanged with another system. The Dublin Core Metadata Initiative (DCMI) maintains DCMES, and "simple" or "unqualified" Dublin Core is a vocabulary of 15 elements, shown in table 8.3, that provide for the basic description of a wide range of information resources. Simple Dublin Core includes elements such as "Title," "Creator," "Date," and "Subject," which are generic enough to apply to just about any resource, no matter the type or format.

This "core" metadata set is expanded by the "qualified" Dublin Core terms, which refine the original set. The sets are not mutually exclusive, and in fact both might be implemented for different purposes. A resource might be described using simple Dublin Core for the purposes of metadata harvesting; the widely used Open Archives Initiative-Protocol for Metadata Harvesting (OAI-PMH) normally collects unqualified Dublin Core. But for display in a local interface, more detailed information could be provided using the qualified Dublin Core refinements. For example, the simple Dublin Core term "Relation" is used to encompass all related resources, but qualified DC allows for the specification of certain types of relationships, when one object "isPartOf" or "isRequiredBy" another. For scholarly works in an institutional repository you might use the "dateCreated," "dateSubmitted," and "dateAccepted" qualifiers, whereas all these elements would resolve to "Date" in simple Dublin Core.

Many Dublin Core-based standards recognize the need for local elements. For example, the Interoperability Metadata Standard for Electronic Theses and Dissertations (ETD-MS), a Dublin Core-based standard for electronic theses and dissertations, employs simple Dublin Core and adds additional elements for theses, such as "thesis.degree.name" and "thesis.degree.level." This standard is not necessarily meant to replace local standards, which may be developed for a particular educational environment, its researchers, librarians, and technical staff;

TABLE 8.3
Basic Dublin Core metadata element set

Element Name	Label	Definition
title	Title	A name given to the resource.
creator	Creator	An entity primarily responsible for making the resource.
subject	Subject	The topic of the resource.
description	Description	An account of the resource.
publisher	Publisher	An entity responsible for making the resource available.
contributor	Contributor	An entity responsible for making contributions to the resource.
date	Date	A point or period of time associated with an event in the life cycle of the resource.
type	Type	The nature or genre of the resource.
format	Format	The file format, physical medium, or dimensions of the resource.
identifier	Identifier	An unambiguous reference to the resource within a given context.
source	Source	The resource from which the described resource is derived.
language	Language	A language of the resource.
relation	Relation	A related resource.
coverage	Coverage	The spatial or temporal topic of the resource, the spatial applicability of the resource, or the jurisdiction under which the resource is relevant.
rights	Rights	Information about rights held in and over the resource.

rather, it can be adapted locally and used when sharing local records with another system.

Another important metadata standard for the library world is the Metadata Object Description Schema (MODS), which is maintained by the Library of Congress. Like Dublin Core, MODS is a general standard that can be used for a wide variety of resources and is easily mapped to other standards. But unlike Dublin Core, which has no native schema for encoding, MODS was created as an XML-encoded element set. MODS takes advantage of XML's hierarchically nested elements and element attributes to allow for richer description and more flexibility for local implementations (see chapter 6 for a more detailed discussion about XML). The schema is made up of twenty top-level elements. Some of these, such as the "titleInfo" element, are container elements for sub-elements, such as "title," "subTitle," "partNumber," and "partName." Element attributes are meant to refine the scope of an element. For example, the "authority" attribute is used to designate the standard or controlled vocabulary from which the value populating the element is drawn. The authority value could be "LCSH" if the term in the subject element is drawn from the Library of Congress Subject Headings; it could be "NAF" if the term in the name element is drawn from the Name Authority File. MODS is highly compatible with MARC, but it uses human-readable rather than numeric tags. It is also not as exhaustive as MARC, which allows for ease of implementation. Finally, for those unfamiliar with XML, which is a very common way of encoding metadata in the digital library world, MODS offers a straightforward example of XML encoding and serves as the basis for learning about XML.

Dublin Core and MODS are generic metadata standards suitable for use in most library or archives-based digital collections. There are many more specific standards that apply to certain types of objects or particular subject areas, and it is useful to at least be familiar with a few of them in case you should find yourself working in a context where they might apply. Metadata choices are shaped by a variety of criteria: the types of resources you are trying to manage (image versus sound), the formats you are dealing with (MP3 versus WAV), the type of digital environment in which you are working (a high-access digital library or institutional repository versus a dark archive or preservation repository), and the type of audience your material is designated for (researchers versus educators).

If you are working with either digitized or born digital images, the Metadata for Images in XML Standard (MIX) consists of technical data elements for the management of digital image collections. This metadata standard allows for diverse systems to exchange and process digital image files, and it is designed to support long-term access, management, and preservation. On the other hand, if you have a collection of text-based digital objects, such as digitized books or manuscripts, the Technical Metadata for Text (textMD) standard allows you to account for textual properties such as language, font, and page order as well as to record information about how the text was processed (what type of Optical Character Recognition), how the text was marked up (what version of the Text Encoding Initiative), and viewing requirements.

Both MIX and textMD are technical metadata standards suited for environments with a focus on preservation. As such they are compatible with the Preservation Metadata Implementation Strategies (PREMIS) Data Dictionary (PREMIS Editorial Committee, 2012). The PREMIS Data Dictionary recommends a core set of metadata needed for long-term preservation and is widely seen as the standard for preservation metadata. As mentioned before, many of these preservation elements are difficult to create manually. Under ideal circumstances they are generated within a preservation repository environment by the technical systems in place. The PREMIS Data Dictionary gives you an idea of the kinds of information that need to be recorded to support preservation, but many of these data elements are not practical or necessary to implement in every environment. For example, if you are working on a digital library that serves primarily as a portal to online educational resources or published scholarship managed elsewhere, this type of metadata may be out of scope. In such contexts, discipline-specific standards that will enhance access based on the needs of users are probably a more worthwhile investment.

There are numerous standards that apply to specific types of content. A few well-established ones are mentioned here by way of example. Learning Object Metadata (IEEE LOM) is aimed at educators to help them find resources that can be used to support learning and help them understand how these resources can be employed. LOM data elements allow for the evaluation of educational resources based on what age level they are appropriate for or what learning style they engage. The Content Standard for Digital Geospatial Metadata (CSGDM) is designed to facilitate the use and exchange of geographic data. It records spatial and time period information such as longitude, latitude, and date range for geographical resources and data sets. The VRA Core is a metadata element set for cultural heritage institutions. It provides for the description of works of visual culture (painting, sculpture, architecture) as well as the visual surrogates (photograph, slides) that document them. It includes elements such as "Cultural context," "Location," "Style period," and "Technique" that are particular to visual arts and culture. All of these content-specific standards attest to the fact that metadata standards are based on what one is trying to accomplish within a given digital collection or environment. Specific standards do not apply all the time, nor are they appropriate to all circumstances.

When considering any content- or format-specific standard, it is important to consider the user communities you are trying to serve. Furthermore, any standard is subject to local needs and limitations. Within an organization there may be a variety of stakeholders invested in a digital library or institutional repository. Metadata decisions are often influenced by the varying objectives of the stakeholders they serve.

One standard that can be applied in almost any context is the Metadata Encoding and Transmission Standard (METS). METS is a standard for encoding the descriptive, administrative, and structural metadata for digital objects, and like

MODS, it is expressed in XML. METS identifies the component parts of a digital object, such as content files, descriptive metadata, and administrative metadata. It specifies the location of these components (where they are stored) and the structural relationships between them. METS integrates different types of metadata as they pertain to a digital object, and therefore encompasses other metadata standards. For example, an object could include Dublin Core for its description, local metadata for administration, and PREMIS for preservation. All of these can be expressed within METS. In this way, METS serves as a kind of metadata "wrapper" that structures the relationship between various metadata element sets with different purposes. METS is widely used by major digital library projects such as the California Digital Library and MIT's DSpace, so although implementation is fairly technical it pays to be aware of the purpose and scope of METS.

FINAL THOUGHTS

Working with metadata requires a balance between familiarity with standards on the one hand, and sensitivity to organizational culture on the other. As someone new to the field, it is your job to bring an awareness of standards, best practices and the library values they represent to conversations about metadata, while at the same time working to accommodate information that local stakeholders want expressed in a structured fashion.

As digital library projects, digital collections, and repositories become more widespread, libraries need people who are comfortable with metadata. A firm foundation in metadata basics—an understanding of metadata theories, categories, and standards—can be applied at various levels in the field of digital librarianship. It applies to those creating metadata and to those managing data entry; it applies at the level of metadata architecture and framework development; and it applies to those who aspire to be digital library project managers. Metadata is also an area of digital librarianship that is evolving, where questions remain to be answered. There is a need for both logical problem-solving and creativity to determine how to make information resources discoverable and available.

Without metadata, the library community cannot meet the needs of current and future users, who expect online access. So whether you are someone considering a career in digital librarianship or someone looking to refresh your skills and get more involved in digital projects, you should be prepared to talk about metadata. If you compare metadata with the traditional description of bibliographic resources, you can find similarities between metadata creation and library technical services and articulate a future for library catalogers. And if you can discuss metadata in terms of its value to various user groups and the tasks they aim to achieve, you can bridge the space between traditional print and modern digital libraries.

REFERENCES

IFLA Study Group on the Functional Requirements for Bibliographic Records. 1998. "Functional Requirements for Bibliographic Records: Final Report." http://www.ifla.org/VII/s13/frbr/frbr.pdf.

PREMIS Editorial Committee. 2011. "PREMIS Data Dictionary." www.loc.gov/standards/premis/v2/premis-2-2.pdf.

Riley, Jenn. 2009. "Seeing Standards: A Visualization of the Metadata Universe." www.dlib.indiana.edu/~jenlrile/metadatamap/.

RECOMMENDED RESOURCES

Dublin Core Metadata Initiative. 2010. "Dublin Core Metadata Element Set, Version 1.1." http://dublincore.org/documents/dces/.

IFLA Cataloguing Section and ISBD Review Group. 2011. *ISBD: International Standard Bibliographic Description*. Berlin: De Gruyter Saur.

Library of Congress. 2011. "MARC Standards." Last modified July 25, 2012. www.loc.gov/marc/.

Library of Congress. 2010. "METS: Metadata Encoding & Transmission Standard." Last modified August 30, 2012. www.loc.gov/standards/mets/.

Library of Congress. 2010. "MODS: Metadata Object Description Schema." Last modified July 10, 2012. www.loc.gov/standards/mods/.

Miller, Steven J. 2011. *Metadata for Digital Collections*. New York: Neal-Schuman.

Chapter Nine

Putting Metadata into Practice

Silvia B. Southwick and Jane Skoric

One of the key challenges you will face as a new digital librarian will be to successfully develop and manage metadata. As metadata is a relatively new aspect of librarianship, the skills that are required come as much from practice and communication with other digital librarians as they do from reference materials. With this in mind, the purpose of this chapter is to provide you with scenarios from actual practice that, hopefully, you will be able to apply to your own situation. Most of the scenarios used are taken from the development of image-based digital collections at University Libraries, University of Nevada Las Vegas. These projects encompass the majority of tasks that you are likely to encounter in any digital library project. For example, we will cover issues related to interoperability among the digital collections of various networked libraries, use of controlled vocabularies, choice of metadata element sets, and other relevant topics.

This chapter presents metadata in practice within three different contexts. We start by looking at developing a digital collection as a project and then move on to developing a digital collection within an organization that already has (or plans to have) a set of digital collections. Finally, we move on to developing digital collections that will be part of aggregated digital repositories. In each one of these contexts we introduce the issues that need to be considered in designing and implementing metadata. The chapter ends with a description of the development of an actual digital collection, identifying the decisions made during the project design and implementation.

METADATA PRINCIPLES

Metadata principles provide a foundation for developing quality digital collections. The National Information Standards Organization (NISO) recommends three principles that are particularly relevant to our discussion:

Metadata Principle 1: Good metadata conforms to community standards in a way that is appropriate to the materials in the collection, users of the collection, and current and potential future uses of the collection (NISO 2007, 63).

Metadata Principle 2: Good metadata supports interoperability (NISO 2007, 76).

Metadata Principle 3: Good metadata uses authority control and content standards to describe objects and collocate related objects (NISO 2007, 79).

These three principles are emphasized in this chapter as we talk about application profiles (APs), interoperability and use of controlled vocabularies, and guidelines for data entry. Adoption of these principles will help prospective digital librarians to have a good start in their new profession.

DESIGNING AND CREATING METADATA FOR A LOCAL DIGITAL COLLECTION

Your organization may decide to build or continue building digital collections to better showcase its unique resources to a larger, online audience. How well your collections are discovered, accessed, and utilized will depend, to a large extent, on the creation of metadata. After reading chapter 8 you now have some understanding of metadata concepts, so let's roll up our sleeves and see what you can do with this knowledge.

Questions to Ask

The creation of a digital collection is a dynamic process consisting of many interconnected steps. One of the first steps to be taken involves asking and answering some basic questions: Why build a digital collection? For whom should you build the collection? What will be the content of this digital collection? Answering these basic questions about purpose, audience, and materials will inevitably lead to many additional questions prior to and during the design and creation of metadata for your local digital collection.

Choosing a Metadata Element Set

As outlined in the previous chapter, there are many metadata element sets from which to choose. Your selection of a metadata element set may be limited by the content management system or other software that will be used to deliver your collection online. For example, CONTENTdm only supports metadata sets that do not have a hierarchical structure. The creation of compound objects within CONTENTdm supports the relationship of a book (parent-level metadata) to an individual page (page-level metadata). It is not currently possible with this system, however, to represent the hierarchical relationships between levels of description that may be captured using Encoded Archival Description (EAD). EAD is a standard that uses a hierarchical structure to describe material organization: from identification of a collection, to a range of numbered boxes, to a named folder, to a dated memo.

The metadata element set you choose will determine what kind of data can be attributed to each item and how that data will be displayed within your collection. Whatever metadata element set is selected, attention must be paid to the rules, conventions, and best practices of that set. You can quickly and easily access information about specific metadata element sets by searching the Internet. Official websites with user support materials are maintained by such organizations as the Library of Congress (METS, MODS, EAD), Visual Resources Association, (VRA Core), and the Dublin Core Metadata Initiative (Dublin Core).

Customizing the Metadata Element Set

Regardless of which metadata element set you select, you will inevitably begin the process of customizing the metadata elements to meet local requirements. Among the first steps will be the identification of those elements that are considered basic to the description and identification of your materials. These elements will generally include *title*, *date*, *creator*, and *subject*. Although metadata element sets usually specify the label for each element (how the element is named in the item record), you may decide to customize element labels and refine their definitions. For example, the University of Nevada Las Vegas (UNLV)'s digital collection, Menus: The Art of Dining (http://digital.library.unlv.edu/collections/menus), contains the metadata element *name of restaurant*, which was assumed to be the *creator* of a menu. Commonly, fields are labeled to assist users in understanding the specific content.

Another step in building your metadata element set will involve the selection of metadata elements that are of particular interest for your specific collection. The topic of the collection, the type of materials, and the prospective audience will help determine whether, for example, it is important to identify people, locations, or perhaps graphical elements. For these, you might need to create local metadata elements, as described below. You must also determine which metadata elements will be visible to the public and in what order they will display in the record.

Finally, keep in mind the notion of balance as you build your metadata element set. Let your objective be to create a set of elements that avoids the clutter of superfluous information, yet accurately describes the items in your digital collection and renders them discoverable. It is imperative that you match resources (funding, time, and people) to your project goals. For example, in the Menus collection because most of the menus were from the nineteenth century and handwritten, the transcriptions of the dishes presented in each menu would require time and effort that were not compatible with the project schedule and staff allocated to the project. Therefore, our project goals did not include transcriptions. As stated in the article "Metadata Principles and Practicalities," "populating databases with metadata is costly, so there are strong economic incentives to create metadata with sufficient detail to meet the functional requirements of an application, but not more" (Hodgins et al., 2002: under "C. Refinement").

Defining Local Metadata Elements

In addition to the elements offered by your chosen metadata element set, your digital collection may require the use of locally defined metadata elements. Such elements will emerge as you consider local needs for access, organization, and preservation. For example, you might decide to use terms from the Getty Thesaurus of Geographic Names (TGN) to describe the items in your collection. There may be locations, however, that are well known locally but not found in TGN. Such terms could be included in an additional metadata element called, for example, *Local Geographical Terms*. For example, UNLV's Historic Landscape of Nevada (HLN) digital collection (http://digital.library.unlv.edu/collections/historic-landscape) includes many items that refer to the Stewart Burial Plot. The Stewart family has historical significance as pioneering ranchers in the Las Vegas Valley. In order to improve discoverability and facilitate access, this term was included in a *Local Geographic* element. In another situation, you might wish to refer to metadata elements that are specific to the material for which you are creating metadata. For example, for a collection of restaurant menus you may decide to create a metadata element for type of cuisine. The creation of this element may be based on the expectations of a target audience, such as hospitality students, concerning terms that they may use for searching.

Selecting and Building Controlled Vocabularies

After customizing your element set, an important follow-up step is to consider the content of the elements and whether the data can or should be controlled. Some fields, such as title, are unique and cannot be constructed from predefined lists. Other metadata elements, like subject, would use terms applicable to various items throughout a collection and may be created using controlled vocabularies (CV). The controlled vocabulary you use generally depends on the contents of the collection. It is advisable, for example, to use a well-established CV such as the Library of Congress Thesaurus for Graphic Materials (TGM) to describe photographs or the Getty Art & Architecture Thesaurus (AAT) for architectural drawings.

There are certain advantages to using a CV. Your users will be able to search for terms without needing to think of synonyms or other variations of the same concept, since resources of a specific concept will be indexed with the same term. Thus, *automobiles* would be used for *autos* and *cars*. Also, an advantage for those creating the metadata is the ability to choose terms from a predefined list rather than rethinking and creating anew each term upon use. As a result, you encourage and facilitate the use of consistent terminology across various metadata creators. If you have fields that include names, for example, you might select the Library of Congress Name Authority Headings. Thus, no matter when or by whom a particular name was entered, it would always be spelled correctly and displayed in inverted order.

There are also limitations to using controlled vocabularies. You may wish to create and implement a set of terms defined by your organization, which would not be found in a CV. In UNLV's HLN collection, for example, TGM was used to describe the *genre* (ex. "correspondence"), while a locally defined CV was used for the metadata element *local genre* (ex. "letter," a non-TGM term). Assigning appropriate CVs to metadata elements will provide lists of standardized terms that can greatly assist users. The degree to which metadata facilitates the searching and browsing of your digital collections, however, will depend on how accurately and consistently the controlled vocabulary terms are applied by those creating metadata.

Creating Metadata

One way to increase metadata quality is through documentation of indexing guidelines that provide metadata creators with rules for data entry (the equivalent of a simple AACR2 for your collection). These indexing guidelines will commonly list each metadata element used to describe the items in your collection, their definitions, and may provide a few examples. Such guidelines are used for training as well as a reference instrument for metadata creators to better understand the data they are to include in each element and how they are to construct the metadata. For example, if you designate date as "required," those entering the metadata understand that a date or date range must be included for each item. Your guidelines would also illustrate that the format of the date is to be entered a certain way, such as yyyy-mm-dd (but not mm/dd/yyyy) or yyyy-yyyy.

Another means of developing good metadata is to provide metadata creators—typically having some cataloging background—with an overview of your digital collection's goals, materials, and audience. Understanding the context and interrelationship of materials included in your digital collection will promote the creation of metadata that is meaningful and useful. The previously mentioned HLN digital collection focused on themes of water supply, water use, and water rights and thus a photograph of a swimming pool would necessitate subject metadata about water. That same image within the digital collection Dreaming the Skyline: Resort Architecture and the Urban Space, however, might include metadata such as *recreation structures*.

As stated above, it is essential that you develop an appropriately sized metadata element set. Likewise, aim towards one that is purposeful. Even before you begin identifying your controlled vocabularies and selecting terms, focus on answering the basic questions of purpose, audience, and materials, as well as funding, staffing, and timelines. The discoverability of your digital collection items could easily be hindered by too few or too many subject terms. Too few subject terms makes it difficult for users to find relevant items; however, an excess of subject terms may also be a hindrance. In order to assign various subject terms, metadata creators might use terms that are not so significant to the item being described and consequently users would need to sift through a long list of items to identify those that are more relevant to their needs. Metadata creation, at its best, integrates precision with creativity.

DESIGNING ADDITIONAL COLLECTIONS

After successfully creating your first digital collection, you might feel confident enough to expand the repertoire of collections offered by your organization using similar steps. While the knowledge you acquired developing the initial digital collection will allow you to achieve your immediate goal, you need to also think more broadly to guarantee that your digital collections will be mutually compatible.

There are many reasons for putting in the effort to ensure compatibility among your digital collections. For example, if the automated tool used for searching these collections allows cross-collection search, you need to guarantee that fields in your digital collections that deal with similar data are designed in the same way. If one of your collections has a field entitled *geographic feature*, using TGN as a controlled vocabulary, it would be important that other collections including similar fields also use the same controlled vocabulary. Another reason for you to create compatible digital collections is to facilitate or enable the implementation of a discovery platform in your organization. Discovery platforms are rapidly becoming an important trend in academic libraries. With such a system, users are given a single search box that allows them to simultaneously look for resources in the catalog, digital collections, electronic journals, institutional repository, and other electronic resources maintained by the library. For such cross-platform searching to work, it is essential that your digital collections be consistent in their design and implementation.

A good way for you to accomplish compatibility among digital collections within your organization is to define an application profile. This will help you to develop a systematic and sustainable way to create and maintain consistency. An application profile (AP) is a specification of a metadata element set to be adopted by a particular application. An application, in this context, could be the system that is managing your digital collections or the system that aggregates metadata from digital collections owned by various participants of a consortium. APs also include policies and guidelines for creating metadata. According to the Dublin Core Metadata Initiative Glossary (Woodley, Clement, and Winn, 2001), elements of an AP can be derived from different metadata sets in order to satisfy the requirements of a particular application.

You may be wondering why you would need an AP if you are adopting a standard metadata element set for your digital collection. Metadata standards, although a very important instrument for achieving consistency among digital collections, are commonly not as specific as most digital collection projects would require. They are susceptible to interpretation. Let's take as an example the Dublin Core metadata element *date*. This element is defined by the Dublin Core Metadata Initiative as "A point or period of time associated with an event in the lifecycle of the resource" (DCMI, 2010: under "The Elements").

As you can see, the definition of *date* is overly broad. If this definition is given to metadata creators, they may choose different event dates for the value of this metadata element such as the date of conversion of the physical object into digital format or the date of publication of the original resource. The Dublin Core metadata elements standard does not provide a way for you to specify the type of data to be used. This problem may be addressed, at least in part, by adopting Qualified Dublin Core. There you can use metadata elements that are refinements of *date* such as the metadata element labeled as *date created*. You might still have to specify how you want metadata creators to express the date: day/month/year, month/day/year or year/month/day? By developing an AP, you will be able to be very specific about which type of data and which format should be used when entering the values for metadata elements. As a general rule, each metadata element of the standard you are adopting needs to be further specified to a level that will help ensure that consistency can be achieved and maintained. Both standardized and local metadata elements will be part of the AP.

Another function of the AP is to specify the properties of metadata. In the Dublin Core Metadata Element set, all metadata elements are optional. It will be important for you to define which metadata elements are mandatory for your collections. For example, you might decide that *date* is mandatory and define it as such in your AP. It will also be important for you to provide guidelines for entering the *date* value, including the situation in which a date is not available for the material being described. One possible rule in this case would be to specify that the metadata creator estimates the date based on specific parameters.

Pre-Application Profile Digital Collections

A situation you might face in your job is digital collections that do not share common standards or guidelines. These collections might have been developed for specific projects without taking into consideration existing collections or best practices. Fields in these collections may share similar names (labels) but may be used for different purposes. For example, similar *subject* fields in one collection may be populated with keywords and in another collection with controlled vocabulary terms. This is not a simple problem to tackle. You need to understand the organizational context and the organization's intention in building these digital collections. You must also analyze their content and identify the target audience. With this information in hand you can start devising an AP that will encompass specific organizational needs. Once the AP is well established, you can audit your old collections and work towards having them conform to the application profile.

Ideally, you would create an AP and use it with your new collections, but every digital collection has its own peculiarities that are not always accounted for in the existing AP. As you revise the organization application profile, you will need to carefully evaluate changes that have the potential to affect existing digital collections or agreements with consortia in which the organization may participate.

METADATA AND THE INTERNET ENVIRONMENT

Our focus up to this point has been on the creation of metadata for digital collections that belong to an organization. Now, let's consider the possibility that you are participating in a cooperative initiative where metadata is aggregated in a central repository elsewhere on the Internet. This provides users with an opportunity to simultaneously search collections developed by diverse organizations. The benefit of this approach is to greatly increase users' ability to discover and retrieve relevant information, which is the ultimate purpose of a digital collection.

In order to participate in cooperative initiatives, digital collections need to be interoperable with other collections. NISO defines interoperability as "the ability of multiple systems or components with different hardware and software platforms, data structures and interfaces to exchange and share data with minimum loss of content and functionality" (NISO 2004, 2). This definition emphasizes the computational aspect of interoperability. Practice has demonstrated that we need to go beyond the computational aspects. Arms et al. suggest that to achieve interoperability among heterogeneous digital collections there needs to be agreement among participants at three levels: technical, content, and organizational (2002). Technical agreements are related to metadata standards, protocol, data security, and so on. Content agreements refer to metadata values and how they are presented, and organizational agreements refer to things like access, authentication, and payment. These agreements form the basis for cooperative metadata repositories.

There are various ways that you can share metadata among collections, the most common being harvesting. Harvesting is typically an automated process that gathers metadata from distributed digital collections in order to aggregate them in a centralized metadata repository. Harvesting is processed through specific protocols. The Open Archives Initiative created such a protocol, the Open Archives Initiative Protocol for Metadata Harvesting (OAI-PMH). The OAI-PMH is a set of information requests that are invoked through HTML (OAI, 2008).

Before going into further detail about the harvesting process, let's define a few terms. Repositories that expose metadata for harvesting are called *data providers*. Repositories that are built by harvesting metadata from data providers are called *aggregators*. Aggregators may or may not provide information services, such as cross-collection searching, with the harvested metadata. When they do, they are also called *service providers*.

Applying this terminology, we can say that in order to share metadata a digital collection needs to become a data provider. There are a few features that you need to incorporate into your digital collection in order to expose metadata for harvesting. First, if you are using a content management system it must implement a layer of the protocol for exposing metadata; most current digital collection systems have this already enabled. Second, you need to choose which metadata set you are going to use to expose the metadata. Dublin Core is the most common metadata set used for this purpose. If you use OAI-PMH, it is mandatory that the digital collection expose its metadata using Dublin Core. However, you don't need to be limited to this metadata set. You could also use Qualified Dublin Core, or any other metadata set that is more specific or relevant to the subject domain area or community your digital collections are targeting. However, choice of metadata element set may be limited by the content management system's ability to deal with structured formats. For example, CONTENTdm, a widely adopted digital collection management system, restricts the metadata sets used for exposing metadata to Dublin Core and Qualified Dublin Core.

The Biblioteca Digital Brasileira de Teses e Dissertações (http://bdtd.ibict.br/), the Brazilian networked digital library of theses and dissertations, is an example of a digital library initiative that uses various metadata sets for harvesting. Most of the data providers within this initiative expose their metadata in three formats: Dublin Core, Qualified Dublin Core, and MTD-BR. MTD-BR is a Brazilian standard specifically defined for exchanging metadata about electronic theses and dissertations (ETDs) within this initiative. The Instituto Brasileiro de Informação em Ciencia e Tecnologia, a Brazilian government agency, plays the roles of aggregator and service provider. It harvests metadata from various Brazilian universities and maintains a central repository that allows users to search in a single repository for Brazilian electronic theses and dissertations. This central repository also serves as a data provider for an international initiative, the Networked Digital Library of Theses and Dissertations, maintained by Virginia Tech. In order to participate in this international initiative, the Brazilian central repository exposes metadata using the electronic thesis and dissertation metadata set, ETD-MS (Atkins et al., 2008). The central repository also exposes metadata in Dublin Core (dc) and Qualified Dublin Core (qdc) for other aggregators that might use its metadata. Figure 9.1 depicts the aforementioned standards in use.

So far, we have been talking about technologies and standards that allow for metadata harvesting from distributed data providers. While these technical aspects are essential for sharing metadata, there is perhaps a more challenging issue to be discussed: content interoperability (or content agreement, as mentioned above). How can we ensure that harvested metadata originating from various data providers is mutually compatible? We need compatible metadata in order to provide good information services across the aggregated repository. Here, we adopt a similar solution to that used in organizational settings—we create an AP in which metadata

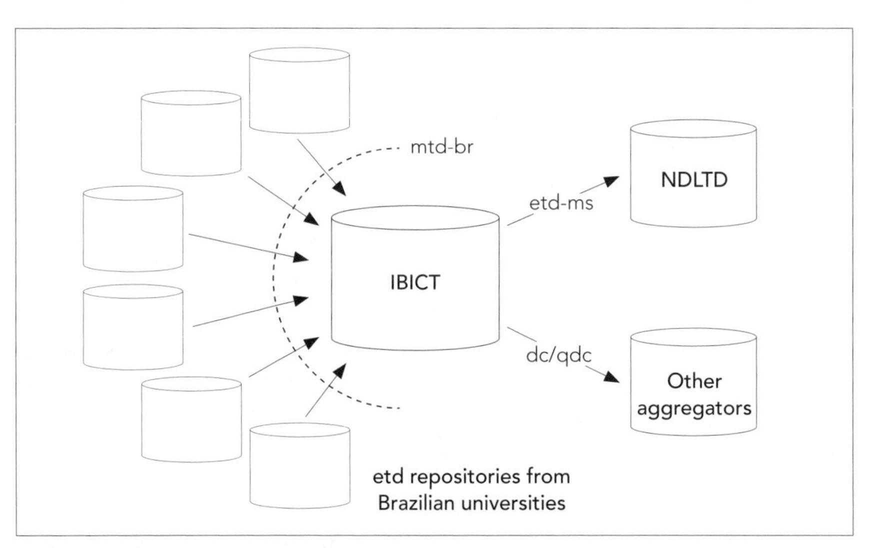

FIGURE 9.1
Example of metadata harvesting using multiple different standards

standards are refined and guidelines for data entry are created in order to increase interoperability among harvested metadata.

An AP in a collaborative environment is one aspect of the agreements made among various organizations with the aim of increasing the quality of the user experience by providing integrated information services. The adoption of a common AP might have some implications for how you work with metadata within your organization. For example, if you have already established an organizational AP, you need to make sure that internal and external APs are compatible.

An example of a consortium AP is the Mountain West Digital Library (MWDL) Dublin Core Application Profile (Utah Academic Library Consortium, 2011). While an AP can generally be based on more than one metadata element set, this particular AP is based solely on Dublin Core. It defines in detail each metadata element and provides guidelines for its content. In order to exemplify the difference in degree of specificity between a metadata standard and an AP based on the same standard, compare the specifications for the same element, *creator*, in the Dublin Core element set and MWDL, in tables 9.1 and 9.2. Some data was eliminated from both specifications as they were not relevant for this comparison.

TABLE 9.1
Mountain West Digital Library application profile for element "creator"

Element Name	Creator
Label	Creator
DC Definition	An entity primarily responsible for making the resource.
Is Field Required?	Mandatory if applicable
Is Field Repeatable?	Yes
How to Use	Person or entity responsible for creating intellectual content of resource such as a person, organization or service. Prefer form of name as verified in the Library of Congress Name Authority File (LCNAF). If name is not listed there, give name in the following format: Last name, First name, Middle initial and period, year of birth and/or death if known, separated by a hyphen. For further help in formatting names not found in LCNAF, consult a cataloging resource such as the Anglo-American Cataloguing Rules (AACR2), Resource Description and Access (RDA), or Describing Archives: A Content Standard (DACS).
Schemes	Library of Congress Name Authority File (LCNAF)
DC Mapping	dcterms:creator

Note that the *How to Use* row within the MWDL AP table provides detailed information on values and formats for entering the metadata element creator. In contrast, the Dublin Core specification does not provide such information.

TABLE 9.2
Dublin Core application profile for element "creator"

Term Name	Creator
Label	Creator
Definition	An entity primarily responsible for making the resource.
Required?	No
Repeatable?	Yes
Comment	Examples of a Creator include a person, an organization, or a service.

Crosswalks

Once the metadata is created according to an application profile, you need to establish a mapping between the metadata set that you have adopted and the metadata set that will be used for harvesting. Frequently, not all metadata elements from a collection are mapped to the target metadata set. You might have various reasons for not mapping some of the metadata elements. For example, the target metadata set may not include an element for the type of data you have in a particular metadata element, or you may have local metadata elements that are unique to that collection. Suppose, for example, in a digital collection of historical photographs, you created a local field to include identified individuals from the photos. You are exposing the metadata using the Dublin Core metadata element set. Since there are no specific metadata elements for this type of information in Dublin Core, you might wonder if you could map it to *description*.

There are various issues to consider here. Does the *description* metadata element guideline allow this type of information? Even if it does allow it, you need to review what else you have mapped to the *description*. A risk is mapping too much data to the element, making it cluttered. It is always good to keep in mind that the metadata you are sharing should be the most significant.

■ CASE STUDY ■

Developing "Menus: The Art of Dining" Digital Collection at UNLV

In this section we explore the most important metadata decisions made during the design and implementation of a digital collection at UNLV Libraries—Menus: The Art of Dining. We focus our attention on those aspects that are more critical for metadata management, and intend to demonstrate some of the concepts and practices that were laid out in previous sections. We don't claim that this collection should be used as an exemplar; our experience has demonstrated that each collection has its own features and the design process cannot be generalized. Our intent is to demonstrate the kind of decisions you may need to make when designing and implementing a digital collection.

Menus: The Art of Dining includes menus from the Bohn-Bettoni Collection, which contains American, Canadian, and English restaurant menus dating from 1870 to 1930. Additionally, this collection includes Las Vegas restaurant menus from 1950 to 1980.

Metadata Set

The first step in designing this collection was to look for possible standard metadata sets to be adopted. At the time this collection was developed there was no standard metadata set specifically defined for this particular type of material. Therefore, the metadata set was locally created and was based on a more general metadata set, the Dublin Core Metadata Element Set (DCMES). Other collections containing similar materials were examined in order to understand their design, including a database of menus created by the Hospitality Management Program students at UNLV, who were a target audience of the new collection. The Hospitality Management liaison librarian was also involved in the design.

Another critical factor affecting our design arose from an analysis of the menus that had been selected for inclusion in the collection. Because the menus could be of interest to a wide variety of users, including restaurateurs, historians, graphic designers, collectors, and the local community, we decided to include as many pieces of information as we were able to find in the menus. The table below shows some of the forty-seven metadata elements used for this collection. As can be seen, we created several local metadata elements to accommodate the information we found in the menus. Many of these metadata elements are not mapped to elements in DCMES. The implication is that these elements will only be available at the local digital collection level. Any aggregator that harvests metadata from this collection will be restricted to fewer metadata elements.

Another aspect of this element set to be observed is the large number of local controlled vocabularies that were created. As mentioned before, CVs allow for consistency among metadata creators, therefore improving search performance. Normally, the number of local controlled vocabularies will be minimal since most of the time you will be able to find well-established controlled vocabularies to index

TABLE 9.3
Partial metadata element set used for menus collection

Metadata Element	DCMES Mapping	Use of CV
Title	Title	No
Alternative Title	Title-Alternative	No
Restaurant or Site Name	Creator	Yes, local
Collection Subject	Subject	Yes, TGM
Graphic Elements	Subject	Yes, TGM
Date Original	Date	—
Entertainer/Performer	None	Yes, local + LCANF
Type of Menu	None	Yes, local
Original Language	Language	Yes, ISO 639-3
Meals Served	None	Yes, local
Illustrator/Designer	Contributor	Yes, local
Chef or Caterer	Contributor	Yes, local
Sommelier/Wine Steward	Contributor	Yes, local
DC Type	Type	Yes, DCMI Type
Rights	Rights	—
Original Collection	Source	Yes, local

your information. That was not true for the menus collection, thus we created several in-house CVs.

Details of Selected Metadata Elements

Title: We created titles that incorporated the most important elements for identifying a menu, such as restaurant name, menu date, and type of meal described, as well as the term "menu." In the case of menus that were created for celebrations or other special events, we added information about the event. Examples of two menu titles are *Thanksgiving dinner menu, Thursday, November 30, 1882 at Union Depot Dining Hall; Ball in commemoration of the silver wedding anniversary of Mr. & Mrs. Harry Marks, supper menu, Monday, July 15, 1895, at Cannon Street Hotel.* Creating such richly descriptive titles increases the chance of finding these digital objects when metadata is harvested and users are searching within an aggregated environment.

Alternative Title: This element was created to incorporate terms in other languages. Many of the European menus had terms in English and French. While the title fields were written in English language, the alternative title used terms transcribed directly from the original. For example, one item has the title *Annual banquet, December 29, 1904 for the Escadron Marie-Henriette held at Le Grand Hotel;* with the alternative title: *Escadron Marie-Henriette banquet annuel du 29 Dècembre 1904.*

Restaurant or Site Name: Since menus do not have a clear creator, we decided to elect the name of the restaurant as the creator. Another collection manager might have decided to identify the manager or cook as creator, and that might be a problem for future interoperability. Since there is not a metadata standard for this type of material yet, our goal was to at least maintain consistency within our own digital collection and then capture other contributors such as managers and cooks in separate metadata elements. Thus, if one day a decision is made to create a standard metadata set for menus, we will be able to conform with minimal effort.

Collection Subject: This is a small set of general terms that are assigned to all records of a collection. They serve the purpose of providing a context for harvested metadata. In the case of *Menus*, the terms used were *menus, restaurants, food,* and *beverages*. These terms help users find restaurant menus in aggregated repositories by associating the term "menus" to others such as "food" or "restaurants." That would eliminate from the results, for example, resources that are about computer application menus.

Graphical Elements: Terms for this element are selected from the TGM (Thesaurus for Graphic Materials) controlled vocabulary. It is mapped to *subject* because the collection has unique and artistic menus from the nineteenth century, and we understand that a user might search for menus that have specific graphic elements; for example, menus that depict angels.

Illustrator/Designer, Chef or Caterer, Sommelier/Wine Steward, Other Contributor: These fields capture all possible contributors to a menu. They are separated but we could have put them together, amended with a role (e.g., Williams, Charles, chef). We plan to make this change in observation and compliance with the guidelines of the Mountain West Digital Library.

Metadata Guidelines

Guidelines for each individual metadata element were created as the project started and continued to be updated as the project developed. They were as specific as possible in order to increase consistency among metadata creators. Although we typically make few adjustments to a metadata set and guidelines as we work, adjustments for the Menu collection were made more frequently. The lack of metadata standard for this type of material caused us to revise our decisions several times. Our intention for making revisions was always to create a better search experience for users and improve interoperability.

Metadata Creation Phases

Metadata quality is essential for a good digital collection. Our experience at UNLV led us to divide metadata creation into three phases: acquiring provisional metadata, revising metadata, and controlling metadata quality. These phases are integrated into the general project workflow.

In the first phase provisional metadata is acquired from the content experts who are responsible for selecting material for the digital collection. It is important to provide them with a tool, such as a database, to acquire the data. Preservation metadata is added to this instrument during the scanning process, such as equipment and software used for creating the digital objects, size of the image, resolution, and so on. The data is then imported to the content management system. At this point, metadata creators begin the second phase: revising the provisional metadata to make them consistent with indexing guidelines.

Quality control is the final phase, but it is a process that occurs throughout the entire project. While quality issues might be detected during project development, to avoid unanticipated quality issues be sure to create specific procedures for quality control after all metadata is uploaded. Consistency is verified at various levels. For example, in the Historic Landscape of Nevada collection which contained various types of materials, we looked at all records of a specific material type to check if titles were constructed the same way or if there were duplications. In the case of the Menus collection, the consistency of the addresses of each restaurant was one aspect verified during the quality control phase.

■ ■ ■

FINAL THOUGHTS

This chapter presents various practical aspects of metadata design and creation. We indicated issues that need to be addressed in each of three contexts (project, organization, and aggregated) as a strategy for showing the progression that should be taken into account as the context becomes more complex. Even when faced with simple tasks, however, you should be planning for the future. In particular, when assigned the task of developing a digital collection, the questions to ask include: how can I design a digital collection that is interoperable? What are the standards that I can adopt to allow such interoperability? How are others designing digital collections in the same content area? Answering these questions will help you build quality collections and will be critical to your success as a digital librarian.

REFERENCES

Arms, William A., Diane Hillman, Carl Lagoze, Dean Krafft, Richard Marisa, John Saylor, Carol Terrizzi, and Herbert van de Sompel. 2002. "A Spectrum of Interoperability: The Site for Science Prototype for the NSDL." *D-Lib Magazine* 8, no. 1. www.dlib.org/dlib/january02/arms/01arms.html.

Atkins, Anthony, Edward Fox, Robert France, and Hussein Suleman, eds. 2008. "ETD-MS: An Interoperability Metadata Standard for Electronic Theses and Dissertations". Networked Digital Library of Theses and Dissertations. Last modified June 25. www.ndltd.org/standards/metadata/etd-ms-v1.00-rev2.html.

Dublin Core Metadata Initiative (DCMI). 2012. "Dublin Core Metadata Element Set, Version 1.1." Dublin Core Initiative website. Last modified June 14. http://dublincore.org/documents/dces/.

Hodgins, Wayne, Erik Duval, Stuart Sutton, and Stuart L. Weibel. 2002. "Metadata Principles and Practicalities." *D-Lib Magazine* 8, no. 4. www.dlib.org/dlib/april02/weibel/o4weibel.html.

National Information Standards Organization (NISO). 2004. *Understanding Metadata*. Bethesda: NISO. PDF e-book. www.niso.org/publications/press/UnderstandingMetadata.pdf.

———. 2007. *A Framework of Guidance for Building Good Digital Collections: A NISO Recommended Practice*. Baltimore: National Information Standards Organization. PDF e-book. www.niso.org/publications/rp/framework3.pdf.

Open Archives Initiative (OAI). 2008. *The Open Archives Initiative Protocol for Metadata Harvesting: Protocol Version 2.0*. Open Archives Initiative. Last modified December 7. www.openarchives.org/OAI/openarchivesprotocol.html.

Utah Academic Library Consortium. 2011. "Mountain West Digital Library Dublin Core Application Profile." http://mwdl.org/docs/MWDL_DC_Profile_Version_2.0.pdf.

Woodley, Mary S., Gail Clement, and Pete Winn. 2001. "Glossary." Dublin Core Metadata Initiative. http://dublincore.org/documents/2001/04/12/usageguide/glossary.shtml#A.

Chapter Ten

Understanding Your Role in the New Scholarly Publishing Landscape

Anne Shelley and Amy S. Jackson

Perhaps you've heard the phrase *scholarly communications* and wondered exactly what it means. It sounds very academic and formal, but it's simply the overall life cycle and flow of information between scholars. By reading this book, you are participating in a scholarly communications cycle between you, the authors, the editors, the publishers, and the venue where you borrowed or bought this book. Faculty members at academic institutions are the scholars you will be most likely to interact with as a digital librarian, although scholars can also be at private research institutions, or unassociated with any institution. Why does a digital librarian need to know about how scholars communicate? In recent years the Internet has transformed how information is published and disseminated, and digital librarians are increasingly being called upon to navigate this new scholarly communications landscape. Open access, institutional repositories, and other alternative forms of electronic publishing are becoming commonplace, and digital librarians are often expected to have expertise in these areas. As an aspiring or established digital librarian, it's to your advantage to become familiar with the nuances of scholarly publishing. This chapter provides an overview of scholarly communications and how changes in the system are affecting libraries and librarians. More specifically, we will discuss traditional and emerging publishing models, the Open Access Movement, data curation initiatives, copyright and licensing issues, and the many roles that digital librarians are playing in the evolving scholarly publishing landscape.

PUBLISHING MODELS: TRADITIONAL AND EMERGING

To grasp the intricacies of scholarly communications, you must first understand the motivations of participating players. Academic librarians, faculty members, and journal publishers all have an interest in spreading knowledge, and have a stake in the scholarly communications discussion. Scholars are focused on achieving tenure and promotion, publishing their work in reputable venues, and increasing the visibility of their research. Commercial publishers want to achieve desired profit margins, and may employ strategies that include increasing subscription fees and claiming certain types of control over the material they publish. Librarians are concerned with providing access to scholarly literature; this has led them to become involved in the creation of new models that support cost-effective publishing alternatives and encourage scholars to assert more control in the process.

As a digital librarian, you might be approached by an academic department at your institution asking the library to host an open access journal. Or you might be contacted by a faculty member who has questions about copyright and his or her work. Your library's administration might even ask you to chair a task force charged with managing research data across the university. These are some of the many issues that have come to the forefront in academic publishing in recent years, and depending on the size and the mission of the employing institution, some digital librarians deal with these issues every day. In order for you to best understand the recent transformations in scholarly communications and how those changes could affect your job, it's important to know about traditional publishing practices and how we got to where we are today.

From the emergence of the first scholarly journals in the mid-seventeenth century to the end of the twentieth century, the printed word served as the vehicle for scholars to communicate their research with one another. In the 1990s, the user-driven push to electronically publish peer-reviewed journals and conference proceedings unsettled both librarians and the research community. Scholars were skeptical that work published in e-journals would be considered in tenure and promotion decisions, and librarians worried about how best to archive and preserve digital material. Many bibliographers—especially those selecting materials for disciplines that are still largely tied to print, such as the arts and humanities—maintain both print and electronic subscriptions to key journals for both archival reasons and user convenience. In light of tightening budgets and rising book and journal costs, print journal subscriptions are often the first cut to be made when electronic options are also available. These cuts have a domino effect that begins with collection development, goes through acquisitions, and eventually reaches the digital librarian's doorstep through the processes described in the rest of this chapter.

An easy way for you to think about the scholarly communications process is as a workflow with five basic categories: formulation, registration, legitimization, dissemination, and archiving. For a long time, the major players and their participation in each category have been clear. The scholar formulates an idea and researches previous work published about the idea. The idea is registered through submission to a scholarly journal, and the peer review process and act of publication legitimize the resulting article. The article is then disseminated through a publisher whose job is to produce, sell, distribute, and publicize the work. Providing access to and archiving scholarly output have been critical functions of research libraries since their inception, and libraries already have well-established systems for storing, circulating, and preserving print copies of books and journals. While we already have this vast and reliable infrastructure for managing print resources, best practices are still taking shape for libraries' management of digital content. Based on how much has changed already and how much uncertainty there is about future changes, your job description as a digital librarian may look very different ten years from now as compared to today. You may be hired to manage an institutional repository and end up developing policies and procedures for data curation!

In libraries that offer journal-hosting platforms to their communities, digital librarians often act as managers for peer-reviewed journals and need to know about the traditional peer-review process and emerging alternatives. Peer review—academia's compass for quality control—is the legitimization step of the scholarly communications process. While peer review has traditionally been an anonymous process in which scholars evaluate each other's work for publication worthiness, some editorial boards are experimenting with new strategies that are arguably fairer and certainly more transparent. Open peer review is a model in which the reviewers' identities are made known to the author and, upon submission, a manuscript is posted online to facilitate an open, public discussion. Often this open discussion occurs only among the publication's pool of reviewers, but sometimes the manuscript is made openly available online, with public commenting enabled. Based on the open feedback the author receives, he or she is then invited to submit a revised version that is formally reviewed. If you manage a journal at your institution, you may want to discuss alternative review options such as these with the journal editor.

Another must-know, widely used method of legitimizing scholarly publications is called the "impact factor." Developed by the Institute for Scientific Information, the impact factor is a formula that measures academic value based on how many times an article has been cited by other academic articles. The quality of both journals and authors is often assessed on the basis of their impact factors, so in order to observe and perhaps increase the reach and prestige of your managed journal or your institution's faculty, you'll want to become familiar with the impact factor and the emphasis that is currently placed on it. Be aware, though, that the impact factor is not the be-all, end-all of scholarly evaluation. The impact factor's reliability and effectiveness is very discipline-dependent, and its measurement is sometimes controversial because journals or authors might be tempted to self-cite in order to artificially increase their impact factor. Other metrics that scholars use to determine the impact of their research include download counts, co-citations, and peak and decay patterns. If you are not already familiar with it, spend some time with Thomson Reuter's *Web of Science,* a subscription database that includes the *Social Science Citation Index*, the *Science Citation Index*, and the *Arts and Humanities Citation Index. Web of Science* is a good product to use to determine impact factors and for bibliometric research in general. The availability and accuracy of these metrics will increase as digital repositories and databases become more interoperable and are better able to exchange and use information.

The Traditional Publishing Paradox

You may notice something odd (or just plain wrong) about this process: an institution invests countless faculty hours in research, authorship, and review, and its library ends up buying the resulting product from publishers. Not only do publishers profit financially, in many cases they also retain most if not all of the author's copyrights to an article. Furthermore, the unrelenting rate at which commercial and society journal subscription costs are rising has taken its toll on static or declining library collection budgets. Publisher mergers and acquisitions perpetuate the problem by creating a handful of massive conglomerates that have significant control over the market and little incentive to lower their subscription costs. Academic libraries have been facing this "serials crisis" since the late 1980s—long before digital librarianship was an established field—when the problem was forecast to become so unwieldy that the membership of the Association of Research Libraries (ARL) voted to create and fund what is now known as its Office of Scholarly Communication (OSC) (www.arl.org/sc/).

A New Model for Scholarly Publishing

The obvious disadvantages of this model have driven libraries into the business of transforming scholarly communications, and academic libraries are assuming a more prominent role in scholarly publishing. More and more, librarians are being called upon to assist in the digital preservation of faculty output, manage the hosting of scholarly publications, and advise faculty on intellectual property issues. Because digital librarians often work closely with faculty and other researchers, they need to have a solid understanding of why scholars choose specific journals in which to publish their work. Scholars are motivated to publish in top-tier journals because, in part, doing so often results in high citation counts and impact factors, and these indicators are weighed heavily by universities in promotion and hiring decisions. Unfortunately, many of these top-tier journals are among the more expensive journals that your library might subscribe to, so your role may include promoting alternative access to scholarship from your faculty through institutional repositories, or alternative publishing models such as open access journals.

Even though as a digital librarian you may not work closely with your library's collection of physical and electronic resources, your work will still be affected by inevitable budgetary challenges to library collections and staffing. The good news is that you are in a unique position to aid your colleagues in and educate your constituents about controlling costs and copyrights. If part of your job responsibilities includes participating in scholarly communications activities, you will want to familiarize yourself with the offerings of the OSC, which collects, synthesizes, and distributes data about issues like publisher profits, journal costs, publisher mergers, electronic bundled package subscriptions, and scholars' evolving communication practices.

The availability of this information has inspired many librarians to advocate to university administrators and faculty constituents for action toward systemic changes. One strategy to consider for managing unsustainable costs, while still providing faculty and students with the resources they need, is to negotiate with publishers at both the institutional and consortial levels. Sometimes negotiations between libraries and publishers involve "big deal" packages in which libraries pay a single fee for multiyear access to multiple journal titles. Such deals can bring down costs for the most expensive journal titles, but the overall cost remains high. In addition, some of the titles that are licensed in these types of deals are not crucial to the library's users, and may be outside the library's collection development scope. You may need to work with your colleagues in acquisitions or purchasing departments on these types of issues.

THE OPEN ACCESS MOVEMENT

The advent of the Internet, which allows for wide, fast, and low-cost dissemination of information, has created significant changes in the scholarly communications landscape. Electronic discussion lists, blogs, and social networking sites are a few of the many new platforms available for scholars to meet and share information, and disciplinary boundaries are now often more significant than institutional and geographical boundaries. The Internet has done many things for us, but it has not solved many of the complications associated with the traditional scholarly communications system. Librarians continue to deal with legal restrictions imposed upon users by publishers, the inability to afford access to the research their own institution's faculty members produce, and decreases in publication and distribution costs that are not passed on to subscribers. By successfully navigating these changes, digital librarians can ensure that libraries stay relevant to scholars' needs.

The Open Access (OA) Movement was created to help alleviate these issues. It focuses on educating consumers of scholarly information about the potential use of the Internet for wider and cheaper dissemination of this information. The Berlin Open Access Declaration states that authors of open access documents grant users a "free, irrevocable, worldwide right of access to, and a license to copy, use, distribute, transmit and display the work publicly and to make and distribute derivative works, in any digital medium for any responsible purpose, subject to proper attribution of authorship . . . as well as the right to make small numbers of printed copies for their personal use" (Max Planck Society, 2003). In order to be open access, this work must be made available in an online platform, such as a repository or journal maintained by an established organization. Copyright holders maintain their copyright when distributing a work through an open access repository, and open access is compatible with peer review. Some studies have shown that open access articles are cited more often than closed access articles, although this seems to be discipline-dependent (Wagner, 2010). Other benefits of open access include increased findability through common search engines such as Google and Google Scholar.

Public funding agencies are beginning to see the benefits of open access for making taxpayer-funded research available to the public. Since 2007, the U.S. National Institutes of Health has mandated that all grantees make published articles available through PubMed Central, an online open access repository, within a year of publication. Additionally, many academic institutions, including the Harvard Faculty of Arts and Sciences and all departments on the MIT campus, are beginning to mandate that faculty publications be made available through open access journals or a disciplinary or institutional repository if the originating journal is not open access.

There are two primary models for delivery of open access articles: institutional and disciplinary repositories ("Green OA"), and open access journals ("Gold OA").

Gold OA

Open access journals, or "Gold OA," are journals that make their content freely available online without a subscription. Since content is never actually free to produce, open access journals have found different funding models to support their publication activities, including charging authors a fee for publication. Many of these journals are supported through an academic institution or scholarly society, and academic libraries often host these platforms. Other journals charge authors a fee to publish a manuscript in their journal, although statistics indicate that fewer than 30 percent of open access journals charge an author fee (Shieber, 2009). Open access journals are similar to traditional scholarly journals in that submitted articles may undergo peer review and may be subject to impact factors. The weight of peer review and impact factors gives prestige to an open access journal in the same way as a traditional journal.

As a digital librarian, you may be involved with starting or maintaining open access journals hosted by your library. There are several platforms designed for hosting journals, including an open-source software product from the Public Knowledge Project called Open Journal Systems (http://pkp.sfu.ca/?q=ojs). These types of platforms include workflows for article submission, peer review, and public display of accepted articles, volumes, and issues, and may even include e-commerce systems for managing subscription journals. You may be responsible for managing the technology, recruiting journals, overseeing workflows including peer review, and administering the entire system.

An important resource for learning more about scholarly publishing in libraries is the Scholarly Publishing and Academic Resources Coalition (SPARC) (www.arl.org/sparc/), which was created by the ARL to provide support to not-for-profit publishers (including libraries) so that they might better compete with commercial publishers. By late 2007, 64 percent of ARL member libraries were already publishing or were planning to publish journals, conference proceedings, or monographs (Hahn, 2008). Journal titles hosted by libraries can be very different from one another. Some titles are newly created, while others are established and have been migrated to the library's publishing system. Some titles are open access, while others are not. The vast majority of these titles are electronic, and their management likely requires a digital publishing system, data transformations, content migration or reformatting, online dissemination, and digital preservation strategies. Given these needs, with a basic knowledge of electronic publishing and metadata management you will be well positioned to play a key role in support of a library's publishing initiatives.

Green OA

Institutional and disciplinary repositories, or "Green OA," are online repositories that host digital content created by members of the supporting community, such as a university. In the Green OA model, a scholar publishes an article in a traditional peer-reviewed journal, but retains or negotiates for rights to deposit a version of the work in an institutional or disciplinary repository. In addition to scholarly materials, institutional repositories (or IRs) often host electronic theses and dissertations, presentations, working papers, technical reports, data sets, and other unpublished or otherwise easily lost "gray literature" from the university. Disciplinary repositories are similar to institutional repositories, but have a disciplinary focus. One of the most successful disciplinary repositories is arXiv (http://arxiv.org/), a repository for preprints in physics, mathematics, computer science, quantitative biology, quantitative finance, and statistics. E-LIS (http://eprints.rclis.org/) is a disciplinary repository for library and information science articles.

Institutional repositories are often managed by digital librarians who oversee maintenance, collection development, and outreach activities related to the library's digital initiatives. One of the biggest criticisms of institutional repositories has been the lack of faculty engagement. When a scholar submits a final draft for publication, he or she normally moves on to another project and is reluctant to devote more time to that article. Managing copyright and embargo periods and uploading the article to the IR—especially if there is no perceived benefit from utilizing the IR—may not be what that scholar feels to be the best use of his or her time. If this scenario sounds familiar to you, don't fret—you have several options! You can lessen the burden on faculty by managing all uploads in the library, or integrating the IR into preexisting faculty workflows, such as the promotion and tenure process or database-driven reports of faculty publications. You can also show a contributor the impact of his or her work by providing detailed usage statistics (how many times an article has been downloaded from the IR in a given time period). Your IR platform may allow you to display the most-downloaded articles on the home page; enabling this option may encourage competition among contributors. Previously we mentioned that some institutions have enacted institution-wide mandates requiring submission of all articles to the IR. Without proper resources and support, though, these types of mandates can be hard to enforce.

Advocating for IRs

In order to populate repositories without resorting to a deposit mandate, academic libraries have developed outreach programming and materials that aim to educate faculty and other authors about the changes needed in scholarly communications. Not all digital librarians have oversight of their institution's IR, but if you do, you will probably find yourself speaking to faculty on cross-disciplinary, departmental, and individual levels about the benefits of depositing their work in the IR. At the very least, your talking points should probably include quick dissemination of research, increased visibility through search engines and full-text indexing, and the convenience and security of having all publications stored in a single location. You will certainly want to inform the faculty of steps they can take to retain certain copyrights of their work, such as use of an author's addendum (discussed later in the chapter) and publishing in open access journals. You may also find yourself working with departmental liaison librarians who have not only disciplinary expertise but also knowledge of the needs and behaviors of certain faculty members. While liaisons' established relationships with faculty can be invaluable, you may need to provide your colleagues with training on scholarly communications issues in order to best prepare them for working with faculty.

The impact of open access on scholarly communications is yet to be determined. Models of promotion and tenure in the academy often rely on the traditional model of publishing, and may discount open access publications, which are often seen as having lower impact factors. Additionally, the slow uptake of faculty deposits into institutional or disciplinary repositories demonstrates that repositories may not have as significant an impact on scholarly publishing as originally hoped for. However, change in the world of academia takes time. Digital librarians can help usher in this change by promoting the benefits of open access publishing to faculty, and by being responsible stewards of content hosted in institutional repositories. Building awareness of open access across our campuses is another way in which we can actively participate in the new scholarly communications model. Because institutions do not yet agree on the value of digital scholarship for academic advancement, digital librarians should work with scholars in the context of their disciplinary and institutional expectations for scholarly output. The three broad disciplines that you are most likely to work with—sciences, social sciences, and humanities—have embraced emerging publishing models at different speeds and with different strategies. You will need to be sensitive to these differences and work with faculty accordingly.

MANAGING, CURATING, AND SHARING DATA

Data curation is a growing area of interest in the library community. As a digital librarian, you may be asked to play a role in your library's data curation activities, so it's important to have an understanding of current data practices (for the purposes of this chapter we consider *data curation* to be defined by the preservation of scholarly data, which is a narrower definition than that given for *digital curation* in chapter 12). Enhancements to online sharing and authoring tools are allowing scholars to manipulate data and collaborate on research at great distances, phenomena that are contributing to the production of large amounts of data. Although scientific data and numerical data sets are the most commonly discussed types of data, all disciplines produce data in some form. Data for a humanities scholar may be in the form of a document text, the physical document itself, or penciled annotations by an author or scholar. Data generated in the artistic fields might consist of images, videos, or audio recordings. A data set is any combination of these types of data, and often supports research findings published in a peer-reviewed journal.

The state of most data sets is largely dependent on the funding of the research project from which they result. While high-profile scientific research, or "big science," has infrastructure and funding behind it, the "small science" data sets created by individual researchers may have little or short-term funding, and the infrastructure may consist of an individual's laptop, or, in the best-case scenario, a department server. When research findings from this type of data are published, other researchers may not have immediate access to the original data set(s) unless they request the data from the author. The author may or may not still have access to the original data sets, especially if several years have elapsed since the data were collected or created. This lack of data organization can make research difficult and inefficient to replicate, thereby limiting the advancement of knowledge. Some data sets may eventually disappear as researchers move on to other topics, or computer hardware fails.

Creating a Data Management Plan

In an effort to round up scientific data, in January 2011 the National Science Foundation (NSF) began to require that all grant proposals submitted to the NSF be accompanied by a data management plan. Such plans generally include information about the types of data collected, standards to be used for the data, policies for access and sharing, policies for provisions of reuse, and plans for archiving this data. Researchers working on grants may call upon you to help write data management plans, and your involvement will give you the opportunity to discuss the benefits of storing their data with the library and possibly making it openly available. If you are asked to take on this role, you should be knowledgeable enough to advise scholars on data storage and sharing options both on and off campus, from institutional and disciplinary repositories to tools like the Open Data Commons, a Creative Commons-like licensing service for data (http://opendatacommons.org/). Some good resources to get you started are listed at the end of the chapter. The website for the Digital Curation Centre (www.dcc.ac.uk/) also has a wealth of resources to help new digital librarians. By actively participating in the research process through development of data management plans, you can learn how data is being collected and used and advise researchers on best practices and national standards.

Your role as a digital librarian may include ensuring that the library is properly curating data, as well as promoting the library's trustworthiness to faculty. You might be involved in making decisions about data curation, including storage, sustainability, and technical support. For example, you will want to weigh the pros and cons of storing the data locally, in an institutional repository or alternate local storage, or remotely, using cloud-based storage options such as DuraCloud (www.duraspace.org/duracloud.php). You may be involved in decision-making steps such as creating a budget, determining technical specifications, and participating in outreach activities. Other technical support decisions you might be required to make include how to best handle aspects like backups, migration, remote access, and other data security issues. By managing the data life cycle at every stage, digital

According to the Digital Curation Centre, the data curation life cycle involves eleven steps: conceptualization, creation, access and use, appraisal and selection, disposal, ingestion, preservation action, reappraisal, storage, access and reuse, and transformation. For more information about the DCC model, see chapter 12.

librarians can help create, preserve, store, and share data, ultimately ensuring that it can be used for further research.

Data Sharing and Linking

In the sciences, it is becoming standard for authors to share data sets either alone or along with a corresponding article, and some journals—notably any title published by the Nature Publishing Group with the word *nature* in the title—require authors to share such data with readers. The social sciences are becoming more data-intensive as scholars mine databases for economic and demographic information. The humanities are focusing on making cultural records more available through digitization and advanced computational models. Your understanding of and respect for these differences will help the library to provide better services geared toward individual disciplines. By actively participating in emerging data curation models, you can help ensure that your library remains relevant in these new types of scholarly curation activities.

One way that libraries help with the sharing of research is through data linking, and these practices are of ever-increasing importance in making scholarly publications locatable and citable online. A data-linking tool that has been largely adopted by commercial publishers is the Digital Object Identifier (DOI), a unique numeric string that is assigned to an article or any other digital object. Similar to an ISBN that uniquely identifies a book, a DOI provides a digital object with an interoperable, persistent link across many digital networks, which increases the article's findability. If your library hosts a journal and does not use DOIs, you may want to consider contracting with a DOI registration agency (such as CrossRef) to assign them to published articles. Another method of data linking that might be more familiar to you is the OpenURL Framework Standard, which links a service point (for example, a database subscribed to by a library) to the most appropriate online resource for a particular user (an easily accessible copy of an article listed in the database). Many link resolver services, such as SFX from Ex Libris, appear in integrated library systems and use OpenURL as their standard.

Because libraries have always been the place to turn to for archiving and accessing information, scientists are beginning to trust libraries as an ally in the effort to archive data sets. By actively curating data, we are becoming more knowledgeable in the area of data management and can help future researchers develop their data plans, which are becoming increasingly more important for grant-funded research opportunities. Although this requires digital librarians to occupy a new position in the scholarly communications cycle, our background and skills make us a good fit for this process.

COPYRIGHT, LICENSING, AND AUTHOR RIGHTS

In the digital environment, traditional copyright laws have been reexamined for relevancy and currency. You should try to stay up-to-date on those laws that relate to the distribution of electronic content. In the traditional scholarly publishing model, the author hands over copyright of his or her work to the publisher, losing all rights of distribution, copying, derivative creation, and archiving. In reality, the publisher only needs the right to distribute the work and receive financial compensation, attribution as the journal of first publication, and the right to migrate the work to future formats (SPARC, 2006). Digital librarians are often called upon to engage in conversations with faculty about these copyright issues (also known as author rights), encouraging faculty to carefully read copyright transfer agreements, and possibly negotiate them, before signing.

Under current United States copyright law, as soon as an original work is created it is automatically granted copyright. Prior to 1978, copyright was only granted after authors passed through a series of rules and regulations for registration of the work, but today registration is voluntary. The copyright protection for every work created today is the life of the author plus seventy years.

Copyright Law

Digital librarians are often responsible for scanning and electronic distribution activities within a library, and should have a good grasp of copyright law in order to understand which scholarly items can be distributed electronically, circulated as a physical item, or reproduced by any means. Items that are in the public domain (published before 1923 or by the U.S. government) may be distributed online without any special permission, but digital librarians should research items that may be under copyright before determining if they can be distributed electronically. Recommended resources for copyright research are listed at the end of this chapter. Unless copyright has been transferred to the library, a library that digitizes an item does not own the rights to the digital derivative unless there is evidence that some amount of creative or "transformative" work has been applied to the digitized item. The copyright of the digitized item still belongs to the original copyright owner, or is still in the public domain if the original item's copyright has expired (this can generally be assumed to be true of items with a copyright date of 1923 or earlier), or if the item is published by the United States government. The "fair use" provision of U.S. copyright law allows for limited use of works that are still under copyright, but does not grant permission to freely distribute items online.

Other areas of copyright law relevant for digital librarians include Section 108 of the U.S. Copyright Act (which allows for limited reproduction by libraries and archives), the TEACH Act, and the Digital Millennium Copyright Act (DMCA). Section 108 allows libraries and archives to make copies of items for purposes such as preservation. The TEACH Act allows certain copyrighted works to be used in distance education, and the DMCA prohibits circumvention of technologies controlling access to copyrighted works, among other provisions. Others in the library may seek you out for expertise regarding copyright as it applies to digital files, and a general understanding of these areas of the copyright law will give you a starting place for further research about specific items and circumstances.

According to current intellectual property law and standard institutional contracts, when a faculty member at an academic institution writes a paper, he or she is automatically granted copyright. When a paper is written by multiple authors, the copyright is jointly owned by all authors. However, when a staff member without faculty status at the same academic institution writes a paper, the work is considered "work for hire," and copyright belongs to the institution. Copyright belongs to these owners until it is signed away, and in the academic publishing environment, it is standard for the copyright to be signed over to the publisher upon acceptance of the article. Digital librarians are often called on to upload works to online platforms, and you will need to ensure that the copyright owner of a work has given permission for the work to be distributed online. Copyright holders aren't always clearly indicated on a work, and the better understanding you have of copyright law, the easier it will be for you to know who to contact for permission. Sometimes, it is impossible to determine who the copyright holder is or how to contact them, and in such cases the work is referred to as an "orphan work." Orphan works are still under copyright, and, because of this, libraries do not have automatic permission to distribute them—however, in many cases librarians choose to put such works online along with a "takedown notice" that provides for their removal if the copyright holder should come forward.

Legislation to remove strict enforcement of copyright on orphan works has been brought before Congress several times in the past decade, but no agreements have been made.

Publishers' Policies

Even if a publisher owns copyright for an article, it may be possible for the author to deposit the work in a repository, depending on the terms of the copyright transfer agreement. If you manage an institutional repository, you will need a thorough understanding of publishers' policies to know whether or not an item may be deposited into the IR. Publishers often have different policies regarding the different phases of a manuscript. The first version of a manuscript submitted to a journal is generally referred to as a *preprint*, while the final version of a manuscript after peer review is called a *postprint*. Preprints and postprints are collectively called *eprints* in the IR environment. Copyright of the preprint belongs to the author, and copyright of the postprint is generally handed over to the journal in the copyright transfer agreement. The journal's final version of the article with formatting, headers, and footers is called the *publisher's PDF* or *publisher's version*. The copyright of this version belongs to the publisher, but the author can often negotiate this. Publishers have different policies regarding uses of articles for which they own the copyright. Some publishers allow an author to deposit a work into an institutional repository immediately after publication. Other publishers only allow deposit after a specified embargo period, or never. Authors can check many journals' and publishers' policies regarding IR deposit at the Sherpa Romeo website (www.sherpa.ac.uk/romeo/). As an IR administrator, you may on occasion need to reject a faculty member's article due to lack of publisher permission. However, this situation can provide an opportunity for further discussion with them about author rights or open access to ensure that future submissions are accepted into the IR.

Licensing Alternatives

Open access advocates and most librarians promote the negotiation of copyright agreements to include deposit into an institutional repository instead of signing over all rights initially. SPARC provides an author addendum on their website (www.arl.org/sparc/author/) that authors can use to retain their copyright to an article. Many other scholarly societies and institutions, including the University of Michigan and the Committee on Institutional Cooperation, also provide author addenda to help faculty protect their intellectual property rights. Links to these addenda can be found in the recommended resources list at the end of the chapter.

Creative Commons licensing is another popular licensing alternative that you can recommend to authors. The Creative Commons organization (http://creativecommons.org/) promotes the sharing of work in an online environment to maximize innovation and creativity. A Creative Commons license allows an author to keep the copyright to their work and dictate how others may use the work. There are six Creative Commons licenses. The most restrictive license allows others to download and share a copyrighted work as long as the original author is properly credited, while the least restrictive license allows others to distribute, remix, tweak, and build upon the work, even in a commercial setting, as long as the original author receives attribution.

You will need at least a basic awareness of how copyright law relates to digitization projects in order to promote open access to faculty, scholars, and other librarians. Many times digital librarians are in the best position to help authors learn about their intellectual property rights and encourage alternatives to traditional copyright and licensing. As the power of wider information distribution becomes better understood and integrated into current copyright law, it is hoped that more scholars will become interested in openly sharing their research online and in open formats.

FINAL THOUGHTS

In order to stay relevant to the scholarly community, librarians must continue to be active participants in emerging communications cycles while having a good grasp of more traditional models. A thorough understanding of all aspects of the process, including the roles of libraries in general and digital librarians specifically, will help you best serve colleagues and patrons at your institution. Through consultations on open access publishing, data curation, and rights management you can help scholars understand new models of scholarly communications and guide them through the ever-changing academic environment. Even if you don't work at an academic library, the issues touched on in this chapter will inevitably affect your job to some degree, whether it be negotiating database license agreements or advising patrons on their rights to reproduce digital content. Digital librarians are fortunate to be at the forefront of innovative library services; every day we get to envision new possibilities for actively engaging with content creators, providers, and users. Participating in the revolution in scholarly publishing can prove to be a meaningful and exciting aspect of this work.

REFERENCES

Hahn, Karla L. 2008. "Research Library Publishing Services: New Options for University Publishing and New Roles for Libraries." *ARL: A Bimonthly Report*, no. 258. www.arl.org/bm~doc/arl-br-258-res-lib-pub.pdf.

Max Planck Society. 2003. "Berlin Declaration on Open Access to Knowledge in the Sciences and Humanities." www.zim.mpg.de/openaccess-berlin/berlin_declaration.pdf.

Scholarly Publishing and Academic Resources Coalition (SPARC). 2006. "Author Rights: Using the SPARC Author Addendum to Secure Your Rights as the Author of a Journal Article." www.arl.org/sparc/author/addendum.shtml.

Shieber, Stuart. 2009. "What Percentage of Open-Access Journals Charge Publication Fees?" *The Occasional Pamphlet on Scholarly Communication* (blog). May 29. http://blogs.law.harvard.edu/pamphlet/2009/05/29/what-percentage-of-open-access-journals-charge-publication-fees/.

Wagner, A. Ben. 2010. "Open Access Citation Advantage: An Annotated Bibliography." *Issues in Science and Technology Librarianship*, no. 60. www.istl.org/10winter/article2.html.

RECOMMENDED RESOURCES

Borgman, Christine L. 2007. *Scholarship in the Digital Age: Information, Infrastructure, and the Internet*. Cambridge, MA: MIT Press.

Crews, Kenneth D. 2006. *Copyright Law for Librarians and Educators: Creative Strategies and Practical Solutions*. 2nd ed. Chicago: American Library Association.

Directory of Open Access Journals (DOAJ): www.doaj.org/.

International DOI Foundation. 2011. "The DOI System." www.doi.org/.

Lynch, Clifford A. 2003. "Institutional Repositories: Essential Infrastructure for Scholarship in the Digital Age." *ARL: A Bimonthly Report*, no. 226. www.arl.org/resources/pubs/br/br226/br226ir.shtml.

Ogburn, Joyce L. 2010. "The Imperative for Data Curation." *Portal: Libraries and the Academy* 10, no. 2: 241–46.

Salo, Dorothea. 2008. "The Innkeeper at the Roach Motel." *Library Trends* 57, no. 2: 98–123.

Society for Scholarly Publishing. 2011. *The Scholarly Kitchen: What's Hot and Cooking in Scholarly Publications* (blog). http://scholarlykitchen.sspnet.org/.

Suber, Peter. 2004. "Open Access Overview." www.earlham.edu/~peters/fos/overview.htm.

Swan, Alma. 2006. "Overview of Scholarly Communication." In *Open Access: Key Strategic, Technical and Economic Aspects*, edited by Neil Jacobs, 5–11. Oxford: Chandos.

Van den Eynden, Veerle, Louise Corti, Matthew Wollard, Libby Bishop, and Laurence Horton. 2011. *Managing and Sharing Data: Best Practices for Researchers*. 3rd ed. Essex: UK Data Archive. www.data-archive.ac.uk/media/2894/managingsharing.pdf.

Van Orsdel, Lee C. 2007. "The State of Scholarly Communications." *Serials Librarian* 52, no. 1-2: 191–209.

Chapter Eleven

Collaborating on Digital Projects

Andrew Weiss

Despite the breakneck speed of change in the digital economy, which has thrown numerous worthy technologies and companies onto the "dustbin of history," one of the most important skills needed by new librarians in the digital age has *not* changed: the ability to work in collaboration with others. Most digital projects are done in teams, or even teams of teams, and require flexible, overarching organizations along with self-directed components in order to succeed. Despite the emphasis on teamwork and team-building exercises in library school classes, short of actual workplace experience it can be difficult to effectively simulate collaboration within the digital projects setting.

This chapter will highlight some of the methods that new digital librarians might employ to improve collaboration in their digital projects. It will address collaborative techniques that arise during the initial development of digitization projects and include a discussion of the issues related to working with certain individuals, such as information technology (IT) specialists, content providers, and consultants. Finally, a case study illustrating the types of digitization projects done by the author will help to round out the discussion on digital project collaboration.

TYPES OF ORGANIZATIONAL COLLABORATIONS

For the sake of this discussion, collaboration has been divided into three types. In the first type, there is intra-organizational collaboration, which focuses on subgroups operating within the library. These groups might include formal committees and subcommittees, as well as ad hoc informal gatherings among library staff. The second type of collaboration involves interdepartmental collaboration. In this scenario a librarian may work with various departments in a university, or with various organizations related to the library, as in the case of a public library collaborating with the Friends of the Library or similar auxiliary group. Finally, the third type of collaboration pertains to the development of partnerships with institutions that exist externally to the main organization. This type includes examples such as an academic library working with a local museum, or a public library working with a local historical society.

Collaborating within Organizations

Anyone who has worked with digital collections knows that they can often take longer than planned. This happens for a number of reasons, but the main one is that numerous variables will arise during a project's life cycle. Some of these variables, such as a physical disaster or the sudden loss of funding or personnel, are unforeseen, but many obstacles can be anticipated with a little teamwork, collaboration, and well-designed workflows. The types of problems that often arise with digital collections include image processing delays (including camera/scanner/computer equipment breakdowns, image manipulation or database software glitches, etc.), copyright clearance obstacles (including the lack of deeds of gift, unclear language in documentation, inability to copy something digitally, etc.), metadata development delays and backlogs (including disorganized workflows, cataloging system breakdowns, "dirty" databases resulting from inconsistent application of metadata, etc.), IT and infrastructure malfunctions (including hosted and non-hosted system architecture updates), project disorganization (including lack of project documentation, workflows, or timelines), and institutional disarray (including contradictory or mixed messages). However, in a healthy organization, that is, one that values the mechanisms needed to foster collaboration and avoid bureaucratic dysfunction, these obstacles need not overwhelm a project and can indeed be overcome.

Seeking Out Natural Alignments

One of the best ways to put an emphasis on collaboration and avoid the pitfalls of the overly bureaucratic office environment is to begin looking at where departments in a library contain overlapping duties and natural alignments. As a new digital librarian, you should make it a priority to seek out similar skill sets and interests that will allow for up-front ad hoc group creation that may later crystallize into an official initiative work group. As each aspect of the digitization process is specialized, becoming an expert in all of them is often not feasible, especially in the beginning.

At an academic library where the staff is quite small in proportion to the number of students it serves, many staff members may have multiple overlapping duties with others in areas such as reference, interlibrary loan, bibliographic instruction, archival processing, and ILS database development and management. Some of these natural alignments among skill sets could be corralled into digitization projects as well. To complete digital projects with a small staff and limited pool of student labor, it may be necessary to seek out colleagues who have similar areas of expertise. If you work with metadata librarians or catalogers, for example, they will likely be well versed in schema such as Dublin Core and MARC. Your organization's archivist may have knowledge of digitization techniques for two-dimensional objects such as photographs, letters, and other small-scale items that are of value in the institution's archives. If you work at an academic library, you might find that the serials librarian has experience with copyright laws and regulations, especially as these librarians often work with vendors to secure access to and licensing of content. Working with the expertise of your colleagues in such a scenario may change your role from that of digitizer to "digitization coach," where you might set down rules and procedures but then consult with others as they perform some of the actual digitization tasks. Nothing is more important in a digital project than the coordination of multiple specialized skills. Therefore, it becomes necessary when you do not possess a skill, and do not have the time to learn it, that you find ways to keep the project moving along. By providing that "coaching" or coordinating role, you can ensure that your digital projects will progress.

Tools for Fostering Intra-Organizational Collaboration

In addition to the creation of work groups, there are various tools for working with each member of the group. One example is to create a checklist that will help all group members evaluate and assess the value of a collection. Table 11.1 shows an excerpt from such a checklist that was developed at Fort Hays State University (FLDCI, 2011). The checklist was filled out by members of the group prior to selecting a collection for digitization. It allows for each member to provide an analysis of a collection from within their areas of expertise and to assign each part of the project a number that will help prioritize it in relation to other potential

TABLE 11.1
Sample FLDCI collection development checklist

COLLECTION NAME:			
Criteria	**Assessment Questions**	**#**	**Notes**
1. Mission			
	Do materials or collection conform to mission and vision of FLDCI?		
	Are materials related to culture/history of western Kansas area?		
	Are materials of significant and unique cultural/historical value to U.S.?		
	Are materials of significant and unique cultural/historical value internationally?		
	Assessment score and recommendations:		
2. Restrictions			
	Is full permission granted to digitize materials?		
	If "No," state restrictions stipulated:		
	Is full permission granted to create multiple versions?		
	If "No," state restrictions stipulated:		
	Is full permission granted to disseminate online?		
	If "No," state restrictions stipulated:		

projects. The Forsyth Library Digital Collections Initiative offers a "digitization toolshed" with other materials useful for collaborative project development at www.fhsu.edu/library/digital/Tools/.

Providing each member a voice in the assessment/analysis part of the digitization process helps to foster a sense of participation and establish personal investment in the project. Additionally, each person's assessment is influenced by his or her respective area of expertise. The archivist, for example, will approach the assessment from the point of view of the physical collection and can answer many questions regarding the condition of the materials. The serials librarian, with her knowledge of copyright and the obstacles it can create, would speak to the legality of digitizing the collection. Finally, the metadata or cataloging expert can provide a good analysis of whether the existing collection metadata is sufficient for the searching needs of patrons, and decide if further detail and granularity are needed.

Collaborating across Organizations

This section will address the particular needs and challenges involved when collaborating with departments outside of the library, but still within the campus or larger organizational community. These challenges include working with overarching units such as a graduate school, which will have ties with multiple colleges and departments, as well as working with smaller units such as individual departments and sub-disciplines within them.

Working with Overarching Units

As a digital librarian, you'll likely be asked to work in a unit that overlaps with other areas. Though both challenging and interesting, the project may be simultaneously helped and hindered by this intersecting of departments and disciplines. In academic libraries, a prime interdepartmental digitization project, and one that truly crosses multiple departments and disciplines, is the creation and management of electronic theses and dissertations (ETDs). Often such projects are carried out in tandem with a campus graduate school, further widening the number of stakeholders and personnel involved.

The main challenge for an interdepartmental project, especially in the case of academia, is that each department adheres to and is influenced by varying normative values that define the protocols of reward and punishment for the members of that group. An English department, for example, with its emphasis on the monograph and printed quarterly journals, will differ from the normative values of a physics department, which places more emphasis on up-to-date data sharing. For the latter, the mandates of open access publishing from governing bodies such as the National Institutes of Health and the National Science Foundation have a profound impact. Conversely, the humanities deal with subjects that are not as greatly affected by the immediate sharing of data. Indeed, incentives for the dissemination and digitization of these works will be very different. Since providing new interpretations of shared, and often old, texts is an imperative for some groups in the humanities, participation in digitization efforts may be hindered by a particular discipline's scholarship customs.

Differing approaches to scholarship and their incentives, which make up the crux of a department's normative values, will have a distinct impact on your work as a digital librarian. Essentially, you will need to analyze and clearly gauge the impact that a digital project will have on the local values that a particular subgroup holds as important. Furthermore, if an overarching unit such as a college or graduate studies department is involved in the project, more complexity will arise.

Mandated policies, such as required participation in an institutional repository or an open access publishing policy, will surely make working with various departments easier. Such policies, which have been implemented at numerous institutions, can have a streamlining effect on project development. However, such mandates generally exist outside the scope of an individual librarian's control, though one can certainly advocate for them. These mandates can also have a negative impact by appearing heavy-handed to scholars and researchers, and may alienate certain audiences, further disinclining content providers and creators from participating in a digital project.

Working with Smaller Units

Although it might appear easier on paper, working with smaller units such as an individual academic department, a museum, or a local historical society can be challenging in its own right. One major concern could be a lack of uniform policies and expectations. A business school, for example, will have different priorities and needs for digitization than an art department. Intellectual and creative output from departments will differ and be subject to different digitization restrictions. Fair use copyright guidelines tend to be less permissive for creative works, for example, and thus weigh more heavily in favor of the creator than they do in the case of factual works. An art department interested in displaying a digital collection of its artwork holdings on campus may run into significant copyright issues that the business department, interested in displaying a self-published journal, will likely not have. The varying values and practices of departments will impact the approach one takes to digitizing a collection. As a new digital librarian, if you work in an academic setting you will need to be aware of the differences among the sub-communities that exist across the college campus; furthermore, if you work in a public setting, you will need to parse the needs of specific user groups in a public or special library.

Another concern when working with different subcultures is the risk of becoming overly specific in any one subject, to the detriment of usage. What interests users in a small sub-community may not interest those in the at-large community. You will need to find a way to balance the specific needs of smaller, and possibly more active and passionate, communities with the more generalized needs of larger communities, despite their less frequent and less vocal participation. A thesis collection at a university will meet the needs of multiple communities and usage statistics will show an across-the-board participation. A larger built-in audience will justify the time it takes to digitize such a large collection of manuscripts. Some relatively small projects, such as a yearbook collection, which usually has no more than a hundred volumes, provide enough varied users among its target group that it would justify the project. However, many small projects such as letters or postcards, or even historical family photos, may not have enough of a built-in audience to justify the effort and cost to digitize. Cost-benefit analyses that weigh potential participation with the project's impact on the general audience are essential to providing a service that meets most users' needs.

Collaborating with External Institutions

Many digitization projects and initiatives will include partners that exist outside of your organization. While this often yields excellent results, there are some pitfalls inherent to this type of collaboration. This section will examine some of the issues that arise when working with an external organization. In particular, three areas will be of interest to new digital librarians: (1) keeping communication lines open and constant; (2) clearly assigning duties from the project's outset; and (3) building flexibility into the partnership to allow for changes in the project.

Open Lines of Communication

One of the main reasons that collaborations fail stems from a lack of clear and consistent communication. It will often be your responsibility as a digital librarian to ensure that lines of communication remain open and clear. Periodic updates and communication of needs and expectations will have to occur at different points during the life cycle of the project. This will include telephone and e-mail communications as well as sending representatives from each organization to meet face-to-face. It is recommended that you schedule regular times to discuss the project and adhere to these times as strictly as possible. Project participants sometimes procrastinate or delay communication with their partners, assuming that discussions are necessary only when a problem arises. However, the more proactive approach of scheduling communication regularly will allow you to head off any potential problems, rather than waiting to react to them.

Clearly Assigned Duties

If you are collaborating with an organization that is providing you with materials to digitize, it will be important to designate early on some of the following: (1) who will choose the materials; (2) who will decide the scope of the collection (i.e., total number of items); (3) who will provide metadata and in what way (i.e., in Excel spreadsheets, databases, or some other format); (4) who will ensure the delivery and safety of materials between institutions; and (5) who will curate or store the archival and surrogate versions of digital objects. Without clear answers to these questions, numerous project goals could fall through the cracks as one side assumes the other will take care of these things. This can happen during all phases of the project, so it is imperative to continually assess and reassess the responsibilities of participating parties. Assigning these duties outright and checking on their progress will ensure that duties do not fall through the cracks.

Built-in Partnership Flexibility

Some problems with external partnerships also arise from the inability of participating organizations to anticipate new variables and alter original project goals accordingly. It will be important for you to address the possibility of changing a project's variables. Some organizations may see deviation from the original plan as a failure or as an admission of incompetence or weakness. This is far from the truth. Allowing changes to your original plan, especially related to benchmarks and timelines, will help you to ensure overall project success. Though missing deadlines can be stressful, having a clear contingency plan for this will serve you well. Assessing what has gone well and what has gone wrong during the project will help ensure that the remainder of the project can be finished.

When partner organizations are unable to allow for changes in project roles or needs (especially when personnel and funding change), projects begin to unravel. It is imperative to allow for flexibility and change in each side's roles. It is recommended that you utilize digital collection preservation and risk assessment tools such as the Digital Repository Audit Method Based on Risk Assessment, or DRAMBORA (www.repositoryaudit.eu/), or the Trustworthy Repositories Audit & Certification: Criteria and Checklist, or TRAC (DCC, 2010) to help you create contingency plans for when projects change in "midstream." These tools are easy to follow and provide clear methods to audit your digital collections using various criteria, including organizational and financial stability, digital object management policies, and technical infrastructure and security. Though meant for large repositories, they can be adapted for the needs of smaller digital collections and projects.

COLLABORATING WITH SPECIFIC PEOPLE

Much of this chapter has focused on the types of collaborative efforts you will likely face when working within an institutional framework. However, only passing mention has been made of the specific types of people you will work with as a digital librarian. This section will focus on those individuals, rather than institutions, with whom you will likely partner, including IT professionals, content providers and collection stewards, and consultants and outside experts. The success of all collaborative efforts, whether they are intra-organizational, inter-organizational, or external partnerships, will depend on understanding and working with these groups of people.

IT Professionals

Although not an entirely separate breed from librarians, IT staff working on digital projects might differ with respect to some of their professional values. While librarians in general adopt the philosophy that information access is of the utmost importance (this is one of the main tenets of the American Library Association), those with a background in the IT industry may not necessarily share this view. In particular, IT professionals who are charged with managing and maintaining databases may be more concerned with data security and integrity. Generally, the two are complementary viewpoints, but sometimes conflicts will arise between system stability and system openness. It can be hard to remember sometimes that information access and information security are not always mutually supportive.

In general, librarians want to share information and provide equal and open avenues for it. However, an IT professional's "bread and butter" lies with authentication, integrity, and preservation. It is therefore vital to keep in mind when working on cooperative digitization projects with IT staff that, even though we might prefer open-access collections built upon open-source share-ware, IT specialists may not agree or may find this problematic in terms of data integrity, long-term system sustainability, and overall platform convenience.

Digital librarians are often familiar with the same subjects as IT specialists, including information architecture and database development (i.e., table creation, using primary/secondary keys, programming with SQL/MySQL, installing and customizing Oracle, PostgreSQL, coding in XML, etc.). Many are able to work comfortably in interoperable library systems as well as in traditional areas such as metadata development, MARC cataloging, and crosswalks. As a result, you may find yourself acting as an intermediary between the library and IT worlds. If you can straddle both realms, it will go a long way toward identifying and bridging philosophical gaps. You may find yourself acting as a translator, interpreting what seem to be different languages and reconciling them into common visions and shared values. Jargon can be a barrier to communication whenever subgroups try to speak outside their cohorts, but a digital librarian is in a prime position to explain differing terminologies to the respective groups. Ultimately, being able to bridge both worlds will improve the results of the collaboration.

Content Providers

There are a number of different types of content providers to work with, almost as many as there are types of digital projects. However, the providers you will most commonly work with include archivists, museum curators, collection specialists, donors, and private collection owners. Each content provider and collection will need to be addressed in terms of individual needs. In many ways, the parameters of each digital collection change depending on the different variables involved.

Curators and archivists often have the same goals as the digital librarians they work with, chief among them improving accessibility to and preservation of unique materials. Subject experts provide a significant amount of insight into the materials they provide and can offer excellent ideas on how to best ensure that a collection's contents serve its audience well. However, it will be important to make sure that responsibilities are clearly demarcated from the beginning. It is often the case that when issues are not spelled out clearly, confusion arises.

When working with donors or content providers who may not have the same level of expertise or even the same assumptions about how to approach the project, delicacy and tact will be in order. While archivists and curators will understand the time involved to process collections, others may lack this insight. It will therefore be important to assess the level of understanding and training a content provider or donor possesses. Some are under the false impression that one can digitize all materials quickly and easily, not realizing that along with the actual scanning of objects there exist the equally important and time-consuming tasks of copyright clearance, archival organization, metadata creation, and long-term digital preservation. Depending on how well organized and documented the collection may be, some donor/content provider expectations may need to be tempered with the realities of digital project management.

Related to these expectations is the common problem of overestimating the need to digitize large amounts of objects. A collection may contain more objects than is physically possible to digitize, either in terms of time or the amount of data generated. It may become necessary to find ways to limit the project's scope and advocate a smaller, more economical or feasible digital collection. This can be accomplished by being adamant that, from the outset, content providers prioritize the items to be digitized. Though they may not be interested in this aspect of the process, or may just want comprehensive digitization, archivists and curators will surely understand the need to limit the project's scope to optimal, representative items in a collection.

Consultants and Other Support Members

Digital librarians may also need to work with consultants whose area of expertise is related to one small aspect of the project. This includes subject specialists, software or web programming developers, and vendors that provide outsourcing services. The benefit of working with subject specialists is that they have in-depth knowledge of their fields of interest. This in-depth knowledge may help to filter out unnecessary items and allow the best specimens of the collection to be emphasized. The specialist can also point out the major themes or issues of the subject, as well as how particular segments of the target audience might use the collection.

At the same time, some discipline-related issues can also arise. Occasionally experts might be partial to a particular subject, or interpretation of a subject, to the exclusion of others. An overly narrow focus in your consultant might result in a collection that does not appeal to a large number of potential users. A balance between specificity and broad appeal must be struck. Too narrow a scope could reduce the audience to only niche specialists; too broad of an appeal will dilute the impact among scholars and could limit the quality of scholarship or educational outcomes. One possible solution is to consult with multiple subject specialists, whose disciplines vary widely and allow for a wider perspective on the collection and its potential impact on users.

Other types of consultants such as software developers or vendors will be useful to your project, but may also pose some challenges. Often, the cost of outside vendors and consultants carries no small amount of sticker shock, yet their work can be done quickly and efficiently, especially if goals are clear and time is limited. One question facing digital librarians is when to call in outside support. This needs to be analyzed based on the potential cost-effectiveness and impact upon timelines and benchmarks. For example, if a project needs someone with PHP skills, it might be in your best interest to bring in someone from outside the organization who can efficiently bring about the outcomes you desire. However, if there is time for others to learn this language without compromising benchmarks or the overall project progress, then it may be useful to have a colleague (or even yourself) learn it in order to keep the work in-house.

Similar issues are at play when deciding whether to work with outsourcing digitization vendors such as ProQuest (for digitizing ETDs) or OCLC (for hosting the CONTENTdm digital asset management system). Similar cost and time analyses need to be conducted to ensure that hiring such vendors will be worth the expense. Deciding whether to digitize in-house or outsource the work will depend upon clear cost-benefit analyses, including examining existing equipment and determining such factors as feasibility of training, current in-house levels of technical expertise, the size of potential labor pools (and turnover rates), the feasibility and applicability of grant funding, and the overall time allowed for the project. Some institutions, for example, have concluded that in-house digitization is worth the investment in equipment and staffing, while others have determined that partnering with outside vendors is a better choice in the long run.

■ CASE STUDY ■

Collaboration at Forsyth Library, FHSU

Forsyth Library provides access services for Fort Hays State University (FHSU), a state comprehensive university in western Kansas, and its 12,000 students (roughly 35 percent on-campus, 65 percent online), faculty, and staff. To meet the demands of the digital age, the library has adopted several strategies to increase the amount of library-related content available online. Emphasis since 2006 has focused on the digitization and online dissemination of archival collections from both within and outside the library, including on-campus partnerships and off-campus initiatives. Collaborations have occurred at the intra-departmental level, the interdepartmental level, and externally to the university. These projects involved library staff, FHSU faculty members in multiple departments including the business, art, and geosciences departments and the FHSU Graduate School, and staff at several museums including the Kansas Cosmosphere and Space Center and the Stafford County Historical Museum. Overall, digital collections grew from less than 100 gigabytes of data to nearly 9 terabytes, and expanded from 2 online collections to 14 within a period of four years, spanning 2007–2011. All collections mentioned below can be accessed at http://contentcat.fhsu.edu/cdm/.

Intra-Departmental Collaboration

Collaboration within the library was primarily achieved through the development of a digital collections initiative and its corresponding work group. This work group was comprised of five library staff members, including an IT specialist (an expert in digital asset management software and Windows platforms), a metadata/cataloging librarian (an expert in Dublin Core), a serials librarian (an expert in copyright), an archives and special collections librarian (an expert in existing FHSU collections), and the digital collections librarian. This group met several times per semester to discuss ongoing issues related to digital collection development, including project management, project prioritization, analysis of project timelines and goals, improvement of digitization projects, metadata development, improving workflows, and technical and staffing emergencies. This work group also developed the collection analysis tools used to aid collection prioritization and develop a project queue to avoid gaps or overlaps in project assignments. Natural alignments and areas of expertise were culled to help guide projects to completion.

Inter-Departmental Collaboration

On-campus partnerships between the library and departments began in a grassroots manner. These interdepartmental collaborations included a partnership with an overarching unit, the Graduate School, and with smaller departments, including the art, business and leadership, and geosciences departments.

Collaboration with the Graduate School primarily occurred with the digitization of the FHSU Master's Thesis Collection, which included roughly 2,900 manuscripts spanning 80 years (1930–2009). Along with retrospective digitization of the theses, in fall 2009 a new mandate for students to provide PDF versions of their manuscripts was implemented. This decision was proposed from both sides of the partnership, and action was taken accordingly. Collaboration with the art department included working with students and faculty to organize, describe and digitize the large amounts of artwork held by and displayed on the FHSU campus. Collaboration with the business and leadership department involved digitizing and placing the digitized articles from their self-published *Journal of Business and Leadership* into FHSU's instance of CONTENTdm. Finally, collaboration with geosciences involved working with professors to digitize Kansas maps as well as the vast fossil collection at the Sternberg Museum of Natural History.

In all of these collaborations with smaller departments unique issues arose, requiring the expertise of outside subject consultants. This was especially true with regard to copyright, as in the case of photographing mainly unpublished artistic works, and the dissemination of sensitive information, as in the case of providing geo-coordinates for digitized fossils.

External Collaboration

Two major collaborations have occurred between Forsyth Library and external institutions. The first partnership was with the Kansas Cosmosphere and Space Center (KCSC), which houses the personal NASA archive of Apollo 13 astronaut John L. (Jack) Swigert. This collection of blueprints and Apollo Operations Handbook manuscript pages and revisions was digitized at Forsyth Library and subsequently placed online in FHSU's installation of CONTENTdm. Issues raised by the collaboration included the need for clearer lines of communication and the assignment of clear duties. Communicative and organizational obstacles were met at various stages of the project, and despite its overall success, the project serves as a cautionary tale about too little partnership policy preparation and infrequent communication (Weiss, 2010).

The second partnership was with the Stafford County Historical Museum, located in Stafford, Kansas. This project consisted of digitizing 2,000 glass plate negatives from the W.R. Gray Photography Studio. In contrast to the KCSC project, however, this project can be seen as a prime example of how to conduct a successful partnership. The Historical Museum project members were archiving specialists and had received a grant from the Kansas Museums Association to pay for their digitization efforts. A clearly defined project scope was proposed, limiting digitization to 7 percent of the collection (2,000 of 27,000 plates), with an intention to expand the project in the future. Clear lines of communication were also established, with constant calling and face-to-face consultations during the project. Duties regarding transport, storage, and metadata creation were also designated clearly between the partners. As a result, the project successfully met its deadlines, benchmarks, and goals, reaching completion in May 2011.

■ ■ ■

FINAL THOUGHTS

This chapter has covered many of the issues related to collaboration in digital projects. For a new digital librarian, coordinating multiple projects, cooperating with different personality types, and accommodating various skill sets is something that must be cultivated over time. While some principles of collaboration and management can be learned in the classroom, certain techniques, tools, and procedures need to be developed through firsthand experience. To be sure, participants in your projects will supplement your digital expertise with specialized skills, but they may also provide significant challenges as well. When teams work well, however, they are greater than the sum of their parts—not merely cogs in a machine, but irreplaceable components in a dynamic system. You should come away from this chapter with a better sense of the complexity and difficulty of collaborating with others on digital projects, as well as an appreciation of the results it can provide.

REFERENCES

Data Curation Center (DCC). 2010. "Trustworthy Repositories." www.dcc.ac.uk/resources/repository-audit-and-assessment/trustworthy-repositories.

Forsyth Library Digital Collections Initiative (FLDCI). 2011. "FLDCI Collection Development Checklist." www.fhsu.edu/uploadedFiles/academic/library/digital/PriorityChecklist.pdf.

Weiss, Andrew. 2010. "Apollo 13.0: Digitizing Astronaut Jack Swigert's Apollo Documents," in *Digitization in the Real World,* ed. Kwong-bor Ng and Jason Kucsma, 470–89. Metropolitan New York Library Council.

Chapter Twelve

Preserving Digital Content

Heidi N. Abbey

We all have them: digital photographs of family and friends, beloved pets, vacations, and other moments in our lives. After the pictures are taken, uploaded from digital camera to computer, posted online, and perhaps printed, what do you do with the original files—do you organize them or back them up for safekeeping? If you are like most people, you may not have considered it important to take such steps until it is too late: your computer crashes and your files are gone. Considering the amount of digital information that we generate every day, it is unfortunate that the average person has little knowledge of best practices for keeping their digital files organized, secure, and usable over time. This is a problem, and it is an urgent one as well. Jeff Rothenberg cautioned in 1995 that "the content and historical value of thousands of records, databases, and personal documents may be irretrievably lost to future generations if we do not take steps to preserve them now" (Rothenberg 1995, 42). As you enter the field of digital librarianship, these are exactly the types of issues and problems that will be at the forefront of your role as a curator of digital content.

This chapter will tie together concepts previously described in this book—digital technology, management of digital projects, and metadata—and discuss the technology, infrastructure, strategies, and standards involved in digital preservation. The topic can be overwhelming and complex, even for seasoned librarians, particularly because it is still a developing discipline. In addition to serving as a digital preservation primer, this chapter will examine topics such as digital curation and digital stewardship that are currently dominating the discourse among experts in the digital preservation community. The remainder of the chapter will address digital preservation best practices, including specific strategies and tools, and provide the key intellectual nuts and bolts to help guide new librarians through the sea of acronyms that are so prevalent with this topic. Finally, a summary of the current digital preservation landscape will be presented with future risks, challenges, and opportunities.

DIGITAL PRESERVATION: THE BROADER CONTEXT

Increase the number of your personal digital files exponentially and reflect upon the number and type of digital objects that are being created, stored, uploaded to servers, edited, resaved, and retrieved by librarians every day. Some of these include scanned interlibrary loan articles, e-books, e-mails, digital audio and video course reserves, electronic theses and dissertations, and digitized primary source materials. In fact, according to the latest study of the digital universe by the International Data Corporation, the amount of digital information created in 2010 exceeded a zettabyte, or one trillion gigabytes, and was estimated to total 1.8 zettabytes by the end of 2011 (Gantz and Reinsel, 2011). Most of this information needs to be managed and preserved for long-term accessibility and use. Information technology professionals such as server and network administrators are essential to this process, but their technological expertise and input are not enough. Understanding how people use and interact with information, thereby adding value to it, is crucial.

This is where digital librarians excel: connecting people with information, regardless of the format. Now more than ever, librarians must work with an interdisciplinary focus, collaborating with experts across multiple disciplines and playing an active role in the long-term viability and sustainability of digital resources. This is essentially what digital preservation entails: the symbiosis of digitization and preservation activities, which results in the "active management of digital information over time to ensure its accessibility" (LeFurgy, 2011: under "A Basic Overview of Digital Preservation").

Many IT professionals, librarians, archivists, and other scholars saw the need for a more formalized approach to the preservation of digital media beginning in the 1990s. Several landmark studies (Conway, 1996; Waters and Garrett, 1996) put a spotlight on the topic within the library and archives communities. In particular, Conway suggested a framework for applying traditional preservation principles, those used for analog materials, to the world of digitization, noting that "many of the core tenets of preservation developed in the analog world can be carried forward to the digital world to continue the necessary roles of stewardship and service" (Conway, 1996). Another key resource in the early development of digital preservation practice was Kenney and Rieger's *Moving Theory into Practice: Digital Imaging for Libraries and Archives* (Kenney and Rieger, 2000). Although focusing specifically on the preservation of digital images, it was and remains today a valuable and practical introduction to the field.

A look back upon my own career as a new digital collections librarian can shed some light on how much the digital library and digital preservation fields have evolved in the past decade. In the fall of 2000 I became the first digital collections librarian at the University of Connecticut, charged with leading the University Libraries' new digital collections program. This was my first real, post-MLS degree position as a librarian, and it was clear from day one that I was starting on an exciting journey and delving into a new arena of academic librarianship. At that time, no one had a blueprint for digital success in higher education. Most digital librarians or digital curators that I knew were figuring things out as they went along, collaborating and sharing best practices as they evolved. It was exhilarating and frustrating at the same time.

Consequently, I spent countless hours in meetings with other administrators, staff, and IT professionals inside and outside of the library, trying to figure out how to build a digital collections program with an infrastructure that was extensible and sustainable, while respecting the capacities of a very limited budget and staffing. Working closely with other librarians, archivists and records managers, I researched image, text, sound, and video file formats, learned about metadata standards, studied the life cycle of digital assets under my care, and took a holistic view of creating digital resources that would stand the test of time. Without knowing it, I was forming the building blocks of a digital preservation program.

Now over a decade later, although I no longer work at the same university, many of the digital projects with which I was involved are still online. However, they look nothing like the resources that I had helped to create over ten years ago. They have been imported into and exported out of different databases and content management systems, saved as different file types, migrated to new servers and networks, enhanced by more robust metadata standards, and given technological face-lifts by virtue of the fact that the basic bits and bytes were preserved by my successors. How exactly did this happen? Who and what technologies preserved these digital files and projects over the years? The answers can be found by examining the current state of digital preservation, digital curation, and digital stewardship.

Digital Preservation: Definitions

Let's examine more thoroughly what digital preservation is and why it is such a critical aspect of digital librarianship. We have already mentioned that it is the merger of theories, policies, and practices from two different fields: preservation and digitization. Although digital preservation has been the topic of many different books and articles over the past decade, there is no universally accepted definition for it yet. There are many different descriptions of the term depending upon who you talk to, be it an archivist or records manager, a librarian, an IT professional, or a lawyer specializing in electronic records discovery. Nevertheless, for the purposes of this book, digital preservation can be described as the active application of dedicated best practices, policies, and resources that ensure the long-term accessibility and use of digital data. If we break down this definition further, we will also discover how pertinent digital preservation has become and will continue to be for the integrity and sustainability of the digital universe.

First of all, digital preservation is an activity. It is comprised of a series of procedures, both abstract and tangible, which result in safeguarding information. Just as with analog materials, you cannot create digital content, copy it, file it away, and then expect it to persist over time without some attention and care. Why? Technology changes very rapidly. The hardware, software, and physical formats (VHS tapes, CDs, DVDs, etc.) that many people own and use today will eventually become obsolete or unavailable. For example, even if you have a collection of VHS tapes, do you own a working VCR player? Right now, you can still buy one online. But if it breaks, who will fix it, and will the repair costs be prohibitively expensive? Chances are you will either lose the data on the tape altogether, or, even if you are willing to pay someone to reformat or copy it to optical media such as a DVD, the resulting disc and its data will eventually wear out over time or fall victim to the same format obsolescence. Technological obsolescence is generally more of a concern than the deterioration of formats and media. The hardware and software required to read the data stored on various formats will more than likely be unavailable long before the media physically degrades.

Second, in order to mitigate data loss it is essential to proactively review and assess the condition of digital files. This requires resources, often in the form of expertise and funding. The management of digital files also includes authenticating them or ensuring their validity and usability. Metadata is often used in this aspect of digital preservation. Administrative, descriptive, structural, technical, and preservation metadata provide contextual information such as the name of the file's creator, the date of creation and history of changes to the file, the file type and size, and the hardware and software used to create it. All of this data assists in the long-term viability of digital information.

Third, a core tenet of digital preservation is the facilitation of data accessibility and use despite the inherent limitations of technologies and formats. All data does not need to be saved. But, for digital content that has enduring value to a variety of different users and stakeholders, digital preservation standards allow for its retrieval and reuse through time.

It is important to note that preservation is not necessarily achieved via digitization. In other words, scanning or digitizing analog information does not invalidate or make the original useless. For example, scanning photographs at a high resolution may minimize the number of times originals are requested and handled by patrons, which can prolong the life of the print. But it can also have the reverse effect through wider distribution to more users who, in turn, would like to view the original materials. Maintaining the digital files over time requires an investment of expertise, hardware, and software to ensure that they remain readable and usable. Without such measures, preservation is not achieved. Another example of this is the digitization of brittle books and newspapers. These materials have been traditionally microfilmed for preservation purposes, and often are subsequently digitized to facilitate patron access and use. There are disadvantages to both approaches, including sacrificing the quality of the original as well as high reformatting costs that leave many organizations simply unable to implement both strategies.

However, regardless of the format in which information is kept, preservation management strategies will be needed to ensure the long-term accessibility and viability of our historical, intellectual, and cultural assets. Digital information continues to grow at an alarming rate worldwide, and technological and organizational strategies for preserving it must keep pace. Otherwise, vast amounts of information and, consequently, parts of our intellectual and cultural heritage may fall into technological cracks and become lost among obsolete hardware and software, heralding what some call a "digital Dark Age" (Kuny, 1998). It should come as no surprise then that digital preservation will continue to play a pivotal role in the library profession.

Digital Curation and Digital Stewardship: Holistic Approaches to Digital Preservation

Within the United States, the U.S. Congress recognized that our nation's digital heritage was in jeopardy as early as 2000. It embarked upon a collaborative approach to managing digital content via the creation of the National Digital Information Infrastructure and Preservation Program (NDIIPP) (www.digitalpreservation.gov/index.html), spearheaded by the Library of Congress. The NDIIPP has been working over the past decade with federal agencies and other organizations across the United States to develop a national digital preservation strategy. Specifically, the program focuses on the following three objectives: (1) ingesting (preparing data and transferring it to a repository or digital asset management system) and preserving data and making digital content accessible; (2) establishing a network of partners across the United States; and (3) creating an infrastructure of information tools and services. Through this program, the NDIIPP and its partners laid the foundation for a more comprehensive view of and collaborative approach to digital preservation.

The NDIIPP and many other practitioners and educators within the library and information science disciplines advocate that digital preservation programs should not exist within a vacuum. Instead, when digital preservation practices and processes are implemented within a holistic context—that is, one that accounts for the entire life cycle of digital assets, from pre-digitization, to digitization and use, through the cycles of storage, reuse, archiving, and disposition or deletion—the result is improved short- and long-term management, integrity, and accessibility of content. This is, in essence, digital curation. Lavoie and Dempsey echoed this new way of thinking when they stated that "the focus of digital preservation has shifted away from the need to take immediate action to 'rescue' threatened materials, and toward the realization that perpetuating digital materials over the long-term involves the observance of careful digital asset management practices diffused throughout the information life cycle" (Lavoie and Dempsey, 2004).

Digital curation involves three other criteria which differentiate it from digital preservation: (1) development of a management infrastructure that facilitates the application of international standards and best practices before digitization even takes place, (2) facilitation of ongoing interaction with data creators, data users, and other stakeholders throughout the digital information life cycle, and (3) incorporation of value-added information such as metadata to ensure the quality, authenticity, and trustworthiness of data. Collectively, these activities promote current and future information discovery, use, and reuse.

While this is a cursory examination of digital curation objectives, many of these concepts have evolved into a more detailed model developed and promoted by the Digital Curation Centre (DCC). In 2008, the DCC launched what has become one of the essential tools for digital librarians, the "DCC Curation Lifecycle Model." This visual representation emphasizes that data (e.g., digital objects or databases) is at the heart of several interrelated digital asset management and planning processes (see figure 12.1).

Surrounding the core data elements in the model are several concentric rings that represent a sequence of activities that may take place at any time during the life cycle of a digital object. This includes the creation of descriptive metadata and representation information, or "the extra structural or semantic information which converts raw data into something more meaningful" (Digital Curation Centre, 2010:

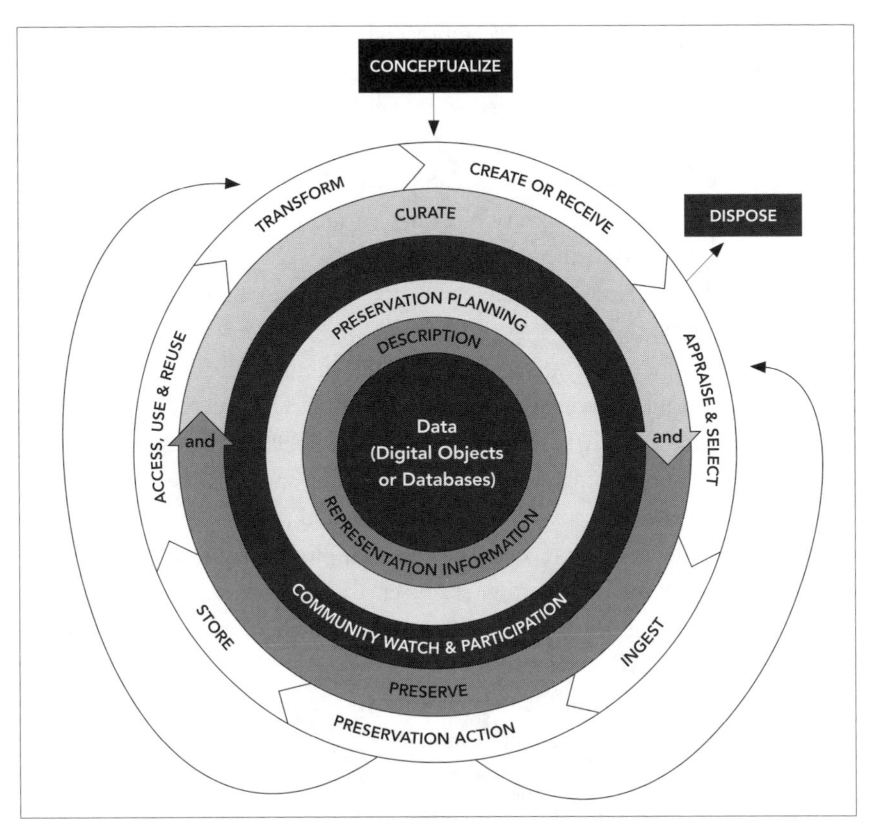

FIGURE 12.1
DCC curation life cycle model

under "What Is Representation Information?"). What the DCC calls "community watch," or keeping up with emerging standards, tools, and best practices, also informs the curation life cycle. Finally, on the outer ring of the model, there are a series of sequential activities that are performed over and over again in the chain of curation. These range from data conceptualization, creation, and receipt to ingestion or transfer, preservation actions to ensure for the authenticity of data, and data transformation.

Radiating around the outermost ring of these activities are the following actions that may be carried out during the curation process: (1) data migration, which entails copying or converting data from one technology platform to another; (2) reappraisal, or determining those materials that are no longer desired for long-term preservation and can be either transferred or destroyed; and (3) disposal, which includes the transfer or destruction of data not selected for retention. These actions further provide for a comprehensive approach to the short- or long-term curation and preservation of digital information.

Another holistic approach to managing digital assets, digital stewardship, has been developing in the United States and is worth mentioning here as it highlights the unique role that digital librarians can play in the sustainability of our digital heritage. In July 2010, the Library of Congress and the NDIIPP established the National Digital Stewardship Alliance (NDSA) (www.digitalpreservation.gov/ndsa/). According to Butch Lazorchak, a digital archivist with the NDIIPP, digital stewardship can be thought of as an overarching framework that brings digital curation and digital preservation together while simultaneously thinking about and having oversight of the cultural, economic, and social contexts in which digital assets reside (Lazorchak, 2011). Like digital curation, digital stewardship includes a focus on collaboration, outreach, community building, and of course, preservation. But the main distinction between digital curation and digital stewardship is that, in this context, stewardship incorporates a much broader cultural and historical responsibility over the life of a digital object. Digital librarians-as-stewards are entrusted with caring for digital assets on behalf of the numerous and diverse communities that value and use them.

As a result of these coordinated national and international efforts to share resources, distribute expertise, and establish best practices, it is clear that digital preservation strategies are most effective when framed and viewed within a larger context that includes both digital curation and digital stewardship. Therefore, digital librarians must take into account the entire life cycle of digital assets over time, engage with communities of data users, and consider the larger historical-cultural and socioeconomic contexts within which data is born, used, and reused.

DIGITAL PRESERVATION BEST PRACTICES: A FRAMEWORK FOR SUCCESS

Now that we have examined the prevailing theoretical framework of digital preservation, curation, and stewardship, let's move into the practical world of ensuring the viability and longevity of digitized content. Where do you start? How can new digital librarians begin to adopt and implement preservation best practices, and which approaches and resources are essential for success? Unfortunately, just as there is no universal definition for digital preservation, there is no magic bullet or one-size-fits-all approach to accomplishing it. There is, however, a continuum of preservation strategies and options that will fit different organizational, staffing, and budgetary needs, and work within the ever-changing landscape of digital technologies and formats.

Perhaps the most often referenced and highly regarded digital preservation tactics are those outlined in the free online tutorial, *Digital Preservation Management: Implementing Short-Term Strategies for Long-Term Problems* (Kenney et al., 2003), which provides an introduction to digital preservation that is approachable for newbie digital librarians. It includes discussions about formats, hardware, and software that are packed with useful tactics for confronting obsolescence, and best practices for everything from media storage and handling to disaster recovery. A concise and easy-to-comprehend synopsis is given of the systems vital to a robust digital preservation program, including a trusted digital repository that adheres to the open archival information system model, and preservation metadata. The tutorial also offers a frank review of the challenges to building a successful digital preservation program and suggestions on how to overcome them.

Digital Preservation Management gives a theoretical summary of three key digital preservation program components advocated by Kenney and McGovern: organizational infrastructure, technological infrastructure, and a strong foundation of sustainable resources (funding, staffing, space, etc.). All of these components center around digital content (see figure 12.2). This echoes the approach of the "DCC Curation Lifecycle Model," particularly because data is still at the heart of it. However, Kenney and McGovern's programmatic model is much simpler overall and therefore, perhaps easier to conceptualize.

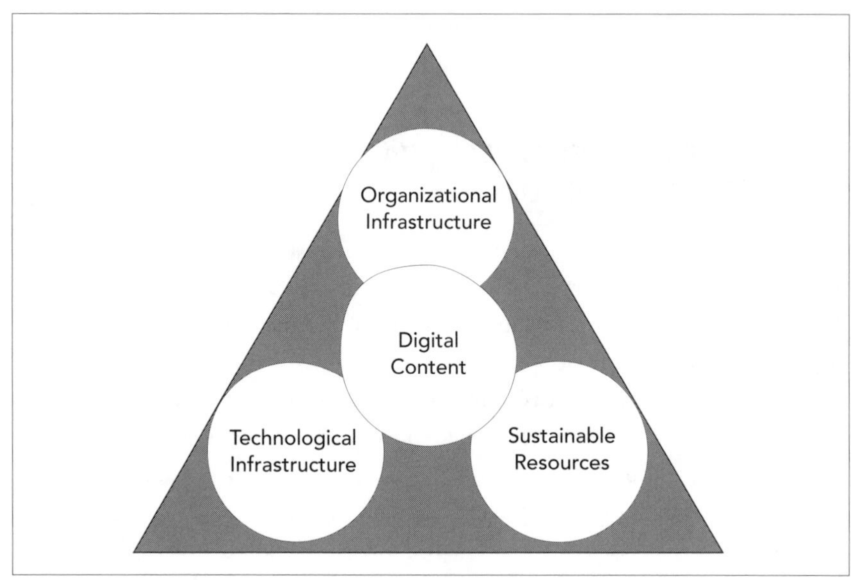

FIGURE 12.2
Three key components of a digital preservation program

The tutorial expands upon the three-pronged method of building a preservation program for digital assets, which is a useful starting point for new digital librarians. This theoretical framework is called the "three-legged stool for digital preservation" (McGovern, 2007) because it symbolizes the necessary balance of organizational and technological infrastructure and required resources that must be achieved to support the preservation of data (the seat of the stool). One leg of the stool represents planning, policies, documentation of standards, and procedures. Another leg represents the tools, hardware, software, and application and management of policies and procedures necessary to achieve stated preservation goals. The third leg is representative of the necessary funding, staffing, and skill sets to sustain the digital preservation program. These three aspects will be used to loosely frame the rest of our discussion about best practices.

Assessing, Planning, and Organizing

The creation of a successful digital preservation program begins with proper planning and organization. Like pouring the concrete foundation for a new house, allocating time and resources to plan and build an organizational infrastructure for digital preservation is essential. But, to continue with our house analogy, you can't build a house without a strong foundation, blueprints, raw materials, proper equipment and tools, and people who know how to use them. The same is true for digital preservation.

The best course of action is to first assess organizational needs and determine resources that are available to make digital preservation possible. This can be accomplished efficiently by using the "Institutional Readiness Survey," which will help in evaluating current resources and those that may be missing (Kenney et al., 2003). The Northeast Document Conservation Center also provides a valuable self-assessment tool for digital preservation online (Bishoff and Rhodes, 2007). After completing a baseline review of an institution's strengths and weaknesses for addressing digital preservation in a sustainable way, the following list of programmatic elements can be incorporated into an organizational strategy:

Mission and vision statements: Make digital preservation part of them. The mission statement should concisely state the purpose of the program, what it does, for whom, and why. The vision statement should embody an organization's aspirations for the future with regard to preservation.

Strategic planning: Develop a preservation strategic plan or at least make digital preservation a priority in an organization's strategic plan, including short- and long-term goals and realistic action items that will assist with achieving the stated goals; continually advocate for implementation of the plan.

Policies, procedures, and best practices: Create and codify detailed documentation that articulates all of these for the digital preservation program, considering all of the life cycle stages for digital content (e.g., appraisal, selection, data capture, ingest, description, preservation actions, storage, use, etc.).

Standards and protocols: Research, select, and document as many relevant national or international standards and protocols as possible. For example, at a minimum, aim to benchmark local, in-house standards against two international standards for digital preservation: the Standard for *Trusted Digital Repositories (TDR),* and the Open Archival Information System Reference Model (OAIS). TDR was recently developed to augment the *Trustworthy Repositories Audit & Certification: Criteria and Checklist from*

2007. Also, incorporate the use of PREMIS (PREservation Metadata Implementation Strategies), which is a data dictionary that outlines the key preservation metadata elements needed to achieve the long-term preservation of digital materials.

Once these foundational policies, procedures, and organizational tactics are in place, we can begin to address the more practical and tangible aspects of digital preservation in the form of technological strategies.

Implementing Technologies and Standards

Continuing with the house analogy, after assessing, planning, and organizing best practices and requirements for digital preservation, we now have a solid foundation upon which to build the framework for the walls and install the plumbing, HVAC, electricity, and other resources needed to make the house livable. In terms of a digital preservation program, these translate into hardware and software to authenticate and curate digital assets, storage media, tools, workflows, and the application of policies and procedures necessary to achieve preservation goals.

If we now consider the "DCC Curation Lifecycle Model," and the technological and format obsolescence of digital media, there are specific curatorial actions that can be implemented after content is appraised and deemed worthy of preservation. The first action is ingesting materials—that is, preparing and transferring them to a trusted repository or archive in accordance with documented policies or other requirements. After ingestion, a preservation strategy must be chosen to continue the curatorial chain of events. But which tactic works the best to mitigate data loss and preserve important digital assets over time? Currently, there are numerous options available on the continuum of preservation strategies, including:

Bitstream copying: The process of making a data backup copy of an original file; this is perhaps the least desirable choice because it is not suited for long-term preservation.

Replication: Similar to bitstream copying, replication involves making many copies of a file and distributing them to many different servers; a well-known example of replication is the LOCKSS (Lots of Copies Keep Stuff Safe) consortial project (www.lockss.org).

Refreshing: Copying data from one medium (for example, an old scratched Mitsui Gold DVD-R) to another one that is similar (a new Mitsui Gold DVD-R).

Migration: Converting or copying data from one technology platform to another, usually because of hardware and/or software obsolescence; this may result in changing the original data to some extent because upgrading from one version of software or hardware to a newer one may require the file format to be altered (e.g., saving 5½-inch floppy disks to a hard drive or VHS tapes to DVD). Critics of migration argue that the integrity of the original file may be compromised, so the validity and authenticity of the file and its data cannot be guaranteed for digital preservation purposes.

Emulation: A digital preservation strategy which calls for accessing data from an old platform by running software on a new or current platform that emulates the original (e.g., websites that allow users to play original 1980s arcade games within a web browser). Migration and emulation are the two most frequently utilized preservation actions.

After data has been ingested and a preservation action like migration completed, digital objects can then be stored in a trusted digital repository or archive. There are many storage options available for digital preservation; they may be commercial (OCLC's Digital Archive), open source (DSpace, Fedora, LOCKSS), or locally developed solutions. Proponents of open source technology, as opposed to proprietary or commercial digital asset management solutions, argue that open standards and open architecture better facilitate an exit strategy—the process by which data can be migrated from one system or storage medium to another. When considering the implementation of any digital repository or archive, having an exit strategy is critical because systems and hardware won't last forever.

Leveraging Other Resources

Now that we have examined the organizational and technological components of a successful digital preservation program, the final strategies needed to complete our framework of best practices focus upon leveraging the necessary resources for sustainability. Returning once more to the house analogy, we need to perform regular maintenance on the property, hire skilled workers to keep the house from falling into disrepair, and identify regular funding streams to pay for these services and ultimately protect our investment. The same is true for digital assets within the context of a preservation program. Because continuing education in the digital library community is so essential to keeping up with new research and developments, funds to send staff to conferences, workshops, and seminars is vital. Digital librarians and content curators need to stay connected with each other, sharing best practices and learning about new and emerging standards that provide for the viability and integrity of digital assets over time.

THE DIGITAL PRESERVATION LANDSCAPE: FUTURE RISKS, CHALLENGES, AND OPPORTUNITIES

Although the national and international digital preservation communities have come a long way since the 1990s, when concerns about the loss of our digital heritage were at their peak, there are still many risks, challenges, and opportunities that will need to be addressed by current and future digital librarians, IT professionals, archivists, curators, and other information management professionals. While there is no one-size-fits-all solution for making sure that digital information will be accessible over time, and considering that technology and the way people interact with it drives most of the variables and challenges that preservation poses for librarians, it is imperative to embrace a culture of collaboration and advocacy to achieve digital preservation objectives. Digital librarians need to continue promoting the importance of their work, highlighting "Digital Preservation as a Public Good" (Kuny 1998, 9), and making the task of safeguarding our digital heritage a wider concern.

The Library of Congress and NDIIPP have already started to make "digital preservation" and "personal digital archiving" household words by launching the "Preserving Your Digital Memories" campaign, which provides the average person with very simple tips on how best to preserve digital photos, audio, video, e-mail, websites, and personal records. This type of outreach and user education is essential for furthering the concept of distributed digital preservation because, given the enormity of the digital universe, safeguarding digital content is in everyone's best interest.

The idea of collaborative strategies that urge organizations to band together to preserve our cultural-historical and socioeconomic heritage has also been gaining attention via the work of the MetaArchive Cooperative (www.metaarchive.org/), the "first private digital preservation network" established in 2002 with the express purpose of building an affordable shared digital repository. Halbert and Skinner summarized this growing concept of distributed digital preservation:

> In the context of this critical need for a new consensus on how to preserve digital collections, a growing number of cultural memory organizations (including those of the MetaArchive Cooperative) have now come to believe that the most effective digital preservation efforts in practice succeed through some strategy for distributing copies of content in secure, distributed locations over time. This conceptual strategy is a straightforward carry-over of the practices that in the chirographic (handwritten) world of antiquity enabled scholars to preserve content through millennia of scribal culture. But in the digital age this strategy requires not only the collaboration of like-minded individuals, but also an investment in a distributed array of servers capable of storing digital collections in a pre-coordinated methodology. (Halbert and Skinner 2010, 6)

Staying abreast of developments such as shared digital preservation projects is a challenge but also an opportunity. Thankfully, resources for continuing education abound: conferences, workshops, seminars, and advanced certificates of study are just a few tools available. In fact, the Society of American Archivists launched a new Digital Archives Specialist Curriculum and Certificate Program in 2011, which will help current and new archivists to gain experience and knowledge managing and curating born-digital records. Graduate students in library school and newly minted librarians will find that more and more jobs require digital asset management and digital preservation experience.

If you really want to keep your finger on the pulse of what is happening in the digital preservation community, start monitoring blogs such as *The Signal* at the Library of Congress (http://blogs.loc.gov/digitalpreservation), and *Digitization 101*, an excellent blog that is regularly maintained by Jill Hurst-Wahl, assistant professor of practice in Syracuse University's School of Information Studies (http://hurstassociates.blogspot.com). If you enjoy Hurst-Wahl's provocative and thought-provoking posts about the future of information access and how it is being shaped by smartphones and video game interfaces and experiences, you just might be ready to jump into a career as a digital preservation librarian.

FINAL THOUGHTS

This chapter has provided you with a basic introduction to the complex but exciting and ever-changing world of digital preservation, digital curation, and digital stewardship. These fields are poised to grow and evolve along with the tremendous amount of digital content being published online, and there is no indication that the digital universe will get smaller, only bigger. The digital preservation strategies, hardware, software, and standards that are in use today may be passé tomorrow. Nevertheless, digital librarians are in a unique position to be agents of change by advocating for the preservation of vital digital data, records, and objects over their life cycles, and by serving a critical role in defining what it means to conscientiously and effectively steward our digital heritage. But librarians will not be able to do it alone. The magnitude of information online today will most certainly require national and international collaborative efforts to achieve any level of digital sustainability. Perhaps Tim O'Reilly summarized it best: "Because as we move to an all-digital world, or a largely digital world, digital preservation won't be just the concern of specialists, it will be a concern of everyone" (O'Reilly, 2011).

REFERENCES

Bishoff, Liz, and Erin Rhodes. 2007. *Planning for Digital Preservation: A Self-Assessment Tool*. Northeast Document Conservation Center. www.nedcc.org/resources/digital/downloads/DigitalPreservationSelfAssessmentfinal.pdf.

Conway, Paul. 1996. "Preservation in the Digital World." Washington, DC: Council on Library and Information Resources. www.clir.org/pubs/reports/conway2/.

Digital Curation Centre (DCC). 2010. "Lifecycle Model FAQ." Digital Curation Centre. www.dcc.ac.uk/resources/curation-lifecycle-model/lifecycle-model-faqs.

Gantz, John F., and David Reinsel. 2011. "The 2011 Digital Universe Study: Extracting Value from Chaos." IDC Go-To-Market Services. www.emc.com/collateral/analyst-reports/idc-extracting-value-from-chaos-ar.pdf.

Halbert, Martin, and Katherine Skinner. 2010. "Preserving Our Collections, Preserving Our Missions." In *A Guide to Distributed Digital Preservation*, ed. Katherine Skinner and Matt Schultz, 1–10. Atlanta, GA: Educopia Institute. www.metaarchive.org/GDDP.

Kenney, Anne R., Nancy Y. McGovern, Richard Entlich, William R. Kehoe, and Ellie Buckley. 2003. *Digital Preservation Management: Implementing Short-Term Strategies for Long-Term Problems*. Cornell University Library and the Inter-University Consortium for Political and Social Research (ICPSR), University of Michigan. Last modified May 2010. http://www.dpworkshop.org/.

Kenney, Anne R., and Oya Y. Rieger. 2000. *Moving Theory into Practice: Digital Imaging for Libraries and Archives*. Mountain View, CA: Research Libraries Group.

Kuny, Terry. 1998. "The Digital Dark Ages? Challenges in the Preservation of Electronic Information." *International Preservation News: A Newsletter of the IFLA Core Programme for Preservation and Conservation (PAC)*, no. 17. http://archive.ifla.org/VI/4/news/17-98.htm#2.

Lavoie, Brian, and Lorcan Dempsey. 2004. "Thirteen Ways of Looking at . . . Digital Preservation." *D-Lib Magazine* 10, no. 7/8. www.dlib.org/dlib/july04/lavoie/07lavoie.html.

Lazorchak, Butch. 2011. "Digital Preservation, Digital Curation, Digital Stewardship: What's in (Some) Names?" *The Signal: Digital Preservation* (blog), August 23. http://blogs.loc.gov/digitalpreservation/2011/08/digital-preservation-digital-curation-digital-stewardship-what%E2%80%99s-in-some-names/.

LeFurgy, Bill. 2011. "A Basic Overview of Digital Preservation." *Agogified* (blog). January 24. http://agogified.com/305.

McGovern, Nancy Y. 2007. "A Digital Decade: Where Have We Been and Where Are We Going in Digital Preservation?" *RLG DigiNews: RLG's Online Newsletter for Digital Imaging and Preservation* 11, no. 1. http://worldcat.org/arcviewer/2/OCC/2009/07/29/H1248893518290/viewer/file2.html/.

O'Reilly, Tim. July 19, 2011. "Keynote Address." Presentation by Tim O'Reilly, founder of O'Reilly Media, for the 2011 NDIIPP/NDSA Partners' Meeting, "Making It Work: Improvisations on the Stewardship of Digital Information" at the Library of Congress. Online video presentation. www.digitalpreservation.gov/multimedia/videos/partnersmeeting-oreilly.html#.

Rothenberg, Jeff. 1995. "Ensuring the Longevity of Digital Documents." *Scientific American* 272, pp. 42–47.

Waters, Donald, and John Garrett, eds. 1996. *Preserving Digital Information: Report of the Task Force on Archiving of Digital Information*. Washington, DC: Commission on Preservation and Access and the Research Libraries Group. www.clir.org/pubs/reports/pub63watersgarrett.pdf.

RECOMMENDED RESOURCES

Bailey, Charles W., Jr. 2011. *Digital Curation and Preservation Bibliography 2010*. Houston: Digital Scholarship.

Consultative Committee for Space Data Systems. 2002. "Reference Model for an Open Archival Information System (OAIS)." http://public.ccsds.org/publications/RefModel.aspx.

______. 2011. *Audit and Certification of Trustworthy Digital Repositories* (draft). Center for Research Libraries. http://public.ccsds.org/publications/archive/652x0m1.pdf.

Cornell University and Inter-University Consortium for Political and Social Research (ICPSR). "Digital Preservation Management Tutorial." www.dpworkshop.org/dpm-eng/eng_index.html.

Harvey, Ross. 2010. *Digital Curation: A How-to-Do-It Manual.* London: Facet; New York: Neal-Schuman.

Harvey, Ross, et al. *Curation Reference Manual.* Digital Curation Centre. Last modified October 2011. www.dcc.ac.uk/resources/curation-reference-manual.

Higgins, Sarah. 2008. "The DCC Curation Lifecycle Model." *International Journal of Digital Curation* 3, no. 1. http://ijdc.net/index.php/ijdc/article/view/69/48.

Hswe, Patricia, Michael J. Furlough, Michael J. Giarlo, and Mairéad Martin. 2011. "Responding to the Call to Curate: Digital Curation in Practice at Penn State University Libraries." *International Journal of Digital Curation* 6, no. 2. www.ijdc.net/index.php/ijdc/article/view/191/256.

Hunter, Gregory H. 2000. *Preserving Digital Information: A How-to-Do-It-Manual.* How-to-Do-It-Manuals-for-Librarians, no. 93. New York: Neal-Schuman.

Kenney, Anne R., and Nancy Y. McGovern. 2003. "The Five Organizational Stages of Digital Preservation." In *Digital Libraries: A Vision for the 21st Century: A Festschrift in Honor of Wendy Lougee on the Occasion of Her Departure from the University of Michigan,* ed. Patricia Hodges, Mark Sandler, Maria Bonn, and John Price Wilkin. Ann Arbor, MI: Scholarly Publishing Office, University of Michigan, University Library. http://quod.lib.umich.edu/s/spobooks/bbv9812.0001.001/1:11?rgn=div1;view=fulltext.

McMillan, Gail, Matt Schultz, and Katherine Skinner. 2011. *Digital Preservation.* SPEC Kit 325. Washington, DC: Association of Research Libraries.

Online Computer Library Center (OCLC) and the Center for Research Libraries (CRL). 2007. *Trustworthy Repositories Audit and Certification: Criteria and Checklist.* Center for Research Libraries. http://www.crl.edu/sites/default/files/attachments/pages/trac_0.pdf.

Skinner, Katherine, and Matt Schultz, eds. 2010. *A Guide to Distributed Digital Preservation.* Atlanta, GA: Educopia Institute. http://www.metaarchive.org/sites/default/files/GDDP_Educopia.pdf.

Walters, Tyler, and Katherine Skinner. 2011. *New Roles for New Times: Digital Curation for Preservation.* Washington, DC: Association for Research Libraries. www.arl.org/bm~doc/nrnt_digital_curation17mar11.pdf.

Glossary of Terms

Aggregator: a repository built by harvesting metadata from various data providers.

Anglo-American Cataloging Rules, Second Edition (AACR2): a set of cataloging rules used for the description of library materials, primarily in conjunction with MARC; currently in the process of being replaced by Resource Description and Access.

Application layer: within the three-tier model of web architecture, the programming layer that allows the presentation layer (web pages) and data layer (database) to communicate.

Application profile: definition of the semantics and syntax of a metadata element set to be adopted by a local application, often containing data elements from one or more schemas.

Art and Architecture Thesaurus (AAT): a controlled vocabulary used for describing items related to art, architecture, and material culture.

Bitstream copying: the process of making an exact duplicate of a digital object.

Cascading style sheets (CSS): a markup language used to format the layout of web pages in HTML or XML by separating the document content from document presentation.

Content management system (CMS): a collaborative software system used to upload, edit, and manage website content via a web browser interface.

Content standard: a set of rules that define how data elements should be used to describe and represent items in a catalog or metadata record.

Content Standard for Digital Geospatial Metadata (CSDGM): a content standard for the documentation of digital geospatial data.

Controlled vocabulary: a consistent collection of predefined, authorized terms or headings with assigned meanings.

Data curation: digital curation as it applies specifically to scholarly or academic data.

Data dictionary: a document that defines the metadata fields to be used for a specific situation.

Data layer: within the three-tier model of web architecture, the "back end" or database containing information the user accesses via the presentation and application layers.

Data provider: a repository that exposes metadata for harvesting.

Database management system (DBMS): software that provides for the creation, management, organization, modification, and retrieval of data in a database.

Describing Archives: A Content Standard (DACS): a set of rules for describing archives, personal papers, and manuscript collections.

Digital curation: a conceptual framework that incorporates the maintenance, preservation, and process of adding value to authenticated and trusted digital data or information throughout its entire life cycle.

Digital humanities: a field of research and scholarship characterized by the intersection of traditional humanities disciplines with computing and emerging technologies.

Digital Object Identifier (DOI): a character string used to uniquely identify a digital object.

Digital preservation: the active application of dedicated best practices, policies, and resources that ensure for the long-term accessibility and use of digital data and information.

Digital stewardship: the process by which digital data and information is managed and preserved, while simultaneously assessing its use and considering the cultural, economic, and social contexts in which digital information resides.

Discovery platform: a system designed to provide comprehensive and streamlined access to all content held by a library, in all formats, within a single user interface.

Dublin Core (DC): a metadata standard consisting of a set of fifteen elements intended for general resource description across many domains.

Electronic theses and dissertations (ETD): theses or dissertations that are published digitally.

Emulation: a digital preservation strategy which calls for accessing or running data on a new platform by running software on the new or current platform that emulates the original.

Encoded Archival Description (EAD): an XML-based metadata standard for encoding archival finding aids.

Eprint: a digital version of a research document, such as a journal article, that is accessible online.

Extensible Markup Language (XML): an open standard that defines a set of rules for describing and sharing data using tag sets.

Graphics Interchange Format (GIF): a standard compressed file format that allows for the storage of images containing up to 256 colors.

Green OA: a scholarly publishing model in which authors self-archive their materials in an online repository while at the same time submitting them to a traditional publication.

Gold OA: a scholarly publishing model in which authors publish directly through an open access journal.

Hypertext Markup Language (HTML): a standardized markup language designed to display data on the Web.

Impact factor: a formula for measuring the average number of citations to articles published in academic journals.

Information architecture: the design and organization of cohesive and effective information structures or computer systems, primarily associated with website design and usability.

Institutional repository (IR): an online system for collecting, preserving, and providing access to the intellectual output of an institution.

Integrated library system (ILS): a computer system that manages library tasks such as acquisitions, cataloging, and circulation and provides a public user interface for the catalog.

International Standard Bibliographic Description (ISBD): a standard for descriptive cataloging that facilitates the sharing of bibliographic records across library communities.

Joint Photographic Experts Group (JPEG): a standard file format with variable compression and unlimited color range, typically used for displaying images on the Web.

Learning Object Metadata (IEEE LOM): a metadata standard for the description of learning objects in an educational setting, maintained by the Institute of Electrical and Electronics Engineers.

Library of Congress Subject Headings (LCSH): a controlled vocabulary used for describing materials by subject.

Linked data: a method for connecting related, but previously unlinked, data on the Web.

Machine-Readable Cataloging (MARC): a set of standards for the representation and communication of bibliographic information in machine-readable form.

Metadata: structured, encoded data that describes the characteristics of an information resource.

Metadata crosswalk: a tool used to map parallel elements between two separate metadata sets.

Metadata element set: a predefined set of metadata elements for use in a given metadata schema.

Metadata Encoding and Transmission Standard (METS): an XML-based standard for encoding descriptive, administrative, and structural metadata for a digital object together in a single record.

Metadata for Images in XML (MIX): an XML-based metadata schema designed for expressing technical metadata for digital still images.

Metadata harvesting: the automated collection of metadata from digital repositories.

Metadata Object Description Schema (MODS): an XML-based descriptive metadata standard that is derived from MARC.

Metadata schema: a framework for representing metadata that defines data elements and the rules governing their use to describe a resource within a specific context.

Metadata standard: a set of rules that define sets of metadata elements for a particular purpose or environment.

Migration: a digital preservation strategy which involves copying or converting data from one technology platform to another, usually because of hardware or software obsolescence

Open access: scholarly literature or research made freely available online without restrictions.

Open Archival Information System Reference Model (OAIS): an international standard which details the technical requirements that must be present in an open archival information system in order to provide long-term preservation for and access to information.

Open Archives Initiative Protocol for Metadata Harvesting (OAI-PMH): a protocol that allows digital repositories to collect and exchange metadata records.

Open source: software in which the source code is made freely available for users to modify and redistribute.

Orphan work: a copyrighted work for which the copyright owner cannot be identified or located.

Postprint: the final version of a scholarly manuscript after it has undergone peer review.

Preprint: a draft of a scholarly manuscript that has not yet undergone peer review.

Presentation layer: within the three-tier model of web architecture, the "front end" consisting of web pages viewed by the user in a browser.

Preservation Metadata Implementation Strategies (PREMIS): a data dictionary that outlines the key preservation metadata elements needed to achieve long-term preservation of digital materials.

Public domain: materials with no copyright restrictions, generally works published prior to 1923 or those produced by the federal government.

Refreshing: the act of copying digital information from one long-term storage medium to another of the same type, with no change in the bitstream.

Relational database: a set of tables consisting of rows and columns that allows for data storage, retrieval, and modification.

Replication: distributing many copies of a digital file to multiple storage locations.

Resource Description Framework (RDF): an XML-based standard for describing Internet resources that enables the encoding, exchange, and reuse of structured metadata; one of the building blocks of the semantic web.

Semantic web: an extension of the current World Wide Web in which data is linked and described in such a way that its meaning can be easily processed by machines.

Service provider: metadata aggregator that provides information services with metadata that has been harvested from other sources.

Standard for Trusted Digital Repositories (TDR): an international standard which outlines in detail the organizational requirements and attributes of a trusted digital repository.

Structured Query Language (SQL): a programming language used to manage data in relational databases.

Synchronized Multimedia Integration Language (SMIL): an XML-based markup language used for integrating multimedia objects into audiovisual presentations.

Tagged Image File Format (TIFF): a standard uncompressed file format used for capturing high-detail images, typically used for storage due to its large file size.

Technical Metadata for Text (textMD): an XML-based metadata standard for text-based digital objects.

Text Encoding Initiative (TEI): an XML-based standard for the representation of digital texts.

Thesaurus for Graphic Materials (TGM): a controlled vocabulary for the description of visual materials.

Triples: the subject-predicate-object expressions that form the syntax of RDF.

Uniform Resource Identifier (URI): a globally unique resource identifier.

Visual Resource Association (VRA) Core: a metadata standard used for the description of images and works of art and culture.

About the Contributors

HEIDI N. ABBEY is the archivist and humanities reference librarian and coordinator of archives and special collections at the Penn State Harrisburg Library. She holds an MLS from the University at Albany, SUNY, and an MA in art history from the University of Maryland at College Park. Prior to joining the faculty at Penn State, Abbey worked as digital collections librarian at the University of Connecticut. She has published in the *Art Libraries Journal* and her work will appear in the forthcoming *Encyclopedia of American Women's History*.

KRISTA E. CLUMPNER is head of technical services and systems at Olson Library, Northern Michigan University. Previously, she worked in a variety of historical libraries in the Midwest involved in aspects of cataloging, control, classification, grant-funded newspaper projects, and preservation issues. She has published in the field of library science and been recognized in the higher education field. She received her MALS degree from the University of Wisconsin–Madison.

IONE T. DAMASCO earned her MLIS from Kent State University and is currently cataloger librarian at the University of Dayton, where her responsibilities are focused on cataloging, metadata and digitization projects, and collection development. She has served on various committees for the Academic Library Association of Ohio and the ALA. She has coauthored two articles on the role of practicums in cataloging education, as well as an article on tenure and promotion issues for academic librarians of color.

JIM DELROSSO is digital projects coordinator for Cornell University's Hotel, Labor, and Management Library, where he is responsible for such projects as DigitalCommons@ ILR, the digital repository for Cornell's School of Industrial and Labor Relations. A digital librarian since 2009, he is also the president-elect for the Upstate New York

Chapter of the Special Libraries Association (SLA), as well as the Communication and Social Media Chair for the SLA's Academic Division.

AMY S. JACKSON is digital initiatives librarian at the University of New Mexico (UNM), where she works with the Institutional Repository and other digital collections. She is active in scholarly communications initiatives and recently served as chair of the UNM eScholarship Committee. Prior to this, she was project coordinator for the IMLS Digital Collections and Content project at the University of Illinois at Urbana-Champaign. She holds a master's degree in music performance from the Peabody Conservatory of Johns Hopkins University and an MLIS from Simmons College.

SOMALY KIM WU is digital scholarship librarian at the J. Murrey Atkins Library at the University of North Carolina at Charlotte, where she oversees the development and implementation of digital scholarship projects in the Digital Scholarship Unit. In addition, she manages the creation of virtual exhibits, coordination of digital publication, and media projects. She received her MLS from Wayne State University in Detroit, Michigan.

CORY LAMPERT is head of digital collections at the University of Nevada, Las Vegas, where she is responsible for management and strategic planning of digital initiatives. Her research interests include digitization best practices and the evolving role of librarianship in a technological world. She is currently serving as the outreach director for the New Members Roundtable of the American Library Association and focuses her service activities primarily on supporting new librarians. She received her MLIS from the University of Wisconsin–Milwaukee.

JENNIFER PHILLIPS is metadata and catalog services librarian at the National Center for Atmospheric Research (NCAR) Library. She has a long-standing interest in the relationship between traditional cataloging and today's metadata services. She works primarily on developing and implementing metadata standards and schemas for NCAR's digital repository.

ANNIE PHO graduated with her MLS in May 2011 from Indiana University–Indianapolis. She is a co-writer and editor for the *Hack Library School* blog. She has interests in digital preservation, metadata, and information literacy. She currently works part-time as a reference and instructional librarian at an academic library.

FRANCES RICE is the director of information systems and digital access at the Roesch Library at the University of Dayton in Dayton, Ohio. Her main responsibilities are planning, implementing, and maintaining emerging library technologies.

ELYSSA M. SANNER is the metadata and cataloging services librarian at Northern Michigan University. She creates metadata and catalog records for both library and archival resources, and provides digital access to archival materials. While a student at the University of North Carolina–Chapel Hill's School of Information and Library Science, Sanner realized that her passion lay with providing access to a variety of materials via metadata creation. She subsequently followed a trail of internship, practicum, and graduate assistantship experiences to her current position.

ANNE SHELLEY is multimedia services and music librarian at Illinois State University. Previously, she was assistant librarian at the University of Minnesota and digital projects librarian at the University of Iowa. Shelley currently serves as the "Digital Media Reviews" column editor for *Notes: The Quarterly Journal of the Music Library Association* and as editor of *Midwest Note-Book: The Publication of the Midwest Chapter of the Music Library Association*. She has published reviews in *Notes, Music Reference Services Quarterly*, *Microform & Digitization Review*, and *Journal of Library Innovation*, and reviews music-related DVD releases for *Music Media Monthly*.

JANE SKORIC received her MLIS from San José State University and is currently cataloging and metadata librarian at Santa Clara University. She previously worked as a metadata specialist at the University of Nevada Las Vegas, as a bibliographic services assistant at California State University, Monterey Bay, and as a member of the Library Task Force at UCLA.

SILVIA B. SOUTHWICK received her MSLIS and PhD from Syracuse University. Her scholarly interests are in the area of digital library development. Topics of specific interest include metadata design and management, and digital library technologies. She has previously held the position of assistant professor in the MLS program at the State University of New York at Buffalo. Her current position is digital collections metadata librarian at the University of Nevada Las Vegas, University Libraries.

ROY TENNANT is a senior program officer for OCLC Research, where he manages projects relating to technology, infrastructure, and standards. His previous employers include the California Digital Library and the University of California, Berkeley. Tennant is the creator and owner of the Web4Lib and XML4Lib electronic discussion lists, and the creator and editor of *Current Cites,* a current awareness newsletter. He has published widely, including a decade spent writing a monthly column on digital libraries for *Library Journal.* In 2003 he received the American Library Association's LITA/Library Hi Tech Award for Excellence in Communication for Continuing Education.

MICHELLE CZAIKOWSKI UNDERHILL received her MLIS from the University of North Carolina at Greensboro. She is a digital project manager at the State Library of North Carolina. She has previously worked as a reference librarian, an electronic resources librarian, and as a solo librarian.

MICAH VANDEGRIFT graduated with an MLIS from Florida State University, where he now holds the position of scholarly communications librarian. His particular areas of interest are digital humanities, scholarly communications, and emerging technologies. He founded and is managing editor of *Hack Library School,* an award-winning blog dedicated to resources by, for, and about students in library school.

LINDA BURKEY WADE obtained her MLIS from Dominican University and earned an MS in instructional design from Western Illinois University (WIU). Wade has been published in the *Journal of Interlibrary Loan, Document Delivery & Electronic Reserve* and the book *Pre- and Post- Retirement Tips for Librarians*. She is the unit coordinator of digitization at the WIU Libraries in Macomb, Illinois, and was recently elected to the Brown County Library Board. She received the WIU 2010 Distinguished Service Award for innovation and dedication to service.

CATHERINE P. WAGNER is a reference librarian for the National Institute of Standards and Technology in Gaithersburg, Maryland. She graduated with her MLS from the University of Washington in June 2011 and found her first job as a digital librarian at the Puget Sound Regional Council in Seattle. In her current role she provides reference services for agency staff and members of the public, and assists with digital initiatives to improve access to reference resources and library collections.

ANDREW WEISS received his MLIS degree from the University of Hawaii at Manoa, specializing in academic librarianship, digitization, and information literacy. He formerly worked for the Japanese Cultural Center of Hawaii in Honolulu, and the Forsyth Library at Fort Hays State University in Hays, Kansas. He currently works for the Oviatt Library of California State University, Northridge (CSUN), as digital services librarian, focusing on developing CSUN's institutional repository, ScholarWorks. His research interests include data visualization, massive digital libraries (including Google Books, etc.), and organizational collaborations.

MATT ZIMMERMAN is a release project manager in the Marketing-Platform Design Department of the Institute of Electrical and Electronics Engineers (IEEE). He is responsible for the deployment of releases and updates for IEEE *Xplore*, IEEE's web discovery system for almost three million full-text documents from some of the world's most highly cited publications in electrical engineering, computer science, and electronics. His past positions include manager of digital services and technology planning at the University of Texas's Southwestern Medical Center Library and manager of faculty technology services at New York University. He holds a BA in English from La Salle University and an MA in English from the University of Georgia.

Index

Page numbers in bold indicate a term in the glossary.

C

D